"Deena Metzger is a courageous and adventuresome explorer who has plumbed some of the most terrifying depths of the human psyche and brought back poems and stories of startling originality and beauty. In this inspiring book, distilled out of her years of writing and healing work, she shows us how to unleash the creative genie imprisoned in the bottles of fear and denial."
—Ralph Metzner, psychologist and author of *Opening to Inner Light*

"Metzger, a poet and healer, writes to bring life and dignity, strength and intimacy to the practice of storytelling. *Writing for Your Life* is an important book that teaches the reader about the relationship between creativity and healing."
—Joan Halifax, author of *Shamanic Voices*

"A truly wonderful way to garden in the soul. Deena's work takes you right down to the roots."
—Jack Kornfield, co-editor of *Stories of the Spirit, Stories of the Heart*

"Invites us step by step into the inner territory of our own creativity. Deena Metzger, a cartographer *par excellence,* provides a road map to the countries of the soul."
—Diane di Prima, author of *Loba* and *Pieces of Song*

"I found myself able to read only a little at a time because I kept picking up my pen and notebook. *Writing for Your Life* is inspiring, a gift."
—Ellen Bass, co-author of *The Courage to Heal*

"This welcome companion to our personal journey applies Metzger's skill—or magic—at helping us to see, and in seeing, to speak."
—Joanna Macy, author of *World as Lover, World as Self*

"[*Writing for Your Life*] is a deep and valuable book about writing and the creative life that stimulates the imagination."
—Linda Leonard, Ph.D., author of *Witness to the Fire* and *The Wounded Woman*

"Deena Metzger is an extraordinary life teacher whose book beautifully and skillfully illuminiates the wonder-filled path of healing and wholeness accessible through the power of story."
—W. Brugh Joy, M.D., author of *Joy's Way* and *Avalanche*

Writing
for
Your Life

A Guide
and Companion
to the Inner Worlds

Deena Metzger

HarperSanFrancisco
A Division of HarperCollinsPublishers

Harper San Francisco and the author, in association with the Rainforest Action Network, will facilitate the planting of two trees for every one tree used in the manufacture of this book.

For workshops and seminars and further information, please contact

TREE, P.O. Box 186, Topanga CA 90290

Grateful acknowledgment is made to the following for permission to reprint material copyrighted or controlled by them:

W. S. Merwin for an excerpt from the poem entitled "Berryman." Reprinted by permission of the author. Robert Bly for excerpts from *The Kabir Book,* 1977, translated by Robert Bly. Reprinted by permission of the author. Alfred A. Knopf for excerpts from *The Magic Orange Tree and Other Haitian Folktales,* collected by Diane Wolkstein, text copyright © 1978 by Diane Wolkstein. Reprinted by permission of Alfred A. Knopf, Inc. Inner City Books for an excerpt from *Body and Soul,* by Al Kreinheder. Reprinted by permission of the publisher. Corey Fischer, Albert Greenberg, and Naomi Newman of A Traveling Jewish Theatre for excerpts from *Coming from a Great Distance,* by A Traveling Jewish Theatre, 1979. Reprinted by permission of the authors. Oxford University Press Canada for an excerpt from "Procedures for underground" by Margaret Atwood from *Selected Poems 1966–1984,* copyright © 1990 by Margaret Atwood. Reprinted by permission of the Oxford University Press Canada. Farrar, Straus & Giroux for an excerpt from *The Storyteller,* by Mario Vargas Llosa. English translation copyright © 1989 by Farrar, Straus & Giroux, Inc. Reprinted by permission of Farrar, Straus & Giroux, Inc.

Library of Congress Cataloging-in-Publication Data
Metzger, Deena.
    Writing for your life : a guide and companion to the inner
worlds / Deena Metzger. — 1st ed.
        p.   cm.
    ISBN 0–06–250612–9 (acid-free paper)
    1. Autobiography—Authorship.   I. Title.
CT25.M48 1992
808'.06692—dc20   91–55323
                                                                                          CIP

05 06 07 08 09 ❖RRD(H) 30 29 28 27 26 25 24 23 22

For Jane Alexander Stewart, who insisted
For Naomi Newman, who asked me to teach this to my friends
For Steven Kent, with whom I discovered the mystery

Contents

Acknowledgments

This is the place to give thanks, and there are many thanks to give.

Everyone who takes a workshop contributes to the community in which the work takes place, taking in what is offered, transforming it, and then passing it on. Leading these workshops has nurtured me, and my students have enriched me beyond measure. Our lives mean little without the rigorous exploration and revelation of self that we practice together. The honesty that becomes eloquence is a gift to everyone.

First, I thank everyone with whom I have worked over the past twenty-five years—all those who have entered the realm of the imagination and verified its significance through their own courageous explorations and writings. I would name names here if I were not so afraid of leaving someone out. So I thank everyone for the work we have done together; I acknowledge all the individual efforts to support this book, all those who gave me their notes, thoughts, encouragement—and their writing.

I am very grateful for the contributions that I was able to include in this book. But these selections comprise only a small portion of what was contributed. I thank everyone who was gracious enough to offer his or her work. One of the joys of writing this book was the chance to reread pieces that I first heard in my workshops. I am grateful for the beauty and the wisdom contained in those pieces and regret that I couldn't publish all of them, for they all merit such publication. I feel privileged to have been able to read them again.

Over the years, I have worked in partnership with several people who, to my great fortune, are also dear friends. In concert, we have been refining and deepening our work and our understanding of the healing power of creativity. In particular, I would like to acknowledge psychologist Jane Alexander Stewart, writer and performer Naomi Newman, and theater director Steven Kent. We have played together in the imagination, developing and leading various workshops that have deeply affected our own lives and out of which many of the ideas and exercises contained here grew.

Barbara Myerhoff was my closest companion. With her, I explored every aspect of imagination, creativity, healing, and the realization of self. If not for her friendship, I could never have written this book.

In the past years, John Seeley fathered my imagination; I thank him for his support and encouragement. I thank him, too, for his awareness that the human being is the one who tells the tale and that this telling, in all its forms, deserves to be heard and acknowledged.

Many people have supported this book. Bronwyn Jones is foremost among them, and I thank her for her many loving efforts and her loyalty. Similarly, I am grateful to Michael Toms, my editor, who enthusiastically supported the book from the beginning, offered his intelligence and heart to its development, and skillfully shepherded it through its several phases. Thank you also to Dean Burrell for his attentiveness and constancy.

I wish to acknowledge my dear friend Nancy Bacal, with whom I have had many rich conversations regarding creativity and the exploration of self. With great respect and admiration, I thank Irene Borger who teaches healing writing workshops for people with AIDS and whose work—week after week—verifies the ways through which the creative can heal our lives. I also wish to recognize my father, who was a writer, my mother, who is a painter, and my many companions in exploring the imagination who, in one way or another, have helped me develop this work, including Vijali, Victor Perera, Brenda Peterson, Regina O'Melveny, Stephen Nachmanovitch, Morena Monteforte, Judith Minty, Peter Levitt, Marc Kaminsky, Eloise Klein Healey, Hella Hammid, Bruria and David Finkel, Ariel Dorfman, Sandra Butler, Alan Bolt, Sheila de Bretteville, and Ralph Abraham.

Originally, Dan Saucedo and I discussed writing the book together. Though circumstances did not permit this collaboration, I am indebted to him for the initial work we did, for his belief in the book, and for his very thoughtful questions and perceptions. I wish also to acknowledge Connie Zweig, who early on offered useful commentary, and Pami Blue Hawk, whose insights, enthusiasm, and laughter have been sustaining.

Barbara Lipscomb has been an invaluable assistant in the creation of this book. At times when I despaired of finishing it, she saved the situation with her impeccable notes, her devoted reading and rereading of the text, her validation of the usefulness of the work, and her willingness to help me with the sometimes fatiguing process of bringing a book into the world.

And I wish to thank my husband, Michael Ortiz Hill, who most carefully, lovingly, and rigorously edited this book. Michael was the eye behind my eyes, without whom—and this is not hyperbole—this book would not have been published.

With very, very few exceptions, everyone quoted in the body of the book, everyone whose work is used as an example, is a friend. This has been a deliberate choice. In these times, alliances are essential; without them we will not survive. I have chosen their work deliberately, not only for its literary merit but more importantly for its integrity. I can attest that each piece arises from an effort to bring into harmony one's life and words. I love these people for their poetry, for the poetry of their lives, for the community we form together, for their wisdom and compassion.

I give thanks here for the opportunity to safeguard the creative by protecting a bit of the endangered territory of the imagination. I do this for my sons and daughters, Marc, Kris, Greg, Pami, and Nicole, for my granddaughter, Jamie Lynn, and for all the children to come.

And in closing, I wish to thank those who will read this book and find something of value in it. To take something from these pages, to transform it in your very own way and pass it on to others, is to complete the cycle of creativity.

Deena Metzger
Topanga Canyon, 1992

Part I

On Creativity

Everyone has the right to tell
the truth about her own life.

Ellen Bass and Laura Davis[1]

There was a little girl who, when she was three years old, wrote, or rather told, her first poem:

> *Tree*
> It doesn't grow in water,
> it doesn't grow in sand,
> but in happy children's hands.

After that she didn't write a poem she liked for over twenty years. When she was three, she knew something that she then forgot and only gradually began to remember over a long period of time. When she was three, she knew the magic of words; she knew that words could create magic, that they were magic. She knew that they could create worlds, could describe worlds, explore worlds, and also be the bridge between one world and another.

In their purest use, words not only describe reality and communicate ideas and feelings but also bring into being the hidden, invisible, or obscure. Words can leave us in the known and familiar or transport us to the unfamiliar, incomprehensible, unknown, even the unknowable. Words, therefore, are the primary route toward knowing both the particular worlds we inhabit and our unique and individual selves.

With words, the little girl at three brought an invisible tree into view. Without her words, that tree might still exist but in another world where she could have no connection with it. Of course, she could not know whether those words constellated something that had not existed until that moment or whether they were the means to confirm the reality of something that had formerly been obscured. In either case, first nothing was there, and then, in a matter of words, something was there for all time. More importantly, there now existed a little girl who saw what others did not necessarily see, a little girl who saw the tree in the hand. And when spoken, these same words made seeing possible for others who were willing to see the tree.

How did the little girl learn of the tree she wrote about? She hadn't been told of its existence. It wasn't in a picture book, a botanical magazine, or the dictionary. It wasn't part of the family folklore. She didn't learn about it in school. But she had to find it somewhere. She was so young, she must have found it in herself. If such understanding was available to her at three, how much more might be available to her later as she grew up and gained experience?

When she was little she saw the invisible tree and announced its existence. As an older woman, when I finally remembered the tree, I remembered the source of the knowledge of that tree, the vastness of the realm of the imagination. I know now that the imagination is the domain of the inner world and that the creative is the way to it.

If the little girl once knew about the tree and intuited what it implied, why and how did she forget? And why did it take years for her to remember and to reconstruct ways to return to a deep familiarity with the world of imagination? How and why have we lost access to this world that is intrinsically ours?

The Words That Are Ours by Right

The way we see a room, a landscape, our awareness of differences and resemblances, the emotions we feel, the ideas we have about ourselves—all of these are embedded in language and in our relationship to words. Some of this relationship is straightforward—we are shown a color and told it is red. But some of it is far more complex. In the course of our development, red begins to attract public and private meanings to itself.

Red flag, red-light district, red-blooded, Red Cross, red herring, red-bait, red-eye, red man, red-hot, red-faced—these are all variations on a theme that goes far beyond the simple association of color and word. To make these images, we must pass the words through our own consciousness and particularity. And in this act of trying to know something else in its specificity, our own particularity is likewise revealed.

Some people fear seeing or feeling anything about which there is no general agreement. For others, it is thrilling to be aware of innuendo, shading, complexity. For those who do not wish to step away from consensus, the creative is useless at best; at worst, it is dangerous. But for those who are intrigued by the multiplicity of reality and the unique possibilities of their own vision, the creative is the path they must pursue. It is the creative and the worlds it opens that we wish to consider here.

The Language That Speaks of Our Inner Selves

We are entering a very singular world together. The world of public discourse—political, social, diplomatic, commercial—has so corrupted language that we are rightly more suspicious of the meaning of words than we are convinced of their veracity. Language has been turned on its head. Still, language contains the possibility of revelation. Those who fiercely pursue the writing of journals, life histories, or autobiographies do so because they sense that the words that have been used to rob them of individuality are the very means by which they can restore dignity and create identity. When truthfulness is honored, describing the world and describing ourselves are the same act. Creating art and creating ourselves are the same act; art, world, ourselves—these are continuous with one another.

How language can obscure or can reveal became clear to me some winters ago. At a particularly dark time in my life, I took myself to Cape Cod for a week of solitude. Winter cold, snow, forbidding winds kept most people indoors. The inns where I stayed were generally empty. The streets were empty. The shops were empty. This pleased me. I enjoyed the silence. During the few hours of sunlight, I spent whatever time I could carefully photographing my shadow, and I spent the evenings writing a series of prose poems that I called, *Shadow Letters: Self-Portrait of a Woman Alone.*[2]

On Saturday night toward the end of this sojourn, I found myself in an unusually crowded restaurant where the tables were set close to one another. Alone at my table in the middle of the room, I was surrounded by excited conversation. Yet from the facial expressions, the body postures, and the snippets I observed and overheard, the talk did not seem to be meaningful so much as it was continuous. As I listened to the chatter, I thought, We are so like monkeys.

In company, it is difficult to be silent. Talk insists itself even if there is nothing to say. The words fill a vacuum. But often the words create another emptiness. That night, I became aware of the chatter in my own head. White noise. A similar babble. I finished my meal quickly and ran back to the inn, not because it was uncomfortable to be eating alone but because I was longing for my own company.

Afterward, my experience shifted. Whether I was alone working on a poem or walking outdoors, I found myself engaged in another kind of language that corresponded to the silence that I was trying to impose upon myself: a language that neither distracted nor beclouded; a language that was mine because it took me directly into, not away from, myself. This is the language of creativity—a language through which the self is carefully reconstructed out of pieces of itself.

> I want to be where the light persists, spending the day hovering in the white spectrum of light, photographing my shadow. From the image, you will never know if I am one of the dark women or become one of the light. The shadow

begins the dream. In the Mysteries, initiates descended into the center of the earth and told—nothing. They said, "She whose Name I will not say . . ." The dream is like the wind. From this window, I know it only by what it moves.

—"*Provincetown, Holly*"[3]

The Forbidden Inner World

For my tenth birthday, my father, who was a printer, surprised me with one hundred copies of a little book of my poems, which he called *My First Ten*. But by that time, the poet in me was already in hiding. What was supposed to be a gift actually mortified me. By the time I was ten, I was judging my poems and was certain they weren't good enough. I was embarrassed by wanting to write poetry. In addition, my father's intense pride in the book somehow subsumed my own efforts and amplified my sense of their limitations.

These feelings are not unique to children. Traveling to the inner realm, even though it is explicitly and absolutely ours, is often forbidden or constrained. Each of us knows the fear that if we speak our minds openly, we will be embarrassed or endangered. The reasons for this are obvious. About the inner world and its revelations there can be neither consensus nor prior definition. The inner world is always, by its nature, every moment, for one's entire life, new territory. And, therefore, the inner world is always outside the prescribed behaviors, outside constraints, rules, and regulations, outside traditional and legislated ways of seeing and behaving. Someone who lives in the inner world and abides by its rules is, almost by definition, an outsider.

And there we have it: the fundamental contradiction and challenge of creativity. If we practice it, if we enter the inner world, we find ourselves outside the perimeter of conventional society—outsiders feeling all the loneliness of that disconnection. And yet we are simultaneously as far as we can get from loneliness because we are, finally, with ourselves.

Furthermore, it doesn't take us long to realize that when we inhabit this inner realm, when we are with ourselves, we are participating in a vast underground world of common understanding and communality some of which may have been with us from the very beginning of time. What Carl Jung calls the collective unconscious— what I like to think of as the creative unconscious (in its communal aspect) or the imagination (in its personal aspect)—is the sea of internal and eternal values, images, cultural memories, and experiences that inform dreams and creative work while, just as often, challenging the prevailing modes of the state, the society, or the community in which one lives.

Another contradiction: while this world we are discussing can be contained within us, it is also vast, endless, and complex. It is the world of worlds. It is infinite. To enter it is to come to know something of it and to learn of the boundlessness of the self. To go within, therefore, is never a diminishment. To stay adamantly without is always a limitation, for the self, the inner world, the imagination, all open out into everything that has ever existed or can ever or may ever exist.

The inner world is for each one of us—novelist, diarist, or diplomat—in our equally ordinary and extraordinary lives the essential territory where everything that might be known resides until it can be called forth into the public arena. Credited or not, the images, inspirations, dreams, nightmares, intuitions, hunches, understandings that arise from the inner world are the *prima materia* from which everything, including ourselves, is constructed. To be willing to live within the imagination is to commit oneself to the gathering together of the pieces that might begin to form a self. To avoid this territory is to avoid the encounters that might validate, inform, or enhance one's experience.

Yet the truth of the matter is that just as the inner territory is proscribed, the self in modern times is also under assault. To go inside is considered solipsistic, narcissistic, small. The smaller intimate history of individuals or marginalized peoples and cultures is not extended the dignity and value accorded to the history of nation-states and canonized philosophic or religious movements. Autobiography, journal writing, and life history are considered lesser forms when compared with the grand sweep of novels, elegies, epics, and biographies of public people. Confessional writing is degraded by the very term used to describe this revelation of one's most intimate story, while objectivity, distance, detachment, and impartiality are valorized. Similarly, the professional writer is often applauded merely for commercial success, while the one who writes primarily for himself or herself is diminished, no matter what the content of the writing, the quality of the search, and the dedication of the effort. The public has prestige over the intimate, the domestic, the interior, yet both the professional writer and the most private journal keeper suffer the same terrors, engage in the same struggles, impose the same disciplines in their encounter with creativity.

Because the inner exploration is so essential to every creative life, we must challenge these attitudes and risk the exploration of these forbidden realms. For despite the prevailing judgments, it is clear that vitality, zest, the very life force itself lie inside and are not to be dismissed, that what is acceptable never has the range of what is still unknown and unexplored, and, finally, that it is the unique vision and exploration, our own subjectivity, that we all secretly seek and cherish.

And so, novice and expert alike, we journey into this territory of the imagination. Like any unexplored territory, it will, each time, turn out to be both strange and familiar. And we go into it, each time, as if we have never been there before and also as if we are coming home.

Let us go with respect and with the commitment that we will not exploit it, colonize it, or decimate it. That we will honor what it offers us, that we will use it in keeping with the principles of the territory, and that we will think of its treasures as gifts to us that we will pass on. In this way we will be able to transform inner exploration into public concern.

Becoming a Writer

When I was quite young, I promised myself that I would become a writer. Later, when I was despairing of this possibility, I threw myself a challenge: if I could write a novel by the time I was twenty-five, I might become a novelist. But if I failed to embark upon this project by that time, then I would forgo the possibility of a creative life. At twenty-five, I had just had a child and was pregnant again. I had started graduate school, was involved in politics, and was trying to be attentive to my married life as well as several friendships. But the challenge remained with me and weighed heavily on my conscience. Ultimately, I started a novel, *Waterwall,* which I eventually relegated to a file cabinet. Afterward, I liked to say that I was blessed by not knowing that the novel was weak and naive because if I had known how undeveloped it was, I would never have written anything more. But something else happened in beginning this novel that was far more important than the book itself. Where formerly I had thought of myself as someone who would never write a book, I now began to think of myself as a writer.

To write is, above all else, to construct a self. Only secondly is it to record one's history, to express feelings and ideas, to create characters, or to communicate with others. Journal entries and life histories, as well as fictions, poems, and plays, are variations on the most fundamental human need to know oneself deeply and in relationship to the world. Beginning that requisite first novel—that commentary on my adolescent life— was evidence of a serious commitment to discover who I was and how I saw the world.

Fifteen years later, I was perplexed by the form of a piece I was writing. By this time, I had learned that the writing, and not I, must determine its own shape and direction. Still, I was uneasy. I didn't know what the piece was. Finally, I heard a voice inside say, "It's a poem."

Another voice, more familiarly mine, asked, "How do you know?"

"Because I wrote it and I have become a poet," the voice whispered shyly.

Those fifteen years were an important period of transition and development. Within that time, I had not only to write but to learn something about the life of a poet—that is, the life that would feed and support the work. It was not easy to do either. Circumstances always mitigated against poetry, and it was difficult to give the work the priority it needed. But ultimately, two things emerged: first, the beginnings of a body of work that seemed to arise from responses to inner urgencies, and second—and just as important—a life that was conscious and aware and that bore the shape of a writer.

Beginning

The first and foremost question a writer, public or intimate, must ask is, What must I say? To begin to know the answer to this question is to begin to know the essential self.

What must I say? What *must* I say? What must *I* say? What must I *say*? And finally, What must I say *to you*?

The beginning. Something wants to be said. We don't know what it is or what shape it desires. An inchoate feeling. A pressure around the heart, perhaps, asking it to open. We pick up a pen or sit down at the computer.

> *This is the moment. Write. No matter what. Write. Don't try to name it in advance, don't call it play, or journal writing, or poem. Don't ask it to have a form, or to be spelled correctly, or to appear in sentences. But write in pen so that you can't erase it, and promise, as a way of showing respect, that it will not be thrown away.*

The beginning. A blank page. It feels as if we will sit before it forever. Then let us sit before it forever. Let us sit before it until we can no longer resist writing.

This beginning is important. It is a wraith we are trying to catch, a swirl of smoke, an inspiration, just the barest breath of something coming into ourselves or going out.

The Journal as a Dialogue with the Self

> *Write anything for five minutes, it doesn't matter what. Write as if you are walking in an unknown woods, attentive to anything you might see, or poking at an indistinct mass wondering what it is, whether it is alive or dead, whether it will snarl suddenly, turn and bite. Keep writing.*

> *Let the writing feel welcome. Keep writing. Don't look back. Don't edit. Don't think of what it might be, could be. Don't think. Only welcome it. Make a place for it to be.*

Later there will be time to be curious. Later we can see what awakened us or what insisted itself. After writing like this for a long time, it will be appropriate to look back and see what has engaged us, what intruded into our daily life, what obsessions or fascinations propelled us. But at this moment, try only to be present and to allow the words to emerge.

If you have never kept a journal, this may be the time to begin.

Keeping a journal isn't so difficult; beginning to keep it is the challenge. It has always been easy for me to keep a travel journal. When I am in a foreign place, I appreciate the journal's familiar presence. It is the close friend to whom I can confide everything and convey my experience. One way to start a regular journal is to imagine that you are traveling. For the first weeks, follow this sequence:

Imagine that your daily life is occurring in a foreign country. Carry a journal with you wherever you go and write in it whenever you have a moment—at the beginning or end of the day, on line in a supermarket, waiting for transportation, in a restaurant, and so on. Write anything and everything: snatches of conversations, observations, concerns, dreams, plans, lines of poems, letters, newspaper headlines. Allow yourself to record anything and everything without judging its appropriateness or meaning.

As this becomes comfortable, expand the journal by adding emotional responses and observations. Enter into dialogue with the things you have seen and heard.

Next, experiment with thinking in the journal, with recording ideas and exploring them.

Finally, consider the journal as a place where beginning fictions or snatches of poems may not only be recorded but explored and developed.

If we imagine that our daily life is occurring in a foreign country, we will be, like travelers, exceedingly attentive to every detail, curious about the meaning of everything, and enthusiastic about experience, no matter what its quality.

At the end of your "trip," you will be able to look back over the journal to discover what you have seen, what has obsessed and fascinated you, and what, if anything, you wish to make of it.

The writing we are doing here may remain in journal form forever. It may occur in the moment and never be considered again, or it may be the beginning of a longer piece. It may be addressed to another individual in a letter or a poem, or to the world, eventually, in the form of a novel. But in this moment, we need think of none of this—only of the words presenting themselves and our willingness to set them down.

Learning to See

In the spring of 1989, I made a pilgrimage to the death camps of eastern Europe. One way that I contained the terror that such a trip induced was to imagine what I would see, creating the story of the journey in advance so that nothing would catch me off guard. It didn't take me long to realize that focusing on what I expected to see left me functionally blind. Like an American tourist who, while traveling in a foreign country, resides only in American hotels, anyone who anticipates and focuses only on the known and familiar finally sees nothing. At first I didn't know how to alter this situation. I wasn't certain how to prepare for the possibility of the unexpected when I feared it so much.

I began by looking at the small. Having spent the two previous years preparing for this journey through my reading, I was already obsessed with the larger and more dumbfounding issues of the Holocaust. To counteract this, I began in my journal to step away from meaning, to relinquish interpretation for the recording of small details that might at some point add up to a larger story.

The color of a wall, a woman and a child staring at me from a window in an East German village, a pebble picked up from a grave, the posture of the Polish nun who opened the door to the convent at Auschwitz, the components of a meal—these became the touchstones of the story that later emerged. I had had one story in mind. This had to be relinquished for the possibility of other stories, the shape and content of which I couldn't even imagine and would not know until long after I had returned. I had to look randomly, to write down everything, relevant or not, to look at things out of the corner of my eye, to hunt images and moments stealthily, to practice slyness. I found myself writing so particularly in my journal that I had no idea if the trip would ever have any coherent meaning. By the time I returned, what I finally saw and understood was far from what I had expected and far more significant than I had imagined. Had I followed my initial inclinations, my journal would have consisted of poor illustrations for a familiar story. Instead, it became the painting, an important story in its own right. But the essential story did not begin to emerge until weeks after my return when I had the leisure to read through the journal and see the patterns that the odd images, moments, unexpected experiences, and insights formed.

The Journal Transforms Itself into Poem, Story, Drama

What is a poem? The poet Eloise Klein Healey says, "A poem is a way of life."

A poem is a penetration into the essence of something. It begins in a moment, is the thing itself as well as the surrounding space. A poem is in the spaces between the words.

Because a poem expresses the inexpressible, it requires to be spoken in the many languages of sound, music, rhythm, and beauty. It is so deep it cannot be told directly, it wants images, it wants metaphor.

Poetry evokes. It speaks to feelings—not emotions, necessarily, but to feelings. Feelings are the way we know experience, while emotions are a response to it.

A poem most often begins with an image—an image that holds a relationship or expresses an idea, an image that has its own power. A bird, let's say. But which bird? How can you tell it exactly? Not any bird, not only this representative of a species, but this bird, this one, here, this morning, now, against the sky, color of . . ., flying like . . ., the one you see . . ., the one you see as no one has ever seen or will ever see again: this bird, this moment, which will never ever occur again. This moment, this bird, this sky, this observer, now . . .

"A bird, a broken wing across the mending sky . . ."

Try it.

Look back into your journal. Find some observations you have forgotten, some images that intrigue you. Think about them.

> *Now, later, tomorrow, or next week, wherever you are, sitting at your desk, at the computer, or on a park bench with the small notebook you always carry, or in a café, or before the fire, or on the train, recall these images. Select one or a few. What engages you about them?*
>
> *You can make a poem of them. Take the phrase or image. Explore it. Go deeper. Bore. Go into the heart of it.*
>
> *Cut away everything extraneous. Repeat what is essential. Find the associations. Leap from one understanding to another.*
>
> *Be aware of the rhythm. Rhythm wants to be repeated. Find the music of the words. Sing.*

It is possible that if you do this again and again, you will soon find that you have written a poem.

After a poem, we often want to write a story. After a glass of wine, a piece of bread.

How did the journal entries I was writing transform themselves into story? Story takes moments, links them together, finds the order inherent in their relationship, and then fills them out. A story has a beginning and an end, has consequences. If the journal is the jumble of raw material—blood, bones, sinews—and a poem is the cell, the impulse, the story is the entire animal.

12

A poem penetrates very deeply; prose or story spreads out, can tell you everything. A poem relies on images, the story or prose piece wants sentences. Even paragraphs. Developments. Insights. Associations. Prose wants to speak to the mind, to
the intellect. It doesn't have to, but it can present ideas. Prose also exists in a time
frame: "She was watching the bird streak across the sky, *when . . .*" Or "The jagged
flight of the bird caught my eye *and . . .*" *And so, when, who, therefore, what, because:*
these are the foundations of a story.

Try it.

Or is it a play? Two voices. Or more. Something that can only be revealed
through conversation or monologue, only through what can be spoken and what is
underneath what is spoken. Through the silences between. Through what is said and
what is omitted. Through the words chosen, through the rhythm of them, through
the vocabulary, the dialect, the intonation. In dramatic dialogue, we play with the way
speech sometimes connects and something glances off, the way we are sometimes certain and sometimes hesitant, sometimes tell the truth and sometimes lie.

"I saw a bird."

Let this be the first thing spoken. The response, then, determines everything:
"I envy you." This takes the play in one direction, while "Was it the blue one
again?" takes us in another. And "At last" takes us somewhere else altogether.

Take the line, "I saw a bird," and begin a dialogue. Allow the two speakers enough
independence to create a miniplay that surprises you.

Now that you have tried different forms, abandon them. Return to the content of the pieces. What were you getting at? What do the forms hold?

Look at what you wrote originally. Don't impose a form on it. Something in
what you wrote will catch your attention, will want to be more than it is. Let it
discover both its meaning and its shape.

Allow yourself to be the scribe for the words that insist themselves. Allow your-
self to be taken, to be passionate, even reckless. Following the clues the work gives
you, go wherever it wants to go. Relinquish your will to its own understanding.

Even when you think you've found a shape, be open to change and new possi-
bilities. A poem sometimes becomes a story, a story becomes a novel, and a novel
can transform into theater.

Or forget form altogether and continue your initial investigations. Seeing the
bird, what other sightings does it remind you of? What bird stories do you know?
What birds do you love? Fear? When did birds become important to you? When
did you forget them?

Ask questions. Discover which questions you want to ask, what interests you. Find a question that startles you. What is it you want to know?

Who we are is revealed, ultimately, by the questions we ask, rather than by the answers we find. What we want to know is a reflection of how we see the world and is a verification that we are looking at it.

So let us begin here: with writing that is completely free and unrestrained, followed by a phrase or image that intrigues, followed by a series of questions, followed by the desire to find a form most conducive to answering those questions or even a form that may, thankfully, raise other questions.

Facing the Fear and Welcoming the Creative

Beginning is difficult. We are afraid of failing. We are afraid we will have nothing to say. We are afraid that what we will say will be banal or boring. We are afraid it may endanger us. We are afraid it may be a lie. We are afraid that what we say may be the truth. We are afraid of succeeding. We are afraid no one will notice. We are afraid someone will learn what we've said—and it may be ourselves. We are afraid there will be consequences. We are afraid we will pay attention. We are afraid we will have to change our lives. We are afraid we won't be able to change. We are most afraid that we will.

It is right that we are afraid. If we are fortunate, we *will* say something, it *will* be the truth, it *will* be eloquent, it *will* have power to it, we *will* listen, and we *will* change our lives.

So, we are afraid. Sometimes fear cannot be distinguished from excitement. The signs are the same: our pulse increases, our hands get sweaty or cold, we feel tense, watchful, anticipatory. We don't know what's coming. Let's call these feelings excitement. What is the difference? When we feel fear we shrink away, but when we're excited we go toward. Let's go toward. Let's go farther. Let's invite the creative into ourselves.

An adoptions worker is coming to your house to interview you on your capacity to adopt the creative. She will ask all the usual questions: Why do you want the creative in your house? What do you know about caring for it? How will you provide for it? How and what will you feed it? Where will you house it? What resources do you have to support it? How will you deal with being awakened at 3:00 A.M.? How will you cope with its needs and urgencies? What kind of community will you provide for it? What will you have to relinquish to attend to it? What will you read to it? How will you hold it? Can you sing?

Imagine the situation. Write it from the beginning, from the adoptions worker's point of view or from yours, or both. Or write from the point of view of an omniscient narrator who sees and knows everything but does not judge. Try not to lie to the adoptions worker, either to pass the interview or to fail it.

Yes, the creative has been assigned to your house. What must you do to prepare? Write the moment in which it arrives. Then write the first day. What are its needs and demands? How can you meet them? Do you meet them? What happens that is unexpected?

Now the creative has been with you a year. How do the two of you live your daily life? What relationship have you established? Again, what is transpiring between you that is unexpected?

My dreams have always been full of infants, and I have come to understand them as symbols of the creative. Sometimes the child is a prodigy, sometimes it is dying, sometimes I've forgotten it in a market or forgotten to nurse it. On one occasion, I dreamed that a social worker brought an invisible child to my door, insisting I take her in. I put her on a couch next to my father, who was also a writer, but she remained invisible. It took a long time and much care before she developed a visible body.

It is useful to think about the creative as a child who has been put into our keeping. This concept challenges the belief that in order to be entitled to work with the imagination, we had to exhibit talent when we were children. To the contrary, the creative may be put into our hands at any time, and no matter when it arrives, we must help it to develop. A writing gift doesn't have to manifest itself in childhood or adolescence in order to exist. For some people, it may well be the blessing of their later years.

The Gift of the Gift

Creativity is a gift. Too many of us refuse it unwittingly. Assaulted by self-doubt, we fail to believe that it has been put into our hands. We diminish it by insisting that we should have been child prodigies. We insist its only proof is commercial gain. But the creative is a gift to us from another realm, and it comes to us when it comes.

The creative is first and foremost for us; this is why creative people are called "gifted." First, the gift is given to us. To recognize that we are gifted—that we have been given the gift of creativity—is to claim parts of ourselves too often denied. But, in order for us to be given to, to be gifted, we must be willing to receive.

Second, we are asked to nurture and develop what has been given, to make something with it. By adding to the gift, we make it more fundamentally ours, and in doing so, we are made more whole.

The third part of the gift is that we must pass it on by offering a gift to others. Something is healed in us through the giving; severed parts are brought together. Exchange occurs and the world heals a little.

Some of these ideas are themselves the gift of Lewis Hyde, who wrote the remarkable book, *The Gift, Imagination, and the Erotic Life of Property*,[4] in which he articulates the difference between a gift-giving and an acquisitive or consumer society. In a gift-giving society, an individual gains prestige and satisfaction by receiving, then by adding to what has been received and passing it on. The society thrives on the energy of the exchange. In a consumer society, prestige and satisfaction are gained through accumulation and acquisition. Nothing is given, nothing is passed on, no energy of exchange exists. Describing several potlatch societies, Hyde identifies artists as members of another kind of gift-giving society.

> One way of knowing who we are is by what we give and what we receive. Write two lists, one of gifts given, another of gifts received. Afterward, imagine that you have found both of these lists and that you know nothing about the person who wrote them. Develop a portrait of the person who emerges from this series of exchanges by examining the nature of the lists, the kinds and qualities of the gifts given and received, and their relationship to each other.

> Reread the portrait. Who is this person? How does she or he resemble yourself? What new perspective does this focus offer you?

> Write a piece about a particular gift you once received or one that you gave. What did this gift mean? Tell a specific story that reveals the nature of the gift.

> How does this story reflect on the portrait you wrote earlier?

In 1938 an odd trio traveled the length of Mexico together: the great muralist Diego Rivera, the renegade revolutionary Leon Trotsky, and the king of surrealists, André Breton. Together they wrote a manifesto about the state of art, which Trotsky and Rivera later disclaimed and only Breton was willing to sign. In this manifesto, however, the three of them had agreed that creativity was innate in every human being and that societies were to be held responsible for crushing the creative instinct. Therefore, they reasoned, a government in the interest of the people would ensure the freedom that would allow the artist in each individual to emerge. Fifty years later, the idea that creativity is innate in everyone is still revolutionary and is still valid.

The next questions are based on this idea that creativity is born in each of us, and they require us to answer with stringent honesty: What are the gifts that we've been given? To deny that we are gifted is, perhaps, to indulge in false humility, which allows us to shirk our responsibility to the gift. But the gift is a sacred trust. It asks something of us. It asks that we accept it and temporarily become its guardian. It asks that we develop it. And then it asks that we pass it on.

So we have to ask ourselves: What is the gift that we've been given? Write a short piece exploring this. Be honest. Tread the fine line between inflation and false humility. Inflation and grandiosity are frightening because they leave us feeling empty underneath our bravado. However, to recognize that everyone, including ourselves, has been given a gift, that it may not be recognizable at first because it may have an unconventional appearance, provides the balancing perspective. Each of us has a unique, modest, but essential gift. What is yours?

Are you confused about the gift? Do your refuse it? Do you dislike it? Is it a burden? Are you afraid it doesn't exist?

Sometimes the dramatic form enlivens what could become a tedious essay. Write a dialogue, a short play with two characters, you and the gift giver. Let the piece develop a life of its own as the characters take off, becoming independent of your ideas and beliefs. Let them say anything and everything in defense of the creative, or even against its existence, or, as may happen, about other subjects altogether. Once these speakers become characters, we have no idea what they will say or do.

Writing dialogue or conversation is difficult because the literal transcription often sounds false. So be aware of the way people actually speak, of the rhythms, interruptions, asides, tones that constitute the discourse. Find language that doesn't violate the meaning or the tone and that reads authentically.

In 1989, I gave a workshop at the Pacific Greens Conference with folksinger and musician Betsy Rose. Concerned as we both are with the fate of the earth, we asked the participants to address the question of their gifts:

For a moment, forget your fear of pride, your lack of confidence, your chronic disbelief in yourself. Imagine the following: The planet is in danger. The situation is dire. It happens that the gods have given you two gifts. The first is great skill in expressing yourself. The second is something important to be said. Meditate for five minutes, then answer honestly: What has been given to you to say? What gifts have been given to you for its expression?

Daring to Write

The unwillingness to accept the actuality of our creativity or to accept the necessity to speak is often a great barrier to expression. Feared, creativity atrophies. Distrusted, it shrivels. Refused, it slinks away. Even when we know that we are to pursue a life of the imagination, we often cannot find the means to do it. Sometimes we feel overwhelmed by the desire to create without any evidence of our ability to do it. Sometimes we simply feel awkward and flat-footed.

This has been my experience: whenever someone has determination, has a clear intuition or belief that he is "meant to write" or that she "has something to say," there is substance to it. Sometimes this intuition occurs without any immediate evidence of the ability to express oneself "appropriately," whatever that means to the individual. Sometimes the something that must be spoken eludes him or her. Still, if the intuition or determination is there, it is probably a reflection of inner knowledge. The task, then, is to find the way.

Cynthia Waring asserted that she wanted to be a writer, but she did not reveal that she was dyslexic. At our first meeting, there was hardly any evidence that she could become a writer, but her inner voice insisted that it was not only possible but necessary. Four years later, Cynthia Waring was beginning to be published. Cynthia's persistence on behalf of her maverick intuition allowed a writer to emerge.

In the first weeks, Cynthia's writing was conventional.

The assignment the first class I attended was: *A place that moved me a great deal.* I wrote: "It's evening on top of a mountain. On the mountain is a very special tree. There are granite steps, three, that lead to the tree. They are flanked on both sides by large, unclimbable stones. The air is so soft, without a breeze or a cricket. There are no shadows as the sun is off this spot of earth and illumines only the high peaks in the near distance. Pine cones and needles cover the ground under the tree and in a ten-degree radius beyond its branches. The dark green needles are in contrast with the golden carpet. A ground squirrel runs up the trunk and off to bed. . . ."

Deena said, "Don't say the squirrel went up the tree and off to bed." I was humiliated.

One day Cynthia was driven to ask me if she would ever reach her depth as a writer. Believing that she had a story to tell that she was ignoring, I asked her to write about becoming a nun. In the beginning, she explored the predictable and prescribed.

I wrote about wanting to be an example, becoming one with God, believing that the ideals of the Order were a good way to spend one's life, that service to others was gratifying. . . . Every time Deena would say, "That's not it." After weeks of this, I went home and wrote the following piece. Finally Deena said, "That's it."

The Nun
On a gray day in January, I walked up the steps of the Order house in Boston and rang the bell. I arrived at that door as if I had been to war. I had no

strength to hope for hope. I was burnt out. If you looked into my eyes, you would see that no one was there. I was desolate, a wasteland, crushed, black and lifeless.

I was leaving behind a lover who betrayed me, a mother who threatened suicide if I entered those doors, and a son, whom I was abandoning. By ringing that bell I left them all. Standing there, I didn't dare think of them. I didn't dare think at all. I didn't have any idea of what the Sisters had meant by sacrifice until the door was firmly closed.

When I was shown the bunk that I would sleep in, I wanted a cigarette. So bad, I thought I would die. But not as badly as I wanted it later that night, lying in my bed after an hour of silence, dinner, two hours of classes, an hour of meditation on my knees, and evening prayers. I lay there waiting until all the sounds in the house were stilled. Then I sneaked out of bed with the fear of being caught, the fear of being humiliated, and a nameless fear that was far more horrible even than that.

I had smuggled in six cigarettes in a special pocket of my black purse and I crept towards them listening to the breathing of the ten sleeping women in the room. I found the matches used for lighting votive candles and crept down three flights of stairs. The fear was great, but the need even greater. I reached the basement without being detected and lit the cigarette. I pulled that smoke into my lungs, a drowning woman gasping for air.

After three drags, I fell to the floor. There on the basement floor, unable to move but totally conscious, I came face to face with myself as an addict. All my lofty ideals of service, of reaching enlightenment, of finding serenity lay there on the floor groveling, cheating, sneaking, ashamed. And this was only the first day.

On my third day, still smoking, I started to detox from alcohol and antidepressant drugs. I only had vitamin B and prayer to get me through, and shame so deep and guilt so tight. I hadn't had the courage to tell anyone, I had drunk a half gallon of wine per day for years, along with taking Stelazine and lithium.

I didn't tell the Sisters, but they mopped my brow, fed me, gave me work I could do, and a sense of self started to grow. As I scrubbed rugs with a hand brush and bucket of soap, polished stairways, rewrote the Bible in my own words, meditated, prayed, lit candles, took communion every sunrise, the addict began to shrink and the Order began to order my life.

This first admission was important. As Cynthia's writing developed, a story emerged with it. Or perhaps we should say, her story emerged, and then her writing followed.

The Masseuse

I wasn't always a masseuse. Before that I was a waitress. Before that I worked in the Complaint Department for a condominium management company. People would call me when the lawn men mowed their welcome mats, when they found a frog in their toilet or their roof leaked. Before that I was a Sister in a New Age Order. Before that I was a nurse's aid, first working in old people's homes and ending up working in the delivery room. Before that I was a devoted disciple of an Indian guru. Before that I was a hippie in a commune which started the first health food restaurant in Boston. Before that I was homesteading in Maine in the Sabago Lakes region. Before that I became a mother. Before that I tried to raise enough funds to save the Biafrans. Before that I worked in Cambridge as a secretary while my husband got his Ph.D. at Harvard. Before that I hitched from Madrid to Istanbul on $5 a day. Before that I married a man I had no business marrying. Before that I was Chief Justice of the college student body and also the first topless go-go dancer in San Jose. Before that I was trying to get through school and do enough drugs to understand and love Bob Dylan. Before that I was singing in bands and school choirs throughout the western United States, entertaining soldiers with show tunes and dancing in tight, sequin-covered outfits with fishnet stockings. Before that, I was a cheerleader in high school, had an abortion in Tijuana, and was madly in love with an up-and-coming opera singer much older than me. Before that I had my first summer job as a file clerk at a title company. It took them months to find anything after I left. Before that I had a horse named Star and could ride her bareback at a full gallop holding my hands over my head. Before that, I dreamed of all the things I might be when I grew up, all the men who would love me, all the places I would go, how big my breasts would get, and if I could ever be rich and famous enough. . . .

This was the beginning. What she has been writing since has brought her enormous gratification. Permission to speak, encouragement to be oneself, support for telling the truth, camaraderie with others pursuing the creative help us to excavate and encounter our submerged voices. The catalytic moment occurred when Cynthia began to speak out about her own life. First, she believed in her need to write; then she began to believe in her right to say what had been given to her to say. Determined to write, Cynthia, like so many others in similar circumstances, found herself capable of acknowledging and honoring a life that the tyranny of convention had demanded she deny. The writing followed from there.

Writing Ourselves

Of course, what is therapeutic does not always become literature. Writing that has a specific goal may be too purposive, may limit the creative. But the creative, when it is pursued freely, is generally therapeutic, is in the interest of the self, even if it disturbs us and arouses fear or despair. That is, there is an intrinsic relationship between creativity and self-knowledge. Ultimately, one informs the other. Soon creativity and self-knowledge will seem like twin sisters, similar but distinct comrades who have a common origin.

When I don't find time to write, I am aware that I am not finding time for myself. When I denigrate what I've written, I notice quickly that I am also diminishing myself. When the writing is banal and conventional, I am aware that I have begun to deny or repress who I am. So when I am disconnected from myself and want to know how I am, I look at what I am writing, or not writing, and then I know.

In the beginning, we must let everything appear without censoring or judging it—both in the very beginning, when we are first experimenting with words, and at the beginning of each creative work. We must ignore all our judgments and beliefs, for, in truth, in the beginning of a piece there is no right way to write, no sentence that is better or worse than another, no formulas that will tell us what is a proper poem or novel. In this part of the writing process, we are mining the creative unconscious, bringing up everything, without knowing what is a jewel and what is dross. Later, when we perceive a direction and an inclination, then we can edit, altering one thing, discarding another, adding here, cutting away there.

Before we edit a piece of work, it is more important that we edit ourselves, editing out whatever impedes or attacks what we've written, what stands between us and the pure word or perception. And what most often stands there is our judgment, disguised in the authoritative voices of standards, prohibitions, and obligations.

In *Toward a Poor Theater,* the revolutionary Polish theater director Jerzy Grotowski distinguishes two ways of making sculpture. The first is to create an armature and add on to it. The second is to take a stone or piece of wood and chisel away. When Grotowski worked with actors, he used the second method. Training with him did not consist of adding to what the actors already knew. To the contrary, his rigorous method was designed to carve away.

As writers, we also wish to begin the process of carving away. After we are naked with ourselves, we can add on, can identify what we suspect may be intrinsically useful and incorporate it into ourselves and our work.

Here are a few fragments from a poem I wrote when I didn't know I was embarking on this process:

I have emptied my house. I think of you in these quiet moments as I walk about with my hands in my pockets, two little fists of stone.

. . . You stand outside a new house I cut from rock. The floor is sand. The roof opens to the sky. Everything is in tones of gray and tan. The tern blends into mud and color is wet sand against dry. Your footprint blanching the mud and the water blowing back dark. You instruct me as I furnish the house saying, "If you must bring in anything, bring in stones, one at a time."[5]

Form Is Content

Form is content. And so form imposes a limitation, a point of view. Invoked at the appropriate time, this limitation enhances the work, but arbitrarily imposed, it can undermine it. Soon every writer learns that beauty, excellence, and power develop through devotion to expressing a particular idea, feeling, or vision precisely and that the essence of the work lies in the rub between the content and the form it requires. The beauty of the rose, like the beauty of the ant hill, lies in its precision, its uniqueness, its perfect achievement of being exactly itself.

"I don't know what I'm writing," wailed psychotherapist Dánahy Sharon Rose. "What are these?" she asked disparagingly. "They aren't poems, stories, articles. They're nothing."

"Call them 'pieces,'" I suggested.

In Pieces is the extremely apt title of the book she is writing about her experiences in a mental institution.

A piece can go in many directions, may resemble a prose poem, may be a meditation, a musing, a review, may incorporate poetry, drama, criticism, anything at all, everything, into it. Nevertheless, each "piece" has a very precise form, determined by the content and the language.

It would be easier to write a story or poem by applying a given set of specific conditions (screenplays often require this), by the accomplishment of a formula, by modeling it upon other works of exactly the same shape. But the use of a formula rarely permits the quality of surprise, freshness, and insight that we desire from a work of art. (We are distinguishing here between applying a formula and using the discipline of a form. The sonnet and the haiku forms, when used skillfully, are not arbitrary restrictions but disciplines that elicit intense originality and sharpness of expression.) So while creativity offers the freedom from indiscriminate restraint, it also challenges us to develop a form or shape according to the lights of the work itself. Here, as in life, freedom implies responsibility.

How will we know, then, when we have found the right form, when the words are right, when the meaning is fully expressed? We will know by the necessity they convey and the beauty and elegance they exude. Beauty, elegance, and necessity are the standards by which complex mathematical theories and proofs are ultimately judged. They can provide useful and difficult standards for what is written, as well.

But what is beauty? I ask this question of myself all the time. Recently, I asked it in a workshop. The answer was overwhelmingly consistent: beauty appears when something is completely and absolutely and openly itself.

And what is necessity? Perhaps it is the meeting place between urgency and harmony, a reflection of the impossibly unique circumstances without which life on this planet could not exist. Necessity is present when something is mandated to exist.

Waiting for the Words to Appear

When you are writing, allow yourself enough time. Sometimes I insist that my hands move across the page, even though another voice is insisting I am empty or have nothing to say. Sometimes the first minutes of writing are simply a process of priming the pump. The act of sitting still with the blank page or of writing as a leap of faith is an offering, a gesture of sincerity that one makes to the creative unconscious. Not always, but sometimes, after much discouragement the writing gushes forth like a geyser from the center of the earth.

In order to write when my children were small, I rented an office so that I could have some uninterrupted writing time. I remember all the days in that office when nothing came whatsoever, though I felt compelled to sit there facing the blank page or putting down words that I was sure I would throw away at some later time. But even while I was sitting there for three days in a row, I believed that something would happen on the fourth day or the fifth. And I was right. Eventually, the writing came. Today, I rarely have to wait so long, but that may be because I have persisted for all these years.

Many years ago, I took a writing class with novelist and short-story writer Christopher Isherwood, in which he revealed his process for beginning a novel. He had been sitting at his desk for days without being able to write anything when, as he described it, his unconscious told him, "You can write another novel if you like, but I won't tell you anything." "They" then sat together for several more days, just as they had in the past, until finally, as Isherwood told it, the creative, either moved by his persistence or overpowered by his tenacity, relented. In any event, words began appearing on the page, and thus the novel was begun.

Writing What You Don't Know

Now, as the writing begins to take hold, set yourself the task to write not only what you know but more especially what you don't know. Let the work surprise you. Leap off a cliff. If the writing is in response to an overly familiar, well-worn question, ask yourself another question or devise a writing task that seems impossible.

> *Tell your life story, write your autobiography in five minutes.*

Impossible? Exactly. That's why it works.

As we do this exercise, we will see that it demands a leap. As we clearly cannot write everything in five minutes—and just as clearly, we can never write everything about anything—this task requires an immediate focus and the choice of a few details or stories that can stand for the whole. It may mean that we start in the middle or at the end rather than at the beginning. It certainly means that chronology cannot be the means to establish order or meaning. But on finishing, we will see that we are revealed by what we have chosen and what we have omitted.

> *Reread you autobiography. What major areas of your life have you omitted? Write your autobiography (five minutes again) using only these outtakes. And write it again. And write it again. And again.*

> *Put the story away. Then, in time, look at it again. Here, as in every other writing, it is important to look at your work with curiosity and without judgment. What have you recorded? Omitted? There is no right way to go, only the way you choose to go. Whatever the creative unconscious offers up is also part of the story.*

> *Did you write about your work? Your schooling? Your feelings? Did you record events? Did you proceed in chronological order? Did you begin with your birth or with the present? Did you take one event or moment as representative of the whole? Did you include anecdotes? Did you include parents, siblings, friends, teachers, lovers, children? Did you speak about your pain or your triumphs? Your dreams? Did you describe your inner life or your outer life or both? Did you discuss your sexuality? Your political ideas? Your relationship to the gods? All or any of these or more are possible—which ones you chose and how you chose to combine them reveal something about who you are.*

Freeing the Imagination

To write what wants to be written not only takes courage but often requires a strategy because language can both restrict and release. Some of the limitations to creativity are inherent in the fact of language itself. The language we are born into has certain qualities and lacks others. My first language was Yiddish, and I am profoundly aware that it has a tone, a certain *tam* actually, that is different from that of English. There are things I can say in Yiddish that I cannot say in English. The unique qualities of Yiddish—the humor, self-mockery, and analysis of character—are different from the lyricism, the poetry, and passionate music of Spanish, the metaphysical precision of German, and the variety and intellectual range of English. Languages are as distinct as people, and they put their stamp on us. To go beyond ourselves often means to go beyond our language. Sometimes this exercise helps:

> *With automatic writing, the task is to write faster than you can think. Allow the words to appear on the page at random, to flow haphazardly. When a familiar word comes into your mind, see if you can write down another one. Write so quickly and so randomly that finally you overcome reason, sense, grammar, form, and, above all, meaning.*

Following these instructions, this is what I just wrote:

Pomegranates, and the flaming cosmos of trees, reconstruction helicopters rescind fragments of elephants, those eyes, another moon, or suave onyx through the backbone of time, another wasteland insistent theocracy. Dim butterflies engraving slate into lagunas of breasts. This body. Colon. Rise, rice and flamboyant pentacles, rings insistent and fragrant. The white lady licks geometry precisely when absinthe sizzles smoke and autumn. I endear myself to prayer, silence of fireflies, lovers, crucifixions, so many hothouses and war without chrysanthemums. Einstein, the lighthouse. Meadows and galaxies, like snow.

For each person who does this exercise, the result is different. Our styles inevitably differ, and even when writing randomly, our own voice is apparent. No matter how we may try to escape ourselves, we find that we cannot escape our imprint. This is useful. As we learn to recognize our own voices, we begin to know ourselves.

Often in the process of automatic writing, the words exude an odd poetry, as if something mysterious and compelling is hovering about them. Something is trying to be expressed, but what it is, we don't yet know. It may be that this process has taken us down into another aspect of self, to the dark waters where poetry might be birthed.

To go against sense, to go against reason, to deliberately deconstruct the world of grammar and thoughtful orderliness is, in effect, to destroy the world as we know it and allow something new to emerge. Grammar is, above all, a system of thought and perception, the way the world is defined and primary relationships are perceived. Some languages, unlike the Indo-European ones, do not separate subject and verb so that an action is never seen as distinct from the actor. Someone born into those languages necessarily perceives the world differently than do those of us who always see an object and an action as distinct. English does not assign gender to nouns, but in other languages, one is surrounded by differentiation between male and female. These conditions influence who we are and how we think. And so our language is a great part of who we are. To see what is possible, we must, on occasion, get out from under linguistic conditioning, and at other times, we must embrace tradition in order to discover our collective voice. Creativity oscillates between what is given and what can be discovered, between what is traditional and what is unique, between the known and knowable and the unknown and unknowable.

Some days after I had written this chapter, I came back to this section and reread the automatic writing exercise. The phrase *Einstein, the lighthouse,* struck me. I put it at the head of the paper as if it were the title of a poem. I gave myself the following task:

> Write a poem based upon an intriguing phrase from the automatic writing. Try to include other phrases from the automatic writing as well.

A poem began to emerge that I include here in its rough form. The italicized words are those that come directly out of the exercise.

> **Einstein, the Lighthouse**
> Climbing the *backbone of time,*
> you first saw light propelled, a knife,
> a thin gash streaking across the sky,
> and imagined glowing *rings,*
> incandescent *fragrance* of the stars.
> That was before the terrible fire of fires,
> before the Milky Way was drawn and quartered
> by the horses of the apocalypse,
> before that *crucifixion* of *geometry,*
> the war that will end all,
> the *wasteland* without sons or *moon.*
>
> Still, the invisible
> calls one electron to another,
> the expanding space in the universe
> is the ether of divine kindness,
> and the tenderness of the Great Mother
> holds the galaxies together in a milky light.
>
> *Einstein, the lighthouse*
> is the *flame* without flames, budding
> on the world *tree,*
> a carpet of *chrysanthemums*

26

from here to infinity
at the feet of the *White Lady*
who forgives all
in the *silence of fireflies,*
meadows, and galaxies asleep in the *snow.*

Write your autobiography in five minutes using the technique of automatic writ-
ing. Keep your inner eye on your life story as you "tell" it in the images and
metaphors that emerge.

This is how my story once emerged:

Trees were behind the walls and still she never hummed or if a bit of bark, only
the glint of the grizzly bear. Then the mirror grieved and she took the spade
and dug determined furrows. He said the great veneration was never under
Mexico. They huddled over those alarming laurel leaves chewed and obscene.
Blood time came. She played nipples. O do re mi. No one had eggplants and
she was purple to the elbows. Why display sergeants when you can rumba? The
trees remained cutouts against her thunder and the cyclades gathered their
amber wings. It hailed and hailed. Why has she eaten storm? The belly anger
of the orangutan was born from the barklined birth trench and she fell up
into the cyclone, all hairy lusting eyebrows. There were never enough tat-
toos. She howled the city, all earthquake. Now in the yoke asking no promises,
she saw the cat's eyes and lapis lazuli, the turquoise of tail, the tippled beak,
this green upon her thigh. She planted the knee becoming sod and did not
empty promises with a sieve. The end of Africa in the coming of Antarctica
with the icy plain and white cells further than dying. Everything will sing,
she thought. I abdicate this to you with trespassing.

Dream time hovers beneath our daily lives. A literal life narrative excludes
the other realities, and soon we lose contact with them and forget that they exist. However odd and arbitrary this piece seems, it actually speaks to the meanings behind the
meaning. Ten years later, I can break the code describing a young woman's relationship
to nature, her discovery of sexuality, separation from her father, her perception of
womanhood, marriage, childbirth, and healing from cancer—in other words, her full
life.

Here is another exercise that insists that we write what comes and also allows
us to play. Play is the very essence of creativity, something that we too often forget:

Write freely for ten minutes, one word following another in alphabetical order.
Afterward, take the word or phrase that is most surprising or unusual for you and
improvise upon it.

This is an example, by Judy Welles, of what came from this assignment:

Able Babies Cradle Diaphragms. Even Farting. Gentle Husbands Invent Jolly Kisses, Leaning Merrily Near Overtly Pulchritudinous Quitters. Reasonably Sane Transvestites Understand Violence, Whereas Xenophobes Yap Zealously.

Reasonably sane transvestites understand violence and certainly Harry considered himself to be more than just "reasonably" sane. After all, he had a certificate *proving* he was sane—his discharge papers from Camarillo State Hospital—and how many other people can boast of a similar authentication of their healthy mental state?

But Harry was still pondering what had happened in the bar last night, his exotically plucked eyebrows knotted in troubled concentration as he poured skim milk over his granola.

Morning sun washed over his breakfast table in a rising tide of rash promises; it was April, the warmest spring day Harry had seen yet, but he couldn't muster his usual ecstatic energy at the coming of spring, at least not as long as he still carried the image of Robert's face dripping with blood, a look of amazement in his mismatched eyes—one green, one brown with a green spot off-center, where his Luscious Life contact lens had been knocked askew. Harry knew Robert had spent thousands on getting his teeth capped but last night two years' worth of beautiful dental work had been destroyed with the butt end of a Courvoisier bottle.

Metaphor as Freedom

When we allow ourselves to write spontaneously, unexpected associations, connections, and relationships occur. We begin to see the network of meaning among things that is otherwise absent in the narrower, linear world of verifiable cause and effect. It is as if things begin to lean one against the other, to highlight each other, to evoke each other in ways we cannot predict. The core of such associations is metaphor. We can say that metaphor describes one thing in terms of another, but more precisely, metaphor finds the hidden, mysterious connections.

One of the ways in which a writer "corrects" the stubborn surface of reality is through simile and metaphor. When we use simile, we are describing one thing by comparing it to another. It is the safe route; reality is not shifted. Nothing happens when we say the bird's wings were blue as the sky. However, when we create a metaphor everything tilts: the bird made of sky . . . That is another matter. We have to wrestle with the meaning of such a description because it alters our understanding of reality.

Our language is full of expressions through which we bypass literalism and its insufficiency. We say we are devoured, drowning, exploding. We say a brook runs and the ocean roars. We say our life feels like hell or that our lover sings like an angel. Then we say we *are* in hell or that our lover *is* an angel.

Sometimes a writer expands or extends metaphor in order to deepen our understanding. Gabriel García Marquez is the master of this technique. In *One Hundred Years of Solitude,* a dead man accompanies his murderer to another village because he would be lonely without him. In his old age, the murderer finds that the dead man who knows his history is his only real companion. This may not be literally true, but what is true is the ongoing relationship between the living and the dead in the Indian-based culture of Latin America.

In one of my first novels, *What Rough Beast,* I entered into the imagined consciousness of a tiger that had escaped from a wild animal park into the San Fernando Valley. As soon as the image had entered my awareness, it transformed into a tiger-man, which happily I did not immediately realize was a metaphor for my life. Whenever I thought of the beast as symbolic, the writing became slack and didactic. The text came alive only when I forgot myself altogether.

In Ariel Dorfman's novel, *Mascara,* the protagonist—a man whom no one ever sees or remembers and who consequently remembers and photographs every face he comes across—falls in love with an amnesiac. This may be an unrealistic scenario for the literal-minded, but it is deadly accurate for those who know how fascism destroys our personal reality and our history. These extended metaphors are the bedrock of imaginative literature.

Writing freely liberates not only our imagination but also our intelligence. It allows us to see what otherwise escapes our rational focus. Perhaps we can say that poets not only use words to describe what they see but they see with words. Words are their very means of vision.

Make a random list of ten or more nouns, participles, and verbs. Arbitrarily create pairs from these words. Then use your madcap fantasy life and imagination to find askew relationships between these pairs or between several of the words.

For example:

stream   flowering   coffee   volcano
night   landscape   bobcat   driving
resistance   beatitude
The night stream flowering in beatitudes.
Coffee driving through my bloodstream, a bobcat alert.
Night flowering like a volcano.
A landscape of bobcats and resistance.

The next task is to discover and develop the meaning of these images.

These seemingly arbitrary associations can lead us back to moments in our lives that we now remember through the qualities embedded in the images. On reflection, I know exactly the experience referred to by the conjunction of "bobcats and resistence" and this phrase reveals an intriguing way to understand that time. These "accidents" of connection may well be revelations. See where your associations take you.

Writing the Seen and the Unseen

Who we are is what we see and what we don't see. After we know ourselves through what we see, we can come to know ourselves equally through what we don't see. What did we miss today? What parts of our lives did we lose through abstraction, distraction, preoccupation? One of the key teachings of Buddhism is awareness. Practicing awareness is as essential to the writer as it is to the monk. Practicing awareness allows us to develop emotional and spiritual peripheral vision, to become aware of the subtleties at the extremities of the familiar. We can recover what we saw but couldn't or wouldn't attend. We can allow these images to enter in our minds again, as if we were suddenly seeing a daffodil appear through the fog. The play of light on the cement, a gesture of caring from a colleague, an emotional interaction we preferred not to countenance, a moment of fear, the welling up of tears, pain, a headline, a spray of color, a conversation with a child—the very substance of our lives often consists of what we have ignored.

When you think you have nothing to say, when your life feels dull and tedious, try writing: Things I didn't see today.

Questions like this are as appropriate to literature as they are to the journal. We can come to know a character by what she didn't see as well as we can come to know ourselves by what we ignored. When I write the words, "I didn't see the sunrise this morning," sadness wells up in me. I can feel a longing to be awake to a beauty that I habitually ignore.

What is invisible to us does matter. Sometimes it drives us and sometimes we are deprived by it. I learned this through reading, "Things I Didn't Know I Loved," by the Turkish poet, Nazim Hikmet, who discovered exactly what he loved while spending years in jail as a political prisoner. Sometimes when we think we are free, we are confined in the narrow place where we forget to love. To remedy this, we make an effort to create awareness, to see what is there to see, to see what we love, and to allow ourselves to be aware of the loving.

Write "Things I didn't know I loved."

Against Silence

This, then, is the beginning: to know that we have a right to the creative and to follow it where it leads. Why should that be so difficult? We know things when we are very young that we forget as we age.

When I forgot what words can do, when the little girl who wrote "Tree" disappeared, I forgot one of the most essential parts of myself. I forgot the part that could see in the dark, that could see the invisible. I didn't forget willingly. This facility was cut out of me. In truth, my heart was cut away.

It doesn't matter quite how it happened, we all know one form or another of the story: for some of us, our hearts, our eyes, what we love, and what we see are cut out of us in school; for others it occurs through the taunting of friends or the impatient ridicule of rationality, pragmatism, or expediency. Sometimes a parent is the conscious or unconscious instrument of this mutilation. Or the pain of remembering or knowing some part of ourselves is unendurable, and as a consequence, everything else that might be intolerable is set aside. Each of us has been undermined and diverted from ourselves by a series of small incidents and assaults from various quarters; from these experiences we learned, carefully and painfully, that it was best to go underground.

Several moments from my childhood established an unnatural and inappropriate silence and awkwardness around words that lasted for a very long time. No doubt the first event was discovering that Yiddish was not the national language of the United States. That the teachers and children in the Brooklyn kindergarten spoke another strange tongue, one that I had to learn quickly and desperately, left me continually uncertain about what I had to say and how to say it. Later, the damage was reinforced when my mother read the crumpled pages of my diary that I had torn out and thrown away exactly because I was afraid that this gift to me of a cloth-bound diary with a little lock and key would be opened behind my back. For a long time afterward, I was only willing to write what was generally known and acknowledged, what was safe for anyone to see.

One of the most gifted women writers I know was told by her teacher, "You must never write about such things," when she wrote a story about teenage pregnancy. It was years until she wrote again or believed her words had some value. An extraordinarily gifted poet was ridiculed by his colleagues and friends after he had spent a year away writing what he had seen in the only words he could find to express his vision. He threw down the manuscript, stalked away, and gave up poetry. Another friend was forbidden as a child to speak at home in his mother tongue, so whenever he spoke afterward he was filled with fear. During a workshop on autobiography, a woman stood trembling as she read her account of returning home from visiting her mother to discover her husband throwing her journals into a huge bonfire on their lawn. She had not written again until this moment, ten years later.

More than our words burn up in such incidents—our souls are burned to a crisp. Afterward, we may not be able to speak again, or at least not in a real way. When my first novel was published, my father held the book in his hand and said, "In my day, we never spoke about such things." My mother often objects, privately, to what I write. "Why do you always tell secrets?" she asks. Because it is the writer's task to reveal the truth, I try to explain.

In 1969, I was fired from a tenured teaching post at a local community college for reading to my students a poem I had written on censorship and pornography. The case soon became an occasion for the advocates of censorship to organize themselves against the students' right to know and the teacher's right to teach. After three years, I was restored to my position by the California State Supreme Court. Of all the painful events in this witch-hunt, what disturbed me most was watching a poet-colleague take the witness stand against me.

When we are told that something is not to be spoken about, we understand this to mean that this something should not exist—should not, cannot, must not, does not exist. In that moment, our reality and, consequently, our lives are distorted; they become shameful and diminished. In some way, we understand this to mean that *we* should not exist. To protect ourselves, we, too, begin to speak only of the flat world where everything is safe, commonplace, and agreeable, the very small world about which we can all have consensus. Soon we don't see the other worlds we once saw, for it is difficult to see what we are forbidden to name.

It is one of the horrors of American history that black Africans were not only enslaved but separated, when possible, from any other slave who spoke the same language. Language, which binds together a common history, a common sense of reality, a vision and understanding of the world, was taken from them. The slave owners had found that when language was excised from the slaves, their spirit was excised as well. The new words, the new language they were given, held the new reality—slavery— and served to enslave them even more.

During times of tyranny or oppression, certain words are often forbidden. After General Pinochet came to power in Chile through a bloody coup that overthrew President Salvador Allende, even the word for the *quena*, an indigenous little wooden flute that carried the melody of so much of the new music of Chile, *cancion protesta*, was forbidden.

Political history is full of instances of words being given and taken away. In George Orwell's novel *1984*, people were controlled through the daily rewriting of history. Today, the increasing governmental insistence that security depends upon secrecy, coupled with the similarly increasing tendency of government officials to lie, is our equivalent of Orwell's Newspeak. Deprived of the knowledge of our true history, our country withers, just as without a personal history, there can be no self.

Without access to language, without the right to speak what we must speak, the self disappears. Access to the word is essential to both political freedom and one's inner reality. To be able to speak is not only a political but a psychological right.

Confronting the Critic Within

The external tyrannies are familiar to us, and we know their consequences and sometimes even how to challenge or combat them. But the internal tyrannies are another matter. I have never met a writer who has not been, at one time or another, sabotaged by the critic within. This actor in our imagination can be as persistent and vicious a despot as any in the public world and is often an introjection of all the external voices that act against or deny us. This inner critic is our own private, personal torturer.

The inner critic is easy to differentiate from the quite different and necessary critical faculty, for the inner critic is never satisfied. No matter how we adjust or respond to what this critic says, he or she finds another way to attack us or our work, unless we find the source of anger or pain and heal the situation.

Marie-Louise Von Franz, the renowned student of Carl Jung, tells how she is attacked by the critic every time she sits down to a new work. "You don't know anything; you can't write; that's stupid" is how the critic belittles one of the most brilliant people of our time. This, she says, sometimes goes on for days. But she persists, to our good fortune, and the work appears. Sometimes there is nothing to be done but sit there.

And sometimes there *is* something to be done. Sometimes the critic can be approached imaginatively. It can be useful to appeal, as one might with any bully, to other aspects of his or her nature. Sometimes I engage in a literal conversation with this critic, either aloud or with pen and paper. Sometimes, I write the dialogue at the computer. First, I extend my respects. Afterward, when I feel that some relationship has been established, I ask the critic to remove himself from the initial creative process, from the first explorations and shaping. In return, I promise to invite him to come back after the completion of the first draft. Then the work will require his expertise and perspective in order to be refined. I am sincere in this negotiation, and the critic often agrees to honor this arrangement.

> *Imagine that the critic, this crabby or abusive voice, has a history, a life separate and distinct from yours, a set of emotions and experiences that have formed her. Who is this person? Write his autobiography. Try to be as open, accepting, and compassionate as you have been with the other writing you have done so far. For in order to know the critic, as in knowing anyone else, you must be free of judgment and preconceived ideas.*

Next allow the critic to speak for herself. How does he see himself? What is her relationship to you, and what does he consider his essential work to be?

Finally, enter into a dialogue; write a conversation in which the relationship between the two of you can be explored and negotiated.

This is an opportunity to practice the voice of the omniscient narrator, one who has a large perspective and has no stake in the outcome. This narrator permits each of the characters to present themselves fully. Using this approach, we can see what is at stake for everyone and what kind of relationship is really possible. Similarly, we can apply whatever we know about conflict resolution, particularly the principles of mutual respect and agreement, so that no one loses. Ultimately, the critic can become an ally, and ultimately we will be strong enough to insist that when he speaks, he speak his mind to us clearly and directly. At some point in our development, it is excellence that we desire, and the critic can help us toward it.

After having fought bitterly with the critic for years or having set ambition aside because of the inability to withstand the inner critical onslaught, we can discover through this exercise that the critic's motivations are honorable but misplaced. The critic may have developed as a protector when we were young to help us avoid situations in which we would have been utterly powerless. If this is the case, we can investigate our fears to discover which are no longer appropriate to our adult or creative life.

Such a confrontation with the critic cannot be not easily resolved. It often takes as much time as it does in our ordinary lives to resolve serious conflicts with others. Sometimes, even after much struggle, the situation remains intractable. Then we must continue as best we can, aided by having brought this inner conflict into awareness.

Important as it is to give the critic her due, it is more important to do whatever we can to bring the writing forth unimpeded. And it will not come forth until there is a safe place where it will be welcomed and accepted for what it is. It may help us here, again, to think of the writing or the creative as if it were a child. Because there are enemies in the world whom we may not be able to contain or convert, we are required to make even greater efforts to provide safety for the innocent one. The last thing we would do with a beloved child is to abandon it when danger is present.

A Safe Place

This takes us to the issue of privacy. Journals have traditionally been written in seclusion to protect privacy or prevent embarrassing revelations from coming to light. But secrecy has another function. It creates a sanctuary for rare and dangerous beasts and monsters, for imaginings and wishes, that eschew the light of day. Secrecy creates a preserve where anything can happen, where anything can be said, where even lies, deceptions, fantasies can cavort without inhibition. It is not only the need for freedom but the danger of premature understanding that makes it imperative to preserve privacy.

The writing that makes us whole, that can heal us, cannot risk hardening the emerging self into a fixed image, even through validation or admiration from others. When writing is fresh and, therefore, delicate, it may be destroyed by premature exposure.

A woman brought a poem to class expecting to be "severely criticized" because it was "flawed." On questioning her, we discovered that it had been ridiculed earlier by a friend. "Do you know what one does with papers like these?" he asked her, gesturing as if wiping his ass.

In truth, it was a good poem, particularly for a young poet. But it was a poem that dealt with personal matters and in which she expressed her pain quite openly. It was the kind of poem that some people don't like to hear. Asking for harsh critique, the young woman was simply asking us to forbid her ever to write again. We refused.

Another danger of exposing the work prematurely is that we may be distracted from going further, thinking the work is done when, in fact, it has only begun. The alchemists knew the necessity of creating the inviolate vessel and giving the elixir all the time it needed to transform into gold. Our writings—that is, our innermost selves—require the same attention, patience, and seclusion.

Another danger is mistakenly using our private writing as coin for intimacy. Too often we read our journals to our lovers and our dearest friends when we are desperately needing to be understood. In that moment, we feel eased in our loneliness, but afterward we may not be aware that the quality of our writing has been changed by subtle restrictions we impose to protect our privacy. If we find ourselves chapped by this overexposure to the elements, we may cover ourselves with a thicker skin, which later even we cannot penetrate.

There is a particularly telling scene in Ingmar Bergman's *Scenes from a Marriage*. The wife, fantasizing about the possibility of reconciling with her husband, reads to him from the journal she has been keeping during their separation. The camera holds in a close-up of her face as she is reading, building up to the unbearable long shot that shows him asleep.

If we can bear to keep our work private until it is really finished, we may find that we are actually seeking intimacy with ourselves. Without that primary relationship, intimacy with others is always disappointing.

—Above all, I have a reality. It is separate from yours. It is mine and I will share it with you when I am ready and not until then. And it is of utmost importance that my reality not be denied—whether I have spoken of it in words or whether I have chosen not to speak of it; whether I have chosen only to show you through my rage. Do not interpret my rage in your words.

Do not expect me to show you my vulnerability because you can show me yours. Do not tell me that you want to see my fear, my hurt, my pain, because you can show me yours, when I can only give you my rage.

I once showed someone my hurt, my pain, my fear. I was tied to the rungs in a closet, by my wrists, naked, and beat until I became unconscious. I woke up in a dark space with welts three quarters of an inch raised. I woke up bleeding, in a clump of old clothes. . . .

I once showed my father my pain at his denial of my pain, and I was thrown across the kitchen floor, my face bleeding into the fucking tile cracks. I have had tile prints engraved into my face.

—I once told my mother I hurt. I was afraid. I was in pain. Before I had words, I told her in tears. I told her through my screams. She took a knife to my genitals.

If I am not yet ready to be opened, it does not mean that I do not have a reality that is mine, behind the rage, that I can only show you, now.

—Ikazo

If, on the other hand—and there is always another hand—we do not reveal our inner selves, we will not have models of honesty and openness and we will be ignorant of the reality of our lives. Speaking openly is the gift we give each other. The women's movement would not have taken the directions it has taken in this half of the twentieth century if women had not decided to reveal the realities of their lives. It has not been a very long time since women began speaking about madness, illness, abuse, sexuality, and other prohibited subjects. What was so urgent for women to speak about is no less urgent for all of us to utter. And so, while we must be careful not to reveal ourselves prematurely, we cannot cloister our inner selves either or we will find ourselves bereft of one of the essential components for the process of transformation: interchange.

In my own life, I once found myself trapped between my desire for privacy and my deepest felt conviction that others would benefit significantly from reading some of my more private writing. I had had a three-year correspondence with my closest friend, anthropologist and author Barbara Myerhoff. We wrote letters to each other several times a month, although we lived only a mile from one another. The correspondence started when I boarded a plane for England while Barbara, unbeknownst to me, was being rushed to the hospital with blood poisoning. In the hospital, she was inspired to write me a long letter that began both with her reflections on our friendship and on dying. Receiving this letter while she was delicately balanced between life and death, I did my best to respond with equal vulnerability and attention to what was important. These two letters set a standard of communication that we tried to maintain that summer even after we were reunited. The letters ultimately became a kind of communal diary, a way of being spontaneous and yet deliberate, a way of recording the extemporaneous. We found that these letters brought our already deeply intimate and bonded friendship to new depths of trust, revelation, and caring and that the process of writing engaged us intellectually and artistically in ways that competed with our usual discourse. So engaged were we both by the correspondence that we would often, not without humor, rush to separate typewriters when we visited each other.

Beloved Friend:

Jesus, this hour is wrung from stone. A thousand "more pressing" demands have been thrust aside. Unbalanced checking accounts. Children's car pools unorganized. Letters unanswered by the carload. Clothes not packed, legs not shaved, notes not assembled for psychiatrists in La Jolla waiting to be turned on to other worlds. No more doubts about priority. No more questions even about whether to write to you, or to engage in active imagination, or attend the dream book. Here is the privacy and here is the totality of my inner voices. Our separate experiences are woven into the fabric of our dialogue. Your vision has become wedded to my dreams. So for me the question of what to do first in the realm of my inner life is simpler than for you. I write to Deena. It's all one, my balance, recognition, sanity, meditation, the myth of my life is here with you.

—*From a letter by Barbara Myerhoff*

During this time, I was organizing a women's writing conference, "Woman's Words," named to honor the last such conference that had been held at the turn of the century. After much debate, considering both our own needs and those of the community, Barbara and I decided to read from the correspondence. We prepared carefully. We were determined to protect the intimacy between us, and we were equally committed to revealing the letters. The experience was overwhelming. Moved by the disclosure of our inner lives and friendship, the women at the conference urged us to publish the letters immediately. We were gratified by this response—and that was the end of the correspondence. We were never able to resume it with the same intensity.

Write a journal entry as if it were a letter to a close and trusted friend. Are there things you can or must say because this person, in particular, is going to read the entry? Are there things you will edit out for the same reason? How might the entry change if you were to write to someone else? Your partner? Your child? Your employer or colleague? A man? A woman? Be attentive to the new depths you are led toward and also the ways and places in which you hide.

Is there someone with whom you might realistically start such a correspondence?

A correspondence between friends can sometimes substitute for a journal. A correspondence between two writers can serve as a writer's journal. I had such a correspondence with Judith Minty during our stay at Yaddo Artist's Colony. Quite often the letters became incorporated into our work.

11/22/1978

This is not a poem. But the response in the moment to your poem. I sit in the rocker. I read your poem. I go home. I sit in the rocker. I read your poem. This has become home. This strange snow. The wild birdstone song on the lake. The haunting cry of something I do not know. I sit with a shawl to my back. Through women I know, I'm home. In the woods I learn not to be afraid. White is an alien time. The red I wear is the shape of the blood we share. The trees have a clear call. I do not want to be alone. A friend is the sound of the woods. You are the woman who has come to be my friend. I say I will never be ashamed to love. The white snake is the most dangerous of all. . . . I read your poem. We stretch each other. We close down into what we are. We are the dark and the bright stars. The tree paws the sky in rough embrace. I will read your poems. I will go home.

This is the poem the letter became:

So Much of Women in This Uneven Grass
This has become home, this snow
and the song of the lake. The ice bird,
the stone loon, lasted for a day. The cry
of what I do not know. In the wood
I learn to be afraid. The tree's call
is clear. A branch paws the sky
in rough embrace. Like blood,
I do not want to be alone.
I say, I am not ashamed to love
and can bed down with the white snake
but the forest is not a place to rest.
I have seen the handprints of stones
break through the ice.

We close down into what we are.
I think I know the way
without the road.[6]

Begin a correspondence with a fellow writer. Perhaps there is a writer with whom you would like to meet regularly, but distance and other circumstances prevent this. Let the meetings occur by mail. Agree to write regularly to each other. See what occurs.

Breaking Through

Some years ago, a poet came to see me. "How do I write a poem?" he asked, having written for years and then having inexplicably stopped without being able to revive the poet in himself. He said he could no longer describe a scene, nothing presented itself to be described, he could not write, didn't know what to say.

I suggested:

Write as if you are a blind man. Write as if you are unaware of any of your five senses. Or write completely from the realm of the senses: as if you are blind but have developed the sense of hearing; as if you are deaf and can only touch; as if your hands, feet, body, skin tell you everything; as if your intelligence is in your ability to taste the world.

He couldn't. He wanted to make sense of his life through poetry, but he was afraid both of the senses and of leaving them as well. He was, it turned out, afraid of what he "sensed" on the other planes of knowing. Also he didn't want to write in the voice of another character. He could not enter into the world of another being, he would not become something he thought he wasn't or use parts of himself that had gone underground.

But there is a blind man in each one of us, and a woman who knows the world through the palm of her hand. Not the limitation but the intelligence and perception of these beings who know the world differently and therefore know different things are in each one of us, ready to enter into the poem, ready to inform our lives. This wisdom, this ability to see what we are blind to in daily life, is available to us. Just as the other senses of a blind person develop to extraordinary sensitivity, so do the formerly buried parts of ourselves become eloquent when we turn away from the familiar.

"I can't do it," my friend said.

"It's not that you can't do it," I suggested, "it is that you are afraid. To discover the enormity of who we are, to go beyond the familiar and often socially or culturally prescribed identity that we accept, is terrifying. You're not incapable. You're simply afraid."

Begin with any line, with any image, and free associate from it.

He did, and it frightened him. He couldn't accept these seemingly random, uninvited, even alien associations, these unexpected feelings and perceptions as the proper realm of the poem. These strangers, however, were his visions, his moments of wisdom. He denied them. Yet he persisted.

Awkward, furtive, tentative images began to appear on the page. They were not like anything he had ever written before. "These are not proper subjects for poems," he said. We were speaking about poetry then, but he was more generally distressed by the appearance of "what ought not to be there." Coming to light were moments previously disowned and disgraced, the simply unacceptable contents of the unconscious.

"Good," I answered. "Now we have a beginning."

Make a list of everything you must not write about. List what you must not write about because:

1. It is not generally important enough from the point of view of literature.

2. It is too private and therefore trivial from the point of view of literature.

3. It would embarrass you to speak about it.

4. It would embarrass or offend your family and associates.

5. It would embarrass or offend the reader.

6. It is taboo.

When he had compiled this list, I continued:

Select the three or four subjects, images, or experiences that made you most uneasy or that hold the greatest emotional charge for you. Then momentarily set aside your inhibitions and concerns and attempt poems on these subjects.

"Afterward," I said, "if the poems still seem inappropriate, you can throw them away."

Within a few months, he had developed a small series of poems about his childhood that pleased him. He had entered into a virgin meadow rich with topsoil from aeons of cycles of growth and decay. He had lived for a short time, because of a wild passion of his father's, on a small farm in upper New York state. The joy amid the darkness of those years gleamed in these first poems like the luminous eggs in the dark henhouse of his childhood.

Eggs
So many eggs we give them away.
My father delivers them after work
To the bar at the foot of the hill.

Then it's always a wild night
Snow snowing down, the road slicker
More treacherous by the hour.

My mother keeps us up late
Crating eggs with her.
Dinner was over hours ago.

Then in the dark, we light a candle
And hold each egg up to it
Illuminating its obscure insides.

—*L. R.*

And so the poems developed, and his understanding of his life with them, the poems feeding the life and then the newly felt life feeding the poems. It was not long until his previously unacknowledged passionate concerns began to filter into his work. Now, some years later, he has given up his commercial work, has left the state, and is devoting himself to his newborn child and a book.

Summer Storm
She huddles us on the root-cellar steps. Upstairs is like the world we enter at birth—flashes of light under the door, loud pounding.

But down here, we're unplugged from the technological age.

We drift on an island far out from our fathers, far out from the mainland where they raise the long bridge of the coming light, the dark spans over which they drive home.

Our mothers consider their greatest of works the egg,

Their most sacred of temples, a chicken coop covered with tar paper,

And their gentlest comfort the warmth under the brood hen where my hand lingered one chill morning in the straw . . . So nice and toasty I drew the rest of myself in and lived my life out there. She cooed sweet songs. She tucked me in under her silk breast when big owls laid low in the sky.

Eventually, the thunder lets up and the rain tapers down to a steady march. I have the feeling our fathers are mustered off to war again. That they're ordered up the washed-out road, and bear down on the seemingly empty farmhouses at the top.

The enemy himself could be lying in wait, who knows? They kick in the kitchen door and the cellar door; they bust into the henhouse. Maybe the enemy's wife and children, or maybe only his hen and chicks which they bash with their gun butts to feed the ravenous men.

—*L. R.*

The Courage to Create

The territory of the self is a vast, unexplored, and prohibited geography. As was said earlier, our experiences, feelings, insights, understandings are often off-limits. As often as we are imprisoned inside ourselves, so often are we actually living in exile outside ourselves. One can say that one of the basic conditions of contemporary life is the unfulfilled longing of the self for itself.

There are many sources of the loss of self: the hidden, shameful knowledge of incest, or child abuse, or other secrets, which one is coerced to abandon in the padlocked dungeon of the unconscious, is one source that, alas, is becoming terribly familiar. But there are so many others. Contemplative and creative experience is trivialized in the following commonplaces: "What are you doing, lazy, lying there all day, daydreaming?" or "Why are you sitting like a stone contemplating your navel?" As a culture we are increasingly separated. Material things are excessively valued over understanding and expression, while emphasis is placed on doing rather than being. From the belief inculcated in most of us since childhood that we amount to nothing, have nothing to say, have never truly lived, to the devaluation of everything that is not commercial and mainstream, there is ubiquitous disdain for the private, particular, peculiar, the perspective of the feminine, ethnic, elderly, the child, the dream world, the occult, and the mysterious.

When the very self is forbidden, then the individual lives under intolerable conditions and the consequences are dire. We suffer inordinate unhappiness and alienation and inflict our dismay, boredom, and ennui, even our rage, upon those we live among.

Above all, then, writing, whether for ourselves or for others, takes courage—the courage to confront ourselves as well as the courage to confront others. Writers, if they are to fulfill their calling, must ally themselves with what we dare to call "truth." To recognize this truth—the reality, the seriousness of any given situation—is difficult enough, let alone to speak it, to be called to stand by it, to write it, to publish it in the world. Perhaps we can say that to be an artist is to be loyal to a vision when it presents itself, no matter how disruptive or disturbing it may be.

Sometimes we write for the sheer joy of it, sometimes to create utter beauty. At other times, we take on the darker calling of telling truths and secrets, speaking out, bearing witness.

> *It is 2:00 A.M. You can't sleep. But you are not tired. Voices within you demand to be heard. If you do not speak, you believe you will die. If you speak out, you believe you will die. What is it that you must say, and who or what is threatening you if you speak?*

There will be words spoken about this unspoken . . . torture.

—*Ikazo*

Bravery does not make a good poem by itself, but when it has a lyric necessity, then the power of the piece as well as the power of the statement is realized. Sometimes it is sufficient to speak what must be said so that we do not remain isolated within a reality constructed of silence. Writing may save our lives, but not unless we meet its challenge:

don't look. I was poisoned once. don't look. It was that simple. don't think. I must say this. don't speak. The poison was strychnine. don't. the poison took a part of my memory. don't. swept away a portion of my childhood the way a wave takes a footprint on the sand, that clean, that final, the way water sinks in sand. Imagine yourself on a beach walking, you turn to face the sea which is dazzling, you see the sea has always meant something, portended something. The sea is heavy with meaning; it is almost unbearable, the dazzle from the sea, the light from the air, the waves of light bouncing back and forth, sea air air sea sky burning blue. who knew how light could hurt you? You bend down and draw in the sand with one finger the number 8. The wave washes up and takes this number. don't. The poison was never so clean; it was for rats. I knew later the sense of being vermin; then I felt only the revolving backward of my eyes, the slow heavy arch of white, turning backwards, the sensation of falling, spinning slowly backwards. nothing could hurt me. Seven. I am down, down farther, and my limbs, I gave them up willingly, take my limbs. I don't want them. I give my body up. Six and no where. now where? where no words are, no words can save me, can't talk myself out of this or into anything . . . words rush apart, words fly off out of my mouth off pages words repel each other the secret force that binds words dissolved, the antiword scatters words there are no words left, Five. None that you can understand. Four. Imagine the stream of a flowing unbroken life in memory, flowing out of a childhood of color. It was not that I had not been hurt. Three. There was some sinew holding my life together, a rope of memory, my life strung along a strand of lights on wire what I remembered a ribbon I felt then I knew everything I ever was. Two. not good, damaged, yes, but continuous, I could remember the earth tones of the squirrel when I was, how old was I? the gaze the perfect clarity, the awful innocence. One. one feels not good but continuous, my life rearing back falling back the heaviness of the poison I've always said, "I don't give a fuck who raped me . . ." it was not that, well, not for more than a few days, it was the ribbon running backwards the reversal of the power of words loss words scattered like leaves the theft my childhood. zero.

—*Marsha de la O*

Sometimes it is not permission to speak but permission to be silent that our soul requires. Sometimes creativity is able to offer us that silence, and that silence can become the ground for creativity.

Once the venerable Zen master, Thich Nhat Hanh, suggested that we bring the practice of meditation into our art form. He suggested that we meditate, write a little, meditate again, write a little, and so on.

This is the poem that I wrote with those instructions.

No Words for Rumi
Silence pours into me
as a cataract of wine
overflowing the sides
of a glass chasm.
If I do not speak
I will die.
If I speak
This silence which has become my breath
will disappear.
How can I pretend
these are not words
or how can I speak
when I am drinking
and under water?

And the order of things,
the wine flooding
down the mountain,
it is so sweet
I fear
there is no end to it.[7]

The Passion of Creativity

To undertake to write is to set out on a journey into the self. It is to be surrounded by all the terrors and resistances that accompany any serious quest. In overcoming one's intractable ignorance, one's fear of the consequences of whatever new knowledge may bring, one enters a process that distinguishes the inauthentic from the authentic self.

Under the best of circumstances, the process of writing allows one to give oneself over to the imagination, trusting that it will act in one's best interests, trusting that the use of the creative, the descent in language into the self, the rigorous scrutiny of the psyche, the inclination to dare the unknown will seriously enhance one's life. For certain groups—the abused, the elderly, the marginalized, women, the physically ill or disabled—the story may be the only way someone can know that he or she exists. Sometimes the simple willingness to explore one's life story asserts the reality of the individual, which is otherwise so often undermined. And as it is almost impossible to disentangle or distinguish the process of writing from one's development as a person, this, in itself, is the beginning of healing.

In May of 1990 I had a dream that aroused and perplexed me:

> I am looking for wrapping paper for a gift which is to be given to me. Ultimately, I realize the gift, a horse, is to compensate me for something, an imminent loss. But then, I am riding bareback on the horse in the late afternoon, passing small houses as I am drawn toward a lonely beach to see the sunset from the bluffs alongside the sea. I am entranced by the feel of the horse between my legs and the dangerous speed at which we are traveling. The light is falling and the horse is dark, burnished black, and sleek. As I feel overwhelming love, unity, and sexuality, I become aware of the presence of a young very gifted artist, who has suffered greatly in her life, behind me on the horse. When I realize she is behind me, I am filled with joy.

These are some of the notes that I wrote in my journal in response to the dream.

The dream of the horse which arouses my passion comes at the beginning of this writing retreat, which I know will be a period of great change. The animal and my creativity are one. The animal, the sexual, and the creative are one. The wounded artist who rides with me resembles the wounded healer. I am reminded that the utter beauty of her work was forged in the suffering she endured. This dark beautiful horse which I have been given to ride is the creative. Riding the horse, I am aroused, inflamed, impassioned. And the wounded artist who can bring the darkness and the beauty together is riding the horse with me. The artist and the creative come together, despite or in response to the wound, until everything shines with an eerie dark light, like the burnished black of the horse of creativity between my flanks, which I have been given to ride.

The creative carries us. It takes us on the journey to wherever it is that we must go. Sometimes the way is arduous, sometimes it is terrifying, sometimes too swift. But these conditions are compensated for by the beauty and meaning that also belong to this journey. In my life, it never occurred to me to reject the gift of the dark horse, no matter what loss I sustained in order to have it. Nor would I reject the presence of the wounded artist within myself, as the wound is one means by which we reach compassion.

Part II

On Story

All suffering is bearable
if it is seen as part of a story.

Isak Dinesen

Stories move in circles. They don't move in straight lines.
So it helps if you listen in circles. There are stories inside stories
and stories between stories, and finding your way through them
is as easy and as hard as finding your way home.
And part of the finding is the getting lost.
And when you're lost, you start to look around and to listen.

*Corey Fischer, Albert Greenberg, and Naomi Newman
of A Traveling Jewish Theatre,* Coming from a Great Distance

Every Life Is a Story

When I ask a gift from my death, it is that at the last minute I will be able to look back over my life and know, without any doubt, the entire story I have been living. As this final gift, all the details and events that I have been relentlessly ordering my entire life will arrange themselves in a simple and startlingly beautiful structure, until meaning—surprising and dazzling—flashes out of the dank, sticky, and entwined chrysalis of daily life. Then I will know, despite pain, disappointment, and limitation, that this life of mine has been a good and meaningful work.

> It seems
> the story of my life
> is the story of trees I've loved,
> some are standing, some fell down.[1]

Every life is a story. Telling the story and seeing our life as story are part of the creative process. Under the best of circumstances, the process of writing allows us to give ourselves over to the realm of the imagination, trusting that within it, we act in the best interest of the self. Sometimes the simple willingness to explore story asserts the reality of the individual, and then the creative process of finding and telling the story becomes part of the way that we construct a life. Our life becomes a story that we are always in the process of discovering and also fashioning, a story in which we both follow and lead—a story that grips us with its necessity, possesses us unmercifully, and yet, paradoxically, that we create and recreate.

In this life, those willing to live in the imagination, walk that odd path between the inevitable and the spontaneous, between the ancient and the unique, between what is given to us and what we make, between what belongs to history—the history of our people and our culture—and what is as quintessentially ours as the sound of our own voice.

The story of our life is the substance of it. And our story is also the cross we bear. It can, simultaneously, be both our joy and our suffering, our enlightenment and our ignorance.

I am in something now. I am in this story of me and my mother. This FIRST story. My story. I need to know this story. In one million ways, I need to know this story.

As much as I hate this story, it is MY story and I have always wanted to know MY story. It is the place for me to stand. The true and deepest knowledge of this story with all of the accompanying feelings, thoughts, emotions, ideas is my foundation. It is the place for me to stand although I cannot even talk about it yet.

—*Barbara Lipscomb*

Not Claiming Our Own Story

There's an old folktale called "The Sorrow Tree": for aeons, people complained continuously and piteously to God. Unable to bear it, God suggested that they hang their sorrow on the Sorrow Tree. Then they were to choose any sorrow they wished from among those hanging there. They circled and circled the tree, looking for the very sorrow that would be exactly fitting and bearable, the one sorrow that would fulfill them. But after much searching, each inevitably reclaimed his or her own pain.

Whatever our story is, we must come to know it. It is given to us the way we are given ourselves; it is the source and the record of our identity. Perhaps story is the only thing we have at the end of our lives, and it is everything.

Imagine that you are at the end of your life. Without hesitating, without thinking, record the story you have lived in five sentences.

It is difficult for us to give up our grief because it is ours and through it we create identity. But sometimes the story, or the sorrow, to which we are clinging is no longer dependable. Story, if we allow it, can also trap us. It can become the treadmill, the rut. It can ravage and reduce us rather than inform and expand our life. One can be as zealous in creating a false story as another might be in discovering the authentic one.

Repeatedly telling a cover story is one of the ways we avoid the one story we must come to know. Offered the opportunity to know the deepest story, we tell the very same cover tale again, ever more ardently, out of fear of being in the unknown, out of self-pity, self-righteousness, out of despair. Refusing to relinquish these misbegotten tales, we find ourselves choosing a life that has nothing to do with our own.

Stalking the Authentic Tale

"Do you have a story to tell about your ethnic background?" I once asked Dan Saucedo.

"There is no story," he said. "My parents are completely assimilated. We never talk about Mexico, and it doesn't matter to us."

Is there a story, then, of their assimilation? I wanted to ask him this question but didn't. He was adamant that there was no story to be told, and I felt it would be disrespectful to insist. But my intuition persisted. The way he insisted on the absence of story sounded like an amputation, and I wanted to know about the missing limb. Over time I suggested there might be a story, and over the same period of time, circumstances alerted Dan to the possibility that another story might be hovering beneath the one he was telling of his cultural neutrality.

Indeed, he discovered that his grandfather had kept a journal at the turn of the century during the first years that he had come to this country from Mexico. This discovery opened a door into story that Dan could not have predicted. It took Dan back into the past, and it changed his future. A few years ago, following the trail of this story, he went to Mexico; there in the remote mountains he discovered, as he told it, "villages of people looking exactly like me."

> The exploration of the Grandfather is a rummaging through the forbidden story, which was admitting I am Mexican. Being born in the fifties meant Mexican was a socially incorrect nationality, especially in Covina. I did not learn Spanish when it was mandatory in the lower grades, because it took me one step closer to the bloodline I was denying. "Mexican? No, no. That's not me." When light-colored blacks passed as white, I passed as Italian. By using my imagination, I was able to approach my heritage through the back door. It was a way of easing into the current without knowing it.
>
> —*Daniel David Saucedo*

An authentic story is open-ended. It can change. It can be transformed, and it has elements of the unknown. It combines all the elements until everything fits. It resembles other stories sometimes exactly, giving us the impression that we have been here before, and yet there is also something mysterious about it, something ambiguous, even contradictory, and that part is equally fascinating. We are consoled by the familiar and intrigued by what we don't know. Here is one way to evaluate a story's authenticity: if you think you know the entire story, you're outside of it. You are in illusion.

The exploration of the Grandfather is a jumbled story with three primary sources: the image of the ideal mentor grandfather; my maternal grandfather, of whom little is known, except that he was an Indian from Mexico who loved to play music and left when my mother was young; and, lastly, my paternal grandfather, who was a working-class property owner from Zacatecas, Mexico, and whom I know through his journal and the stories my father tells.

In your workshop, my imagination was freed to create a composite grandfather. My maternal grandfather left twenty years before I was born, and my paternal grandfather died eight years before I was born. Thus, knowing something of them, but not too much, gave my imagination a foundation and the freedom to explore the prism of heritage. The three images fused into a single character—the teachings of one, stirred in with the mysticism of the second, infused with the practical world of the third.

By submitting to the trance of creation in the grandfather stories, I was not distracting myself from the exploration of heritage, because I did not realize heritage was the topic I was uncovering. I was having a good time being intimate with the images the imagination provided. I was having fun as a writer. The stories did not lead to an epiphany of acceptance that I was Mexican. They were more subtle. They opened the possibility of traveling through Mexico in search of my grandfathers' homes. Somehow, through the cycle of writing and exploration in the real world, the stigma of being Mexican was erased. Somehow, there became value in being Mexican. I could tell people I was Mexican without worrying that something bad would happen. My acceptance of being Mexican was a by-product of the work, not the quest. The value of the work is not the epiphany but the intimate engagement of the imagination which subtly opens the doors of possibility.

If admitting I was Mexican was the forbidden story, I think the key word is Story. In your class, the imagination is used to engage material which cannot be approached directly, partly because too many real-world details limit the subconscious power of the imagination. The importance of telling story after story, either from the imagination or the real world, is that this kind of work/writing we engage in is an archaeological dig. Getting to the real story and doing the real work is an excavation filled with tremendous discoveries; and just when we think we have it down, we discover an unknown culture buried beneath the city we have been painstakingly excavating. That may be why some of our profound stories, in my case the forbidden stories, take so long to discover; they were so well hidden that we never knew they existed.

—*Daniel David Saucedo*

All the Possible Stories

There are different kinds of stories. There are our own stories about who we are and what has happened to us. There are stories about other people and events that happen to them. Sometimes the focus is on character and sometimes on the event. Sometimes the story reveals a person, sometimes it describes a mood, and sometimes it explores circumstances. Exploration, description, revelation are at the heart of story, as they are at the heart of authentic or vital lives.

Some writers never write about themselves because they are private, or because they do not believe it is possible for one to say anything objectively truthful or valid about oneself. Other writers never write about anyone but themselves, for the same reason: because they do not believe it is possible to say anything truthful or valid about another. We have all had someone say to us, "I don't know you at all," while someone else has said, "I know you better than you know yourself." Some of us use microscopes, some of us use telescopes; some look within, some look without, but all serious writers, private and public, are engaged in a common task: to see something as it is and to reveal it without distortion.

Whether we are using ourselves and our personal experience or we are creating fictions, what we write must derive from something we know deeply. It is not necessary to have experienced it directly, but it is necessary that we refrain from falsifying reality and that our intelligence, intuition, and heart validate what we write.

In some ways, whether we set it on the page or not, it is necessary that we know our own story before we attempt to understand others. Knowing ourselves can be a useful measure through which we can approach others. It is not that we expect anyone to resemble us exactly but that self-knowledge activates and substantiates our knowledge of the world.

To write, we must know ourselves. But in writing, we *make* ourselves known; we not only come to understanding but we make something. At its best, writing is a completely creative activity—something exists afterward that was not there before. Accordingly, there are consequences of even the most fanciful things we write, especially if we allow ourselves to illuminate and give voice to unconscious, unarticulated, unenacted aspects of self.

"You gotta tell the people whatcha gonna tell 'em. Then, you gotta tell 'em. Then you got to back up and tell 'em what you done tole 'em," says the wise storyteller Junebug

Jabbo Jones, played by writer-actor John O'Neal. And he does tell us three times, because the story matters so much, we must know it in all its nuances or we will know nothing. Until recently, every culture had storytellers who knit together the fabric of society with their yarns, recollections, and parables. Sometimes these bards were saints, but they were just as likely to be rascals upon whose flamboyant honesty the society depended.

Those storytellers are gone, replaced for the most part by the hucksters of commercial culture. Stories surround us, but they are not stories upon which we can depend, for we do not demand that they be the fruits of lives deeply lived. With alarming frequency, those who select or promote the stories we read or see refuse the complex or disturbing tale for something far more simple, even simplistic.

American television, in particular, and increasingly American publishing— alas, most commercial media—have the tendency to reduce life to the flat and pat. This pervasive trivialization dominates the postmodern world, where life models itself on superficial images and four dimensions are increasingly reduced to two. Soon we become oblivious to the consequences, which are our constricted and unsatisfying lives.

Joseph Chilton Pearce, who recalls a girl who preferred radio to television because "the pictures were so much more beautiful," also informs us that "the Jungian psychologist Frances Wickes found that many later childhood dysfunctions resulted from a lack of storytelling, fantasy play, and imaginative ventures in the prelogical years."[2] It is possible that deprivation in the postlogical years is even more dire. As economic goals begin to shape literature, formulas developed to ensure commercial success have little relationship to things as they are, and the truth and meaning of our lives cannot be contained within such limitations. Whatever motivates the distortion of reality, it is not literary. Genre fiction—murder mysteries, spy novels, horror stories, and the like—are designed to avoid considering what it means to hunt or be hunted, to inflict pain, to kill; in contrast, these are the very concerns of literature. Regularly entertained rather than confronted or confounded by death, we acquiesce to the gradual erosion of meaning. We buy designer plots and designer jeans. Stories so fashioned, so essentially predictable, are amoral.

> *Have you ever met a true storyteller? The proverbial old salt, the wanderer, the old wise woman, the beggar, the bawd, the troubadour, the raconteur, Scheherazade? Remember one of his or her stories and try to write it in the appropriate vernacular with all its subtlety and innuendo. And if you have never met one, imagine yourself as the storyteller in your community. Write down a story from your life as you might tell it, with all its bravado and flourishes.*

When we tell a story, we wish to tell more than meets the eye. The bare account might be journalistic, accurate, informative, but not story. Story develops through an amalgam of insights and images from many realms and speaks through a blend of content, form, and language. The shape of the story and how we tell it are intrinsically part of the story.

A story not only has a shape but *is* its shape. It is the pattern through which otherwise random, isolated, and sometimes inconsequential events or experiences are organized. We enter a story through perceiving this intrinsic configuration, understanding that the elements belong to each other, follow from one another for reasons other than chronology. The pattern beneath the tale may be recognizable—an archetypal grid—or it may be unique, but this underlying motif or design tells its own essential tale and is pleasing in ways that have nothing to do with the content.

In story, we are moved by the relationship between the events in a way that each individual event or experience cannot or does not move us by itself. When we perceive beauty, fitness, and grace in the coexistence of the elements of the story, independent of its content, we recognize the necessity of the story.

In a good story, a story that is absolutely right for the components, all the necessary elements are present and all the extraneous elements have been removed—nothing is forced or arbitrary; it has an organic form. Then we experience the shock of recognition of some truth or rightness; we are struck, beyond our ability to doubt, with the absolute presence of meaning. A story has necessity. It pleases us because it exists. When we hear a genuine story, one of our responses is "yes."

Meaning is at the core of the creative process and of storytelling. It is both the goal and the attribute. When it is our own life story we are telling or a story from our lives, we become aware that we are not the victims of random and chaotic circumstances, that we, too, despite our grief or feelings of insignificance, are living meaningfully in a meaningful universe. And, again, the response to our own story, as well as to the stories of others, is "Yes. Yes, I have a story. Yes, I exist."

The Shape of Stories

To know a story is the beginning; to write it down, to shape and refine it are another story altogether.

One evening under the stars, the mathematician Ralph Abraham was explaining the enormous significance of making a model, an artifact, of our knowledge. "People watched the stars turn about the heavens for aeons knowing that they turned, understanding the principle of rotation," he said, "but when they were able to transform this understanding into a model—the wheel—their entire civilization changed."

Similarly, knowing our story, understanding our psyche, and seeing the patterns take us only so far. When we can actually make the model, create the artifact, invent the wheel—write the story in its complexity—we find ourselves in an evolutionary place. On one level, the story, like the picture of the solar system, is an illustration of what we observe. But like the wheel, it is also an artifact in its own right. The formed story can act in us as a wheel acts, as our means of transport—it literally takes us to new places.

A written story is a history. Recording the story gives permanence to what is otherwise eroded each minute of our lives by the nature of time passing and by society's essential indifference to the meaning of private experience. But when written down, a story, no matter how private it remains, also becomes part of the public record.

> *Take an event from your life and write it in the first person: "I went to . . .," or "It happened . . .," or "When I was . . .," and so on. As you write, hold the belief that your life is a story or is composed of several stories. Remember that your story develops from what you tell and what you leave out, that there is neither right nor wrong, nothing that should or should not be included, no place more appropriate to begin or end than another. Write about this for five to thirty minutes.*

> *When you are finished, put the writing away. Sometime later, retrieve the piece and look at it again to discover what the piece is about. What story have you been trying to tell? Are there details that, on review, seem to have been included simply because they occurred and not because they are germane? Were there interesting details or asides you excluded because they seemed oblique? What would emerge if you excluded many of the chronological details but included some of the other images—if you were loyal to the emerging story rather than to the actual details of the event?*

The Story Has Its Own Mind

When the writer's voice begins to resound, it brings with it an urgent desire to tell the truth and a sensitivity to the necessity of story. Even when writing about ourselves or an event that we know well, we sometimes find that the story itself is going elsewhere, that associations are entering that are surprising us, that it is taking a direction we never expected. As it is always possible to come back to the known, it is politic, under these circumstances, to see where the story wants to go.

It is not our task to determine the meaning or substance of a story in advance. Thinking about it is as likely to take us away from its essence as toward it. In telling or writing a story, it is best if we can get out of our own way to find a rhythm that elicits the story in us. Often when we are able to do this, randomness disappears, the unseen becomes visible, and fate, providence, or some mysterious shaping power makes itself known through the certainty of form.

The rational mind can be the greatest enemy of creativity, despite its belief that it is the most important element within us. The direction of the story is often the battlefield between the creative and the mind, between inspiration and willfulness. The mind is an impediment when it cannot separate itself from will. That coalition prohibits understandings that arise from areas beyond its ken. Thinking, like the critical faculty, can inform, enhance, and enrich writing and may sometimes—not always—inspire or instigate writing, but it is not the primary mode of the artistic process. The rational mind cannot work in a field of unlimited variables. It must, as science must, limit the possibilities in order not to be overwhelmed. This limitation, necessary to the logical mode, is deadly to creativity and to the imagination, which thrive on infinite possibilities. Thus, we must try to be aware of those times when the rational mind is limiting our expression. In the battle between creativity and mind, it is worth seeing what happens when we allow creativity to win:

> *Write a story using only the elements that you have eliminated from the previous assignment, a story that emerges from the outtakes.*

> *Next do the opposite: write a story that obediently follows the direction of your mind and will. In this instance, avoid asides, intuitions, bewildering inspirations. What happens when you follow an outline rigorously?*

> *Compare these two with the first story. Which technique is most appropriate for you, and which is most appropriate for the story? Compare the three tales to see the merits and consequences of each of these three directions.*

Just as the mind can distract us from what we want to say, so can the desire to chronicle the literal truth. Omission is one of the primary ways to create falsehood, but including every detail is another way to lose the thread.

In Jorge Luis Borges's story, "Funes, The Memorius," a bedridden man discovers that he has the ability to remember everything. Today he remembers everything he saw and remembered yesterday, even to the configurations of the clouds, and tomorrow he will remember everything he remembered today, which includes everything he remembered the day before, and so on. We can quickly see the dreadful consequences of this prodigious capacity.

Every time we speak, write, or act, we sacrifice completeness. There is nothing we can do fully or perfectly. Given that things will be omitted, moments will be truncated, experiences will, at best, be rendered partially, we learn to communicate through silences and absences as well as through disclosure.

Sometimes we have to override accuracy to create verisimilitude. And sometimes we have to "invent" details to communicate the story fully. In the privacy of our writing studio, we can honestly determine whether we are fabricating to reveal or to conceal. Then we bring ourselves, again, to the discipline of revelation. It's often easier to do this when pretending to be writing about someone else.

When we write stories in the first person, we have the most direct communication between self, writer, and audience. But in the beginning, it may be easier to tell stories in the third person to overcome self-consciousness or inhibition. Writers who are shy of their intelligence when speaking in their own voices about themselves can use the device of a narrator speaking about someone else to stay close to the material. A narrator can bring another perspective altogether to the work.

> *Choose one version of the story just written. Rewrite it in the third person as if you are writing about someone else: "When she went to . . ." or "It happened that he . . .," or "When she was . . ." Or write another version, telling the story from another narrator's perspective. If necessary, fabricate in order to support the emerging direction of this new story. Omit details that undermine the story. Once you have an inkling of what the story might be about, allow the story to lead in the rewriting.*

Organic Form

As you are writing this story again, find the patterns it contains, the shape that seems authentic. Rather than cause and effect, follow coincidences, relationships between images, subtle affinities, repeating metaphors; all of these illuminate the tale.

In *To the Lighthouse*, by Virginia Woolf, the lighthouse itself determines the shape of the novel. A beam of light falls on the story, illuminating one character or event and then another, leaving the former in darkness. There is, in this novel, an intrinsic relationship between the content of the book and its original narrative shape.

However, we can't impose patterns arbitrarily on our lives and hope that they are valid. The pattern we are searching for is the authentic one. It can only be discovered. When we impose a pattern, we are "making something up," and this undermines the work. If Virginia Woolf had arbitrarily imposed a pattern, the novel would not have the same beauty or eloquence. As written, the pattern emerges organically, as if discovered by Woolf at the same time that the excursion to the lighthouse is experienced by her characters.

My early writing was both brazen and hermetic; I was caught between the passion to reveal and the injunction to hide. A style developed from this. I can even say that I learned to write through the rub of these contradictions against each other. Predetermined conditions or forms would probably not have contained this paradox; something would have been omitted—the very essence of the dilemma that ultimately generated the work.

A story is like a lens or a frame: it gives focus, it unifies, it organizes diverse images into a coherent meaning. Without the frame or focus, the events would be random and disconnected. Story provides the relationship, the links, the connections. One of the reasons we tell stories is that the existence and the nature of relationships become clear in the process of telling.

There is a story in the smallest moments and in the largest. There is a large story that each one of us is living into which all the other stories fit, like one Russian doll into another. It is the shape of this story that I would ultimately like to see before I die. But this larger story has other component stories, has parallel stories, has stories within stories, all of which coexist with our one life story. One story does not cancel out the other story. Nor does the coexistence of several stories, sometimes contradictory, mean that one or the other is inauthentic. Whether we see the small story or the larger story that contains it depends only on our perspective. What might be a detail from one perspective becomes the subject of an entire story from another.

A story is enlivened by details, by the insights and associations that flesh it out, take it deeper, give it a larger perspective, put it in another context, relate it to other experiences.

> List four things that happened to you today. If it has been a particularly uneventful day, you are fortunate, because you have the opportunity to discover that story resides in the smallest and quietest moments. Free associate on these four events until each event is connected with at least three other events or moments, whether current, past, future, or imaginary.
>
> Next, list three often peripheral or oblique moments, observations from today's experience; that is, connect at least three other contemporary events or experiences to the original four.
>
> Examine all of these events, moments, or associations as if they were completely neutral phenomena. Is there a pattern that connects any of them? What affinities exist among the several associations? What relationships emerge?
>
> Make a story from these connections, fleshing them out until they form a whole.

Barbara Lipscomb's List:

I. I sat on the couch with Colin and Sarah watching a music video as they drank their bottles. I said something about Sarah's tummy as I changed her diaper. Colin lifted his shirt and pointed to his tummy.

Lori's doctor couldn't find the embryo on the ultrasound, only the placenta.

Geoff came home early.

II. How nice it must be for them to have parents like ourselves. Lori and I in high school together. I couldn't wait for Lori to come home.

How many things one must learn to do at one time when one is a mom.

How irresponsible a doctor can be: "If we can't find it Monday, we'll schedule a D & C." Thank God, she got a second opinion. The anxiety of waiting until we know if everything will be OK with this pregnancy.

Thank goodness! I am drained and want to leave.

I need real day care. Exhaustion.

III. The gardeners working outside.

Photos of Sarah and her grandparents on the neatly arranged shelf.

I wanted to call my mom. I wanted a mom.

I really wanted to go home and take a nap.

I wondered if I could ever handle two kids.

I loved doing the dishes and straightening up the toys.

I loved Colin caressing my arm while he was drinking his bottle. He won't always sleep in a crib.

I wanted to write a piece that has been jelling, but there was too little time.

Should Lori have to go through this after the miscarriage?

This is the piece that emerged from these lists:

It began early. Our days always do. I stole one edge of the diaper bag for my journal and a book I am reading, placed them in there neatly just in case both kids napped at the same time. Just in case I had a moment to myself today.

Sometimes I really wonder how fit I am to be a mom. Things are easy at Lori's. Things fall into place there. I look around her house. It is neat and clean. There are photos of Sarah and her grandparents on the shelf. There are videos, Nintendo, a gardener, a garage with tools. There is a dining room set, a cordless telephone, clean carpets, a memo board with emergency numbers, toys, an extra key. My apartment is not this way.

After lunch, I love to wash the dishes, wipe the counter, run the disposal, wrap the leftovers, clean the high chair. I love to cluster the toys, connect the train tracks, and throw all the garbage away. I am amazed that everything falls out when there is a baby or two around.

How can Lori possibly be ready for another baby? Will I ever be ready? Things will fall into place for her. That is how it is with Lori.

I wonder how people get to be one way or another. I wonder if it gets a lot easier once you realize you are different than most of the world.

—*Barbara Lipscomb*

This is how a story develops, from small moments and insights that cluster together, the way a life is organized from the bits and pieces of our days. The random events, the random thoughts become a whole through the understanding of the imagination.

Return to the writing suggestion from the first chapter: that you write your life story in a short period of time. Take thirty minutes to write your autobiography this time in the third person as if you are telling someone else's story. Remember that you can't tell everything, not even everything that matters, for if you could it would take forever.

Afterward, consider not the story so much as the subjects you have chosen to address. You may have followed chronology and started with your birth, or you may have written about love, parents, friendship, work, or schooling. Perhaps you chose to tell one moment, allowing it to stand for the whole, or perhaps you recounted several events and allowed yourself to emerge through their relationship. There are an infinite number of ways in which we can approach ourselves; each is valid and legitimate. For some, it will seem as if the story is incomplete, as if some areas—dreams, suffering, sexuality, politics, spiritual practice—are omitted, while others will have different concerns. Here it is not only the specific details that concern us but the categories of interest that reveal something of who we are and the new perspective which emerges from the point of view of the "narrator."

Listing the Stories

I like to make lists. Once it amused me to keep a journal with a formal title—"The Book of Lists: A Writer's Journal." The lists became a catalogue of ways in which I could approach my life, ways to remember experiences by categorizing them. In that book, I kept lists like the following: stories about my body; synchronicities and miracles; visions; childhood friends; mentors; recurrent dream images; stories about my children; gifts received. This last list began:

> A velvet cloth tightly rolled about lavender, camphor, cloves, and spices; snake earrings with lapis lazuli eyes; four friends appearing at dawn, singing; the femur of an elk; a 100-page handwritten response to a novel I had written; the set of knives I coveted for years, a gift from my children; a talking stick; a cup with the inscription, "Storytelling is at the heart of human experience."

Recently I added a category: lists of lists to be made. Here I included: losses; death stories; memories of nature; stories that help me survive; teaching stories; bird stories; wolf stories. Needless to say, the lists overlap. But when the same story possibility appears on several lists, the story itself is altered by the different perspective of each list.

Under each category I wrote the names or a few words or a sentence to capture the particular event. Under body stories, I included: "stepping on a spike on the beach when I was ten; wading in the grand indoor fountain of the Ambassador Hotel; knowing the instants Marc and Greg were conceived." Under stories about my children, I wrote, "The milk coming in just after Marc was born. Playing cards in the labor room without realizing Greg was crowning. The three of us in yellow rain slickers and black boots walking together in the stormy night."

I once heard someone say that the mind is one part of the brain telling a story to the other part. Perhaps the self is the composite of all those stories told.

Here is a list of lists that you might amplify. You may wish to begin these lists at once, adding stories to them as you think of them, or you may select one category and concentrate on it, choosing another category another time.

Stories from your childhood.

Stories your parents and siblings tell about you. (My parents like to recall that I called a cow a "moo" when I first started speaking.)

Stories your parents, siblings, children tell about their lives. (When my father was living in England, he had an accurate vision of his brother dying at the Russian front.)

Morality tales your parents tell in order to shape your behavior. (My mother tells a story about going to school in poor, worn-out shoes stuffed with newspaper after her brother insisted that she had to study.)

Stories you habitually tell about your parents, siblings, children, lovers.

Family stories. The stories that are traditionally repeated at family events, the ones that create social cohesion and are the ways of sustaining family history and culture.

Stories that you tell strangers about your family in order to create intimacy and reveal character.

Stories you tell to strangers, to new acquaintances, potential friends in order to introduce yourself.

Stories you tell about love, travel, and adventure so the high points of your life may be known.

Cultural tales. Teaching stories, inspiring stories, ethnic stories. Stories you tell in order to illustrate your values, to sustain you and others, or to bind you to your ancestors, your people or tribe.

Stories that reflect your beliefs, your family's beliefs, values, fears, understandings of the nature of people, the world, the universe. These may be stories you've heard and cherished or events from your own life.

Stories for your most intimate associates. Those moments that you will tell to a prospective lover or potentially dear friend to reveal yourself, to see if you will be accepted.

Stories so intimate you believe they will bind you to someone forever.

Lies you tell so often they have become truths.

Stories you will never tell anyone.

Stories you will never tell, not even to yourself.

I began this list with family stories because these earliest stories determine what we later recognize as story. These stories are the origin of our unique minds; they shape our understanding of experience and establish how we see and know the world. The smaller stories of our personal lives and that of our family are amplified by the larger stories of community and tribe. In the movement from the personal to the collective, opinions become values and responses become encoded as ideas. What we think and what we believe are formed as much by the stories we've heard as by the books we've studied. Indeed, unless we examine these stories, we may not be aware of the ideas and convictions that regulate our lives. Once we recognize these influences from the more public world, we can return to studying the very uncommon person that we are.

Relevant knowledge of the self rests in this dynamic between the individual and the world. For some of us, our sense of self may develop from our commitment to certain ideas or ideals, while for others it may derive from a passion for the color blue. In either case, it is the commitment and the passion that want to be known.

> *After you finish one or a few lists, read them aloud to yourself. You may be surprised by the portrait that emerges from this shorthand record of a life.*

When my husband, Michael Ortiz Hill, himself a poet, read this section, he told me he'd once written his life story through his associations with fire. As a young boy, he had burned down the garage during the time of the Vietnam war and the Watts riots. The "fire next time" had resonated through his childhood; he had believed that everything was combustible.

Now it occurred to him to retell his life three more times, one for each of the remaining elements: water, air, earth. The last intrigued him most for it would include childhood adventures with ant hills, getting lost in caves, his affinity for enclosed places. "Earth," he says, "is about darkness, about the body, about the ambiguity between being planted and being buried."

> *Tell your life story through your relationship to the four elements.*

Sometimes all we need to begin writing is a title that will open a path. It was the title "The Man Who Saw Fire" that inspired Michael Hill to write. These lists we've made, the stories contained within them, lend themselves to a series of titles that could become pieces.

> *Translate the items on the list into titles. Then write a series of portraits or self-portraits based on the stories on the list: "The Woman Whose Mother Said . . ." or "The Man Who Always Heard . . ."*

Making a list serves two purposes. The first is that, willy-nilly, the list comprises a self-portrait of who we are. The second is that it can sustain us in those dark times when we are afraid we have nothing to say. Young or aspiring writers are often plagued by variations on the fear of having nothing to say: that nothing has happened to them and they have nothing to say; that they are not interesting and they have nothing to say; that they are not thoughtful enough and have nothing to say. Sometimes one is even tortured by the passion, longing, or determination to write about the abysmal feeling that one has nothing to say but is stymied because of feeling one may not even have anything to say about this. Making the lists is one way to address this problem.

The Dream Police

One of my favorite exercises, based on list making, alerts us to the essential particulars from which we make a self.

> *Suddenly there is a knock at your door. A trusted friend enters to warn you that the Dream Police will arrive in twenty minutes. Everything, everything in your life, that you have not written down will evaporate upon their arrival. You have a short time—twenty minutes—to preserve what is most precious in your life, what has formed you, what sustains you. Whatever you forget, whatever you have no time to record, will disappear. Everything you want must be acknowledged in its particularity. Everything, to be saved, must be named. Not trees, but oak. Not animal, but wolf. Not people, but Alicia. As in reality, what has no name, no specificity, vanishes.*

We are what matters to us. Our identity materializes through images, memories, events, and through things. In this exercise we select what is essential to us, what has formed us, what we cannot live without; this as often includes grief, losses, and failures as it does joy and triumph.

Once I found that I couldn't do the exercise because I couldn't bring myself to exclude the Holocaust. If I included it, I would feel responsible for its existence. If I excluded it, I would be positing a fool's paradise. This dilemma was so strong, I chose to write about it at length. By default, I claimed the Holocaust as I investigated my preoccupation with it.

Barbara Myerhoff collected "survivor's stories" from elderly Jews in Los Angeles. One story concerned a young Polish Jew who was told by his mother to pack a shoe box with what was important to him so that he would be ready if they had to leave suddenly. Because he couldn't decide what to take, he packed two shoe boxes, one with a comb, a handkerchief, some food, socks, gloves, and another box with his treasures, a few letters, photographs, books, and mementos. One day, his mother entered the house, shouting, "Now! Run!" He picked up one shoe box and ran. When he opened the shoe box on the train, he was bereft. "How useless these things are. What am I going to do with them? How will they help my life?"

When I was going through Barbara's papers after her death, I found this story among others in her file. But I found two versions of it! In the first, the boy chose the box of photographs, but in the second version, he chose the items of daily life. It is easy to understand how his dismay was applicable to both boxes. For many years, I agitated about the story. Which choice was the correct one? But however much I agonized over the solution, when I had the opportunity to ask the original storyteller which version was correct, I kept silent.

It was through the Dream Police exercise that I discovered I couldn't live without history. My list included the life of Socrates, the writing of the Bill of Rights, and the French Revolution, as well as the afternoon I washed my hair in a downpour, then rowed through the water lilies on a mountain lake. I remembered the performance of *Waiting for Godot* on Broadway, roller skating when I learned that FDR had died, seeing fabrics wildly thrown from the windows in the New York garment district as World War II ended in Europe, and the solemn moment when I learned the atom bomb had been exploded. I remembered huddling before a television set in Jerusalem as a Hebrew-speaking commentator rhapsodized incomprehensibly about the astronaut walking on the moon. I recorded walking across the field on my wedding day and the awesome rainfall that caused floods in Topanga where I live. And, to my great distress, I forgot music. Each time I do the exercise, the list changes. If I were to make a list today, I might only record, after those people I love, the names of animals, birds, and trees.

In one class, a woman listened to our lists with astonishment. When it was her turn to read, I understood why. She had been afraid to imagine a life without the structures and institutions of urban living. She spent the entire time listing her life-support systems—the bank, her bank account, the stock market, grocery store, pharmacy, gasoline station, her car, garage, department stores, credit cards, and so on. I am afraid that she will have to take care of all of us in the future, for in all the time I've been suggesting this exercise, no one else has ever attended to the business of life.

After you have made this list, put it aside for a while. Then examine it:

> As earlier, imagine that you are an anthropologist who has unearthed this list of "possessions" that once belonged to some "unknown" person. Write a portrait fleshing out that person, speculating on his or her character and life.

On one occasion, the "anthropologist" studying a list wrote:

> This is a marginal woman. She is afraid the police will come and take everything from her. Still, when she prepares for flight, she takes nothing substantial. Perhaps she had very little. Perhaps she only had rituals—blowing out candles, prostrating herself before a holy icon. When she started menstruating, her mother slapped her "so she'd always have rosy cheeks." Then as now, women were concerned with their appearance. Rosy cheeks were important to that society. Each year her mother brought her a dish of the first snow to wash her cheeks so they'd be rosy forever. . . .

—Clara Bowles

All the Voices Within Us Become Story

I think about story arising from or developing around character. Some people think of plot first, of moment and event, but for me, story has a person at the heart of it: the one who undergoes an ordeal or is altered by experience, the one to whom something happens or who makes something happen. Even in my second novel, *What Rough Beast,* it was the tiger protagonist who was the focus rather than the conditions or events that surrounded his existence. When I write, a character always leads me through event. Creating a portrait can be the beginning of finding or learning the story.

The characters I write about are and are not based upon myself; I am not the only person within myself. Our familiar selves are not the only ones we have to work with nor the only ones we explore. Each of us is an exceedingly complex being, containing so many selves that we are more like communities or large populations than single individuals. These different selves, so many of whom are unknown to us on a conscious level, are those whom we must contact as we struggle toward self-knowledge and toward a deeper and more authentic means of understanding others. They are the basis of our understanding of ourselves as well as the core from which fiction emerges. Here again, the writing process that takes us in also leads us out. We build the same bridges to reach the inner and outer worlds.

> *Listen to your interior voices in order to identify them. Allow the different parts of yourself to coalesce into characters. Imagine that they are part of a community—a family, a village, a city. Then imagine that you, the writer, are approaching this community for the first time. Which individuals are most compelling to you? Seek out a few with whom you wish to acquaint yourself. Enter into their homes. Let them speak to you. Record the dialogues. Allow them to interact. A story can be told in many forms. Write about their connection in any form that seems appropriate.*

> *A story need not be confined to the story form. You may find yourself writing a play like* Our Town *or a long poem like "Spoon River Anthology" or small terse interior monologues.*

Who do you become when you identify yourself in this way?

To discover the nature of others inside us may require a creative ruse or literary sleight of hand, even though the task is not different from understanding others in the world. The ability to enter into the psyche of another being, real or imaginary, is the root task of creativity and an essential requirement for being in relationship and living in the world. If we cannot imagine and feel the experience of another different from ourselves, then we are not in dialogue or vitally connected to others. There is nothing more lonely than to discover that one has, despite all one's efforts, only been talking with or about oneself.

The Story That Holds Our History

Story has a collective as well as a personal function. At the end of what we might call the century of psychology, it is not theory but stories that are informing us about human nature. Alarmed by the grave threat to cultural diversity through the dominance of an increasingly monolithic global culture, many find an antidote in gathering stories and pursuing life histories. The reemergence of the storyteller in her traditional role of cohering society is a sign of the conviction that stories can sustain us. Stories provide a bulwark against the erosion of our personal and collective histories.

It was because Barbara Myerhoff was far less interested in the data than in preserving the stories of the Huichol Indians in Mexico that the shaman Ramón Medina Silva agreed to pass on his knowledge to her, much of which she subsequently published in *Peyote Hunt.* It was also her great passion for story that created a link with a group of elderly Jews in Venice, California, whose tradition has always been encoded in stories. Her book, *Number Our Days,* in addition to rendering and even preserving this culture through the gathering of its stories, has also become a basic text on the significance of life history and storytelling. Similarly, because the writer Victor Perera was interested in story, he was able to persuade the venerable Chan K'in of the similarly endangered Lacandon Indians to pass on his knowledge and that of his people, which Victor published in *The Last Lords of Palenque.*

What was clear to both tribal seers has taken most of us so long to understand: that it is in story that the teachings lie. This is in part the theme of the extraordinary novel, *The Storyteller,* by Mario Vargas Llosa:

> Talking the way a storyteller talks means being able to feel and live in the very heart of that culture, means having penetrated its essence, reached the marrow of its history and mythology, given body to its taboos, images, ancestral desires and terrors. It means being, . . . one of that ancient lineage who . . . roamed the forests . . . bringing and bearing away those tales, lies, fictions, gossip, and jokes that make a community of that people of scattered beings, keeping alive among them the feeling of oneness, ... constituting something fraternal and solid.

In our culture, the grandmother who tells her story feels the imperative to give meaning to her life by passing it on to others, while the grandson who collects the story is himself substantiated by this gathering of his history. Teller and listener become partners in the insistence that individual lives matter.

For some people, the desire for history has come too late, after relatives have died or have become inarticulate. For some, the few stories that are transmitted are inadequate to convey the texture of the life that went before. Then the inquirer is left with the dilemma of the fiction writer, the need to create a layered, detailed narrative out of bits and pieces of memory, anecdotes, random conversations, faint particles of history. Sometimes we have no alternative but to make up a history or remain bereft. Although this approach goes against everything we've learned about research, objectivity, and the scientific method, the disparaged imagination remains capable of rendering a convincing fabric from a few disconnected threads.

When we ask ourselves to speak in the voice of the other, we do just that; a voice emerges that is very different from our own. The longer we stay in the other's voice— the more we aid the process by taking on the posture, speech patterns, body, and character of the other—the more completely we can enter that person's psyche, understanding, and perspective. Things we don't know we know emerge. Words, ideas we would never expect to utter are spoken by us. Sometimes the transformation is so complete, we might imagine we are possessed. But it is the opposite; perhaps it is we who possess the other.

> *Enter into the body of your grandfather (or grandmother). Imagine his body, the clothes he's wearing, the feel of his skin and bones. Watch your posture change. What feelings accompany the shift? Move carefully through the decades of his life, as you remember or imagine them, until you come upon him in his old age. Look at his old hands. Put yourself into those hands. When you recognize them as yours, acknowledge the history that has accumulated in them. What is it like to have such hands? Ask him to "speak" about his hands. Ask him to remember an important moment: the onset of puberty, his first job, coming to this country, his marriage, a moment of defeat, a moment of triumph, how it felt to believe what he did, what wisdom he would like to leave with you. . . . Enter into the moment before his death. . . .*
>
> *Allow his voice to take over, evoking the rhythms of his speech and the particulars of his vocabulary. Disappear into the emerging character.*

After you read what you have written, you may well wonder where this fictive voice originated. Certainly, it is possible to construct a character from the observations made and knowledge accumulated over the years. But there is often a sense, when we give ourselves over to the imagination, that what we write is the expression of something we know from within. When the character who emerges is both so very particular and so very genuine, we cannot help but believe that an actual person has spoken. And where might that actual person exist but within ourselves?

I was working on this '29 Model A pickup. Wonderful car really. Convertible cab wood spoke wheels original paint. Found the engine in a farmer's barn outside Omaha when Margaret and I were driving back from Indiana after visiting my brother Charles. I was just about finished with it and ready to walk on over to Tom Ake's so he could help me start it up when I found that one of the cylinders was defective. Boy that pissed me off. Lugged that part halfway across the goddam country. Never would have even bought it if I hadn't been out visiting Charles. Screw him anyways. What does he know about California? Things are different out here. There aren't any freebees. We don't all grow up and live on the same land. Things aren't handed to you like a glazed ham. You got to dig for your opportunities. Ply your trade. Shit, I got more power burying stiffs in the ground than he'll ever have owning the courts in Columbia City!

Then this pain shoots through my arm. The one that I'm leaning on to look under the hood. And it hurts so goddam bad that I'm chewing grease off of the manifold, face down in the engine before I know it.

And I know what's up. The doctors told me for years, "You can't go through life eating oysters and weighing 280." But all I can think of is Margaret. Me in this warehouse in Newhall full of dead antiques and feeling like I'm about to become one and she at home on the other side of the valley.

I start to feel a little bit better but I know it ain't for long. My body is sweating through the grease. So I make it over to my car. My damn pink Cadillac. "A living classic," I had always told Margaret. I roll up the windows, blast the air conditioning (paid for it in cash), and pull into the fast lane on the 405 south. And this is beautiful. I'm heading home. . .

But halfway up the Sepulveda Pass, my eyes go white with pain and my hand feels like it could tear the steering wheel off without me even wanting it to. Cars honk as I swerve across two lanes. I'm goddam scared. Sweat's dripping off of me like a squealer in front of a full union hall. I'm scared I'm not gonna make it home.

I do. I swing that Cad into its place like I've always done. I don't even notice that the space next to mine is empty. I just know that Margaret is gonna be there. She'll know what to do. I scream for her as I burst through the back door and the mynah bird on the counter screeches back at me from its cage. I scream for her again in the kitchen and the bird screeches back. And I know that it's just me in this big fucking house. Me and a caged black bird watching me die. Mocking me under my own roof.

—*Tucker Gates*

There is no line that separates writing for self-discovery from fiction. Self-discovery clearly informs the writing process, and making fiction educates us regarding ourselves. The awareness that is at the core of personal development must be at the core of creativity.

Stories Construct a Self

Stories heal us because we become whole through them. In the process of writing, of discovering our story, we restore those parts of ourselves that have been scattered, hidden, suppressed, denied, distorted, forbidden, and we come to understand that stories heal. As in the word *remember,* we re-member, we bring together the parts, we integrate that which has been alienated or separated out, revalue what has been disdained. In other words, self-discovery is more than gathering information about oneself. The gathering, the coming to know, has consequences. It alters us. We re-store, re-member, re-vitalize, re-juvenate, rescue, re-cover, re-claim, re-new. Writing our story takes us back to some moment of origin when everything was whole, when we were whole. It takes us back to the moment, in kabbalistic lore, before the world-vessel was shattered and the divine sparks scattered helter-skelter. We are like that broken vessel, and story has the possibility—becomes one of those deeds, *tikkun olam*—of gathering us up again.

But here is the irony: satisfying and sustaining as the consequences of creativity may be, the actual involvement is often difficult, even frightening. To reconstruct a self, an old self may have to be shattered. Sometimes the world-vessel must be pulverized. To discover who we are, we may have to divest ourselves of everything, go beyond the imagined limits of ourselves. We may have to leap out of the familiar, jump off a cliff, go to the very edge of the world where all the dragons live.

Even though the writing exercises in this book are just that—exercises—they can still provide real challenges. If we write them only *as if* they are real, we will get writing that reads only *as if* it is real. If we accept the imagination as a real place where real events in our real life occur, then the writing will have that authenticity as well.

Up to this point, we have been thinking about creating ourselves through processes of construction, but deconstruction may be required first. The next two exercises are designed to divest, to shatter the extraneous, to reduce us to essentials. However small or shaky the ground we stand upon when everything is stripped away, it is *our* ground and needs to be known.

Imagine that you are being confined to an iron lung where you will spend the rest of your life. Enter into the reality of the situation both as writer and character.

Where are you when the news comes to you? How do you respond to it? What do you feel or think immediately? Later? Who is with you? Why has this circumstance occurred? What do you imagine your life will be? What experiences have you had that make this situation unbearable? What experiences have you had that may help you?

This is the first day in the iron lung. What happens as you enter it? How do you spend the day? Who is with you? Who are you?

You have been in this situation for several years. What is the content of your life? How do you spend your time? Who have you become? How do you sustain yourself, if you do? What meaning, if any, does this confinement have for you?

In a ritual giveaway, I recently received a snake ring from Anne Herbert. While I was opening the gift, she told the following story: her life had become bare. While moving to a smaller place, she realized she had divested herself of almost all her possessions, retaining only the very basics she needed to survive. Faced with the giveaway, she asked herself what it would be like if she were left with nothing—nothing extraneous in her house and nothing extraneous on her body. That is how she came to give away the ring that was her only adornment. A question engaged her: Who would she be when she had nothing—that is, when she had nothing but herself?

This next exercise is a variation on the same theme. These are the underlying concerns in this exercise: Who are we when we are stripped of everything? Do we exist without mobility? When we remain immobile for a long time, who do we become? Who are we when our freedom is seriously circumscribed, when we are stripped of our normal life?

Imagine that you have been sentenced to spend an indefinite amount of time in solitary confinement. What circumstances, external and psychological, have brought you to this?

Enter into the experience of one day in solitary confinement. Describe your life in minute detail. Write a piece that captures and details your inner life under these conditions. What do you love?

How are you already living your life as if you are in jail? In solitary confinement?

Prison literature attests to the extraordinary ability people have to survive, even thrive, under the most limited circumstances. Often we do not know who we are or who we can be until we are reduced to the essentials. Without this knowledge, we can never know our complete story. When we understand ourselves on this level, it's possible to address that ultimate and most important question: Now, what do I love?

> *Make a list of what you love, and then create a portrait of a person from these details.*

How we care, what we care about, what we care for are the qualities that reveal character. As Rabbi Abraham Twersky writes, in *Living Each Day,* it is not by one's sins that you know someone but by what the person celebrates.

We often make a fetish out of our failures, losses, and inadequacies. As a consequence, we rarely come to know what gives us joy, what we love, what and how we celebrate. And yet, at the core, we are our passions and our commitment to what we love.

> *Writing "Things I love" can be a useful meditation, to be repeated frequently.*

The process of self-discovery is a meandering one. We set out in one direction and then turn back to another. We move from the need to know ourselves to the need to know others. As important as it is to know oneself bare, so it is equally important to discover the parts of ourselves that have not yet come to our awareness. Sometimes we strip ourselves down to the essentials, and sometimes we add to ourselves that which is missing.

Creating a Usable History

I had a client whose life story had a hole in it that she could not fill. At fifty, L. M. found herself still unable to enact her life. She felt that she had little time to waste, but whenever she explored this situation therapeutically, she fell into the pit of motherlessness and could not get out. Her father had left or died when she was an infant, and her severely depressed mother was a recluse and an alcoholic, so L. M. grew up virtually without parents, deprived of the basic support and knowledge necessary for entering the world successfully. Under these circumstances, some children develop street smarts, but she didn't. She withdrew. Though intelligent and gifted, she found herself living a severely curtailed life. She had no *usable history* from which to draw.

One day she mentioned an aunt who had appeared infrequently when she was a young girl. Something in her tone of voice, a whisper of longing, perhaps, alerted me. Remembering that I had formed myself as a child on the basis of books I loved, incorporating them into my life as if they were my real history, it occurred to me that an imagined story might serve the same function. Was it possible to live a story in the imagination so that it served one in the manner of a remembered event?

We decided to experiment. I asked her to tell the story of her childhood and adolescence in detail. We located the place where her mother's condition deteriorated and where L. M.'s loss began. Into this story, we carefully inserted the existence of an imagined aunt based in part on the scanty memories she had of her mother's sister.

At first, the portrait of this imaginary aunt was a barely disguised fantasy of how L. M. herself wanted to live her life. The aunt appeared as a sensitive and daring artistic woman, living a busy and exciting life in Manhattan. But soon, as my client acknowledged her growing longing to have a relationship with this aunt, she focused on the aunt's regret that she was childless. And from that moment on her writing changed.

My client began imagining moments when her aunt came to visit her. Because she needed to create a usable history, she wrote about these moments in great detail; this was the essence of her writing task.

At first she remembered her actual life as precisely as she could. Then, through writing, she "re-remembered" it. That is, she constructed a relationship with an imagined aunt who became a surrogate mother.

With the painstaking care of a novelist, L. M. imagined this woman, her apartment, her lover, her work, her life. When she knew as much as she could about her, she imagined the aunt visiting at crucial times, helping her when the need was great, and finally inviting her to live with her in Manhattan. Soon L. M. had "documented" a year when she lived with this aunt and how this year and the times they spent together afterward had significantly changed her life. By the time she wrote about the aunt's death, she was in real grief.

After a while, L. M. began believing in her aunt, the way a novelist believes in her characters, knowing they are fictions but living with them, nevertheless. Soon the fictions are out of the control of our will. When characters take on a life of their own, we fall into relationship with real if incorporeal beings. As L. M.'s writing progressed, her aunt became more complex and contradictory—more real and human—and her impact on L. M. increased.

Eventually L. M. began testing the experiment. She told stories about her aunt to some friends. When she spoke about her life to new acquaintances, she incorporated these stories until they became part of the body of her life. The stories took on substance; in time they had an equality in her imagination with what had really happened. Soon the aunt took on a reality that was almost equal to the reality of other memories.

I don't think L. M. ever forgot that she had created this aunt, but she did allow herself to ignore this fact. Her aunt thrived in her imagination and supported her life. Over a period of time, L. M.'s life changed. She dared to do things that she couldn't have dared before. She became energetic, motivated. She saw herself as capable. The last time we met, she showed me a portfolio she was taking to the movie studios, arguing for the need to present images of older women in the media. "I never could have done this without my aunt," she said with a wink.

> *Create a usable history. Examine your life. Had circumstances been different, might you be more satisfied, more fulfilled, more capable of enacting your potential? Is there some lack or loss in your life that acts as an impediment to your development? Write a piece in which you review the nature and particularity of this lack or loss.*

> *Embed an imaginary event or a character into this period that would have altered your life considerably. To the extent that these imagined circumstances give you a foundation from which to work, write about them until they become familiar.*

The First Meeting with My Grandfather

It was raining at the Greyhound station in Weaverville. Across the street there were stacks of logs that went for blocks. This is where I first met my grandfather. My bus had arrived half an hour early, so I kept looking out to see if I could see myself, or my father, or my Uncle Mark getting out of a pickup. I was gathering my bags and typewriter when he entered.

He walked across the window looking like my cousin Ernie, who doesn't look like me, or my father, or my uncle.

Riding along the Trinity River with raindrops falling into the water around the rocks, we went further and further into the mountains. I don't remember exactly what we said, only that after all these years he was glad that I finally came to see him. I watched his hand on the wheel and looked at his eyes watching the road. He had dark skin and a thick jaw. There was the scent of pine and wet dirt.

As the weeks went on, he told stories, some about growing up in Zacatecas, fishing in the lake with his grandfather. He left when the revolution came. He said his house had walls three feet thick. I asked if it was for insulation against the heat. He said it was to stop the bullets. He had ridden a freight train north to El Paso. He sat in the open door of a boxcar in the Arizona desert, his train stopped at a spur while the passenger train raced by. He saw porters, linen, and silverware, and set a dream of starting a family. He promised himself he would take them on vacation by train and feed them in the dining car.

—*Daniel David Saucedo*

There is a time in each of our lives when a relationship with someone else— a teacher, a mentor, a fellow artist, someone who has walked a path we are considering—can be crucial. Without such a person in our lives to guide or sustain us, to introduce us to new experience or encourage us in our work, we might not have the confidence or ability to go where we must go.

From the time I was young, I wanted to be a writer, but it always seemed as if other priorities interfered. When I was thirty, a working mother, a woman with two children, I met the writer Anaïs Nin, and we maintained our friendship until her death. During that time, she taught me, by example, how to be a writer, encouraging me to trust the inner life and my own voice. Had I not had that friendship, I might not have had the courage to become the writer I am.

But not everyone has the advantage of such a mentor. And yet it is difficult to learn our art and craft without one. There is a particular wisdom that a writer can offer a writer or a painter can offer a painter that is like no other. But if we cannot find such a mentor in our external daily lives, there is no reason to believe that we cannot have it through the imagination.

Once when I was lonely as a writer I spent a week in my imagination with Eugene O'Neill. I pictured myself as a teenage runaway, a woman young enough to follow O'Neill around Provincetown, eavesdropping on his conversations with the old sailors, drifting along the foggy dunes, watching intently as he struggled with a play. Unlike Anaïs Nin, who had been so gentle and nurturing, he was tough and demanding. He had no patience for someone who did not devote herself entirely to the muse. He berated me, he mocked me, he taunted me. And then when I wanted to defend myself, he turned away to his own work. Perhaps if I had not "met" O'Neill, I might not be so fierce about my work today. When I actually went to Provincetown, it did seem as if I had been there before. This "first" visit was a second visit. I walked the streets trying to "remember" how it had been when he and I had strolled there together. And I was able to speak to him in my mind again, to say that I had heeded him, although he had thought I hadn't been serious enough. As I was telling him about a play I had written, *Dreams Against the State,* I realized that it had been greatly influenced by his work.

We will speak again about the need for a mentor and the way to create one in the imagination in a later chapter. What we are trying to do here is establish the legitimacy of appealing to the imagination when we are in need.

To become a full partner with the imagination can take us far beyond our expectations, increasing the quality and the dimensions of our lives. But it may require that we challenge conventional ideas. I taught a class called "Diaries, Autobiography, and Life History" at California Institute for the Arts in which I asked the students to *write lies.* They objected. They sweated. They protested. They said they wouldn't; then they said they couldn't. Then they wrote.

This is an excerpt from a letter I wrote about that experience:

1/29/75

In class today, my students break their habits of thinking. We write lies. Everyone writes so very, very well. M.'s lie is that the U.S. is making peace in Chile and Brazil. All the clichés turn inside out to allow her to say what she needs to say without sounding sentimental or fanatical. Because of the ironic tone, we can't dismiss what she says. It is a strong piece. Another woman writing about her neat, organized conventional home reveals the home she really comes from. J. goes against his basic feeling of safety and trust in the world by writing about torture. Another young woman writes a piece about not caring at all for art or people. I myself begin writing: "First of all I am a man. I've always known it and knowing it have secretly longed to be a woman, but never succeeded."

How I love these words: "First of all, I am a man. But secretly longed to be a woman." Oh, that longing. Something revealed here—my longing for the feminine in myself.

These lines have the same strength as M.'s lines: "My friend refused a rock concert engagement in Brazil. . . ." We are aware of how profoundly betrayed M. was when her friend actually accepted a "tour" in Brazil, pretending that Brazil is a country like any other and that her own allies were not being tortured there. "My friend refused," M. wrote, knowing she hadn't refused.

This is how I introduced the assignment:

Write against patterns. Go against the devils. Write what you never write. Lie. Validate what you don't validate. Indulge what you don't like. Wallow in it. Write the opposite of what you always write, think, speak. Do everything against the grain!

We remove the grid of language by speaking nonsense, remove the grid of ideas by lying, the grid of tyranny by breaking patterns, the grid of "ought" by indulgence, the grid of meaninglessness by finding an image, and remove hesitation through wild invention.

"But I am afraid it *will* be a lie," a student protests.

"You are choosing the lie," I say. "It is still your choice. Your lie. And so it is you. The mask you choose is your mask."

Nothing is arbitrary. Everything reveals. It is really impossible to lie.

Sometimes we have to lie in order to tell the truth. Fidelity to the actual details of an experience or to its chronology can kill a piece. It is not what happened on the surface that engages us but what happened within—within us, within the relationship, or within the event. We search out the essential truth—avoiding the distortions of the literal—and commit ourselves to it. Not telling everything can be a way of lying.

Telling everything exactly as it happened may be another kind of falsehood. A writer searches for the essence of things; preoccupation with actuality is not necessarily the way.

> *Write an elaborate lie about yourself. Be as specific as possible. Allow yourself to be carried by the lie. Tell it with such care that even you may forget that the story is imagined.*

Once, I bought something so beautiful I couldn't say that it came from a shop. When a friend asked where I had gotten the five-foot camel made of embroidered Indian mirror cloth, I lied, saying it had come from a stranger.

"This is how it happened," I said. "I was crossing Pershing Square when a polite foreigner asked me directions to the same hotel where I was going. Walking together, we became acquainted. I confess, I found him very intriguing. When we arrived, he asked to see me again. I explained that I was married. He began insisting while I resisted. Finally, when I couldn't withstand his entreaties, I played for time.

"'If you send me the most beautiful thing in the world, I'll see you again,' I said. I gave him my address and forgot about it. Two months later, this camel arrived. There was no return address on the crate. And the man never called."

My story was so convincing, I began to believe it myself. But now the secret is out. This has been my favorite lie. I've told it for years. It is an old friend, which speaks about beauty, magic, and generosity. I treasure this lie.

Now that I've confessed, I will continue to tell this story as if it were the truth. To some extent, this confession feels like a lie. Before this admission, a magical gift existed; now there is a little less magic in the world. We were better off with the lie of the gift of the camel. So when someone asks me again about the camel, I will speak about the mysterious man from southern India who appeared bearing gifts.

This story is a variation on the tall tale, on the fisherman's story of the one that got away. Wonder is at the core of these stories, and when we tell them, it is to this quality of wonder that we aspire.

Stories from Our Imaginings

I don't think I would have become a writer if I hadn't imagined myself as one. When we fail to imagine our lives, we may live someone else's life, becoming the victim of another's imagination—advertising has such an effect—or we may live out something that only passes for a life, is less than a life. When we begin to imagine our lives, we discover that it is our life, our whole and entire life that we are imagining.

A life lived only in the so-called real world is only part of a life. Our spirit wants so much more that only the imagination can satisfy it. Many issues that cannot be resolved in the material world can be alleviated through imagining—even such an issue as time.

There is never enough time to write. A writer never has enough solitude. The days or the nights are never long enough. The poem or the journal piece wants its own time and its own rhythm. It does not want to be interrupted. It wants to be able to watch the birds midparagraph. It wants to be able to take a walk and have time to come back and work with the thoughts that arise while hiking in the woods, walking through skid row, or climbing rocks in the desert.

Sometimes we feel as if we'll never master the art because we are so enmeshed in daily life. We sandwich writing, reading, or walking in between work, family, and chores, and nothing gets done. There is no continuity or development. We imagine what it is to be a writer and assume that it is different from how we are. We come to believe we will never know how to do it, even if we have the time and opportunity. We are afraid of the solitude and the concentration we believe may be required.

How do we get the time? Sometimes it is hard enough to get an hour a day, let alone a day a week, a week a month, a month a year, or a full uninterrupted year.

> *Imagine that you are given a year off from your life. This year off will have no impact—unless you choose for it to—on your domestic, professional, or financial life. There will be no sacrifice required in order to take this year off, and you will be able to provide yourself with everything necessary. However, there is one condition that you must accept in order to take this year off: you will have to spend it entirely alone, without speaking to anyone.*

This exercise, like several of the others, depends on your willingness to enter the reality of the imagination. After working with the questions that follow for some time, you may discover that your daily life will begin to reflect the imagined experiences. When you finish writing this series, you may have transformed yourself from someone who dreaded being alone to someone who thrives in solitude.

Consider responding to the following questions as if making journal entries during your year away. At the end of the writing, you will have something resembling a journal of the year. Or write these as small stories, which, again, at the end of the writing, will become the larger story of the year in solitude.

1. *Imagine that you have a year to pursue your inner life in silence. You will live alone without telephone or visitors, in the utmost simplicity.*

   Where will you go? What solitary environment will suit you? Do you prefer the mountains, desert, islands? Are you inclined toward mild or rigorous weather? Do you want to create your own shelter, or must you find a place that can house you? What basic necessities are you taking with you? What things will you leave behind? *Describe the environment you have sought for this time. How does it resemble your present living situation, and how is it different?*

2. *Write a letter to your loved ones explaining why you're going.*

3. *Describe single days in your new environment or life during the first week you're away, during the middle of your retreat, and during the last week.*

4. *What are you writing during this year? What creative work are you doing? What did you expect to do before you left? What did you actually do?*

5. *What are your fears? Your discomforts? Your anxieties? Tell some anecdotes that reveal the difficulty of the situation. What has been the worst part? What has been the greatest gain?*

6. *Imagine this retreat in a city rather than a rural area. Which city do you choose? What does it mean to live in solitude in an urban setting? How do you live a solitary life in a large city? Compare the rural time with the city time. What advantages does each have? What difficulties do you encounter in the city? Describe the urban environment specifically and your particular daily relationship to it.*

7. *Write the first and last paragraphs of the piece that you complete during this year.*

8. *What has it been like to be completely alone? Not to speak? To be completely dedicated to your work?*

9. *What were your most significant experiences?*

10. *Describe your return to your usual life. How have you changed? What difficulties and joys do you encounter as you return? What have you gained? What are your regrets? Who are you now?*

The Fictional Story Wants to Come Alive

When we address questions such as these and pursue the story in them, we travel the borderline between fiction and life. Most often, life edges into fiction, but sometimes fiction wants to come alive. This is often the case with this exercise, which confronts us with our fear of solitude and our confusion about our lives.

Isolated from others, freed from distractions and responsibilities except those for our daily care, released from the white noise of our daily life that is ever increasing, we have the opportunity to attend to our real selves. This writing can duplicate the experience of retreat or *sesshin*, effectively stripping away daily concerns, preoccupations, and illusions so that we can commit to what is essential. To the extent that we are broken down by this process, we feel devastated; to the extent that we discover our neglected inner core, we are restored.

This is a warning: after spending a year away in one's imagination, the longing for solitude and uninterrupted work may not be eased. A story about solitude may not satisfy the desire for the real thing. After we addressed these questions, Cynthia Waring announced that her mother had given her the means to take a year off to write. Although she did not write the book she hoped to write, she did write every day and, consequently, began to identify herself as a writer. When she returned to her life, she began a book on which she continues to work now.

This year, Cynthia asked me how one sets up a writer's retreat in one's own home. "I took a year off, and I wrote a little, but it wasn't what I had intended. This time I really want to become a writer through devoting myself to writing for an extended period of time."

Setting up a Retreat

A little diversion from story is needed here in order to answer Cynthia's question and address how to create the environment in which a story can be written.

A time of retreat has a shape, is rounded by silence. Our communities, the city, our houses are all noisy, and so our minds are noisy, full of distractions, demands, urgencies. Retreat is a sabbath in the midst of worldly cares. The sabbath that comes after creation is also the sabbath before the next creation. It is the still center from which the new world emerges. The Kabbalah says that the omnipresent deity, the *Ein Sof*, withdrew in order to make a place for creation. And we do likewise. We withdraw, not only from the world and its preoccupations but from the incessant monologue and concerns within ourselves, in order for something else to come into being.

We think of retreat as going away, but it need not be a physical act. Each of us can find our own way to silence. Ritual is required. Laying in supplies. A goal and a willingness to adventure. But we can only prepare so much. Ultimately we will have to confront something we didn't expect and for which we are not prepared. Something will come out of this, something surprising. But be still, or you may miss it.

We withdraw and the inner world appears, so we learn to follow its direction and laws. Retreat involves discovering those laws, then trying to live according to them. It is like settling into a foreign country.

Setting up a retreat for oneself in one's own environment, rather than going away or attending a writer's colony, is challenging. Having a particular project to accomplish may help, but it may be just as satisfying to make retreat itself the goal, to connect with the magic of writing rather than with the business of it.

In retreat one will be alone for hours, days, or weeks. Ritual can enhance rather than minimize solitude and its gift, which is the ability to pay minute attention to the details of living. Oddly enough, this focus alleviates loneliness.

> *Before beginning retreat, contemplate the following: How will you live each day? How will you organize your living space to accommodate aloneness rather than company? How will you keep from dying of loneliness? What gives you pleasure? What engages your mind? What do you wish to read? What work do you wish to do, and what do you need in order to accomplish it? How do you need to prepare? What supplies do you need?*

If you do not have days or weeks for retreat, you can retreat regularly for an hour at a time. The same questions apply. I advise new mothers to learn to write in ten-minute segments. My friend, Marc Kaminsky, writes even as he runs from the subway to the bus. I always picture him flying through the streets of New York, pen in hand, papers falling out of his pockets, in a whirl of poems.

The attitude with which we approach this time influences the experience we will have. It is easy to impose so fierce a discipline that one feels punished rather than liberated by the retreat. Fears that we will not succeed and be productive can completely overwhelm the moment. When setting goals, if these are to be set at all, discover what will nurture the work, support you as a writer, then organize the time and space to provide it.

> *Arrange or rearrange your work space and desk with carefully chosen books and images so that you have a view and places for contemplation, reading, and hard work.*

The awareness that everything you are doing is focused upon the creative process—whether you are picking a flower, hiking, or preparing a meal—can, by itself, transform the space and the most mundane of activities.

Choose your books as carefully as you would choose a companion for such a delicate time, for they are the only ones to whom you will speak. When I was at Yaddo, I created a ritual of reading poems aloud each morning before I started writing. This broke the silence of the night. Soon I was in dialogue with the poems I was reading, using lines from them as titles for my own poems.[3]

> *What does the writer in you need? What has he been longing for? This is the time to do what you have little time for in daily life—the hikes you've been planning,*

the music you've wanted to study, the letters you want to answer. You can arrange the day to accommodate several passions—meditation, studying a new language, yoga, wandering in the woods or on unfamiliar streets, planting bulbs, writing letters, exploring with a camera, making masks, drawing. In this way, you frame the writing time with other pursuits.

Lay in supplies. Decide on a project, select work to be edited. Plan simple meals and try to shop in advance, or set aside occasional short periods of time for silent forays into the public world. Retreats in one's home in urban centers are difficult, but they at least allow us to shop for food at midnight when we are less likely to be distracted by the hustle and bustle. Put the phone machine in another room, check it very infrequently. Sort the mail; open only what is urgent or interesting. Store the radio, hide the television, discontinue the newspaper. Become a monk— contemplative or ecstatic. Awake at dawn, watch the sun descend, follow the waxing and waning of the moon. Greet the stars. Whistle to the mockingbirds. Consult the I Ching, the runes, or Tarot, read tea leaves, find the auguries in clouds. Light candles. Build a fire. Learn the languages of birds, animals, and trees. Pray. Write and write and write.

A year after we imagined a year off, my dear friend Barbara Myerhoff died. Alerted to the suddenness of death, I regretted how consistently I had subordinated the inclinations of the imagination to more practical concerns, and I determined to take time to redefine and recommit myself. Despite difficulties, I quickly arranged to take an extended leave from my work. For the first time in my life, I had time to write, and the writer within, who had always had second-class status, became a full citizen with a newfound ability to determine the course of her life. Priorities and considerations that had been determined previously by the roles of mother, breadwinner, and teacher were reconsidered and renegotiated.

Most of us who live in this culture experience the pushes and pulls between our inner and outer lives. Often the inner life does not know how to be its own advocate. Allowing the inner life its own story, giving it a full place, albeit in the imagination, establishes its legitimacy. Afterward, we are more capable of knowing how to act in the world in authentic ways.

My life changed in three stages. I was affected by the exercises on solitude, I actually took a year off, and then I discovered that the experience had changed me drastically. Since then, my engagement with teaching and healing has not diminished, but my commitment to the writer has been strengthened. Before the retreat, I did not know that I could maintain two absolute commitments; afterward, this seemed possible.

Stories of the Selves We Never Met

It had been difficult for me to commit myself to writing because there was a split inside me. The writer was in constant conflict with "others"—the teacher, activist, therapist, healer, mother, and so on. The more I thought about this, the more I realized how divided I was in all areas of my life. There was within me a very gregarious woman and also a hermit. There was someone quite outspoken and someone extremely shy. An anarchist and a legalist, a free spirit and a drone, a sophisticate and an innocent, a crone and a child. I once put it the following way: "Always wanting to be Zorba, I've discovered I'm the Englishman."

The more I thought about this and spoke about it to others, the more I realized how many of us at one time or another feel divided among the different people within us. Such splits are endemic to our society and keep us in a constant state of anxiety. Listening to others, I became aware of a range of splits that seem to torture us: the priest versus the magician, the martyr versus the hedonist, the poet versus the teacher, the public person versus the private person, the introvert versus the extrovert, the king versus the fool, the thinker versus the feeler, the intuitive versus the rationalist, the masculine versus the feminine, the ascetic versus the sensualist, the Apollonian versus the Dionysian, and so on. As I listed them, I realized they reflected the basic schisms in the society between the masculine and the feminine, culture and nature, law and instinct, human and animal, body and mind; it is, therefore, even more important that these splits be healed. As they are addressed through the imagination, rich, complex, and contradictory characters develop.

List the splits, the inner conflicts, that are within you. Select the pair that has the most "heat" for you at this time.

Select an incident in your life that required you to respond from one part of yourself, suppressing the needs of the other part. Write the incident twice, as if it had happened to two separate people, each of whom would respond differently. Because one member of this pair may be severely suppressed, you may have to imagine circumstances in which she acted and expressed her proclivities.

Commit yourself to working with a specific split, one in which you recognize a wound that has not healed. At what times in your life have you felt this conflict most acutely? What events or experiences may have contributed to creating this split? How does the split live within you now?

Create a fictional character whom you like and respect and who embodies one half of the split. Write about this character in the third person. The task is to bring subjectivity to something that is both omnipresent and abstract within us. Give her a past, a culture, a personal history, and, most important, respect. Tell a story in which this dominant characteristic is active.

Do the same for the other half of the split.

Let them speak in their own voices.

It is so difficult to create characters such as these without judging them. For though we are divided among different aspects of self, we often believe that we favor one while we are beholden to or tyrannized by the other. This may be a fiction, but it sets one self against another. Creating two characters of equal stature who embody two opposing qualities in ourselves allows us to confront and accept some of the choices we have made in our lives.

Return to the characters and deepen them, asking the important question: Who is this person? What sustains her? What maintains him? What are the limitations in her life? What are his passions? Around what necessities, what callings, is the character formed?

Because anxiety often accompanies the split, we may not know these parts of ourselves well, and we may feel pulled away by one each time we try to approach the other. It helps, therefore, to look for the particulars in creating the characters:

How does he earn a living? What is her ethnic background? What are the tragedies he's sustained? What brings her joy? What is his kinship network? Social class? Who are her friends? How does he spend time? What is her deepest calling?

While writing, be aware of the moments in which you feel pulled apart, when you resent identifying with the character, can't abide his strength or her intelligence. The writer's allegiance to the authenticity and autonomy of character can help you avoid stereotyping or judgment. Do what you can to create a character you respect, different though she may be from your sense of self.

Imagine a traumatic event that is extraneous to who these people are. Imagine that the same event or same kind of event happens to each of them—for example, that each is involved in a car accident, or each loses a lover, or each is deprived of his or her livelihood, or has to confront death. Write a story, a moment in which the characters—first one and then the other—experience this kind of situation and respond to it. The responses must come from the quality in the character that represents the split.

Compare the two stories. Why did each of them act the way he or she did? Presume that each action was ultimately in the best interest of everyone and everything involved. How does this change your original analysis?

At the end, write a story in which the two characters meet, experience the conflict between them, and cannot be reconciled.

Write another story in which the two meet, experience the conflict, and are reconciled. Be certain that this latter story is completely convincing. (This may take weeks to accomplish.)

As the characters in this study developed, it was heartbreaking and rewarding to see the struggles that emerged in the individual members of the class. A woman who was in the process of remodeling a very elegant house was, simultaneously, writing about her "sister" who was living on the street. Another woman found herself caught between a rambunctious teenage tart and a cool designer who had sacrificed her private life to achieve the perfect line. A man was torn between a character who was devoted to family while another aspect of himself holed up in a remote cabin daydreaming. A woman who spends her daily life restructuring education for disabled children lost herself in the character of a middle-aged American geisha who ran a house for lonely and respectable middle-aged men.

When Carolyn Flynn joined the workshop, she was beginning to recognize the conflict between two parts of herself. The organized, efficient, urban woman was confronted by a woman who wanted to write poetry and speak to trees. When we began writing about the split, she created two fictional characters: a man who was focused, outspoken, and extroverted and a woman who was musing, silent, introverted.

This is how the pieces began:

7/18/89

He was positively happy. He left the library, famished and tired, but content with the morning's work. He had put off lunch till 2:30, but he'd gotten through all thirty-four boxes of Jane Abbott's papers, helped by the exquisite cataloging accomplished by the archive's staff. . . . He couldn't help but believe that this next folder, the one in his hand, would be the one that held the key. Of course, it hadn't happened this morning, but still he was positively happy.

This work engaged a part of him that reveled in mindless but engaging tasks, like cleaning marijuana by hand, or drafting an architectural design, the old-fashioned way of twirling a pencil to keep the line the same size all across the page. For some things he had endless patience, and when he sat down to a day of note taking, a new yellow notepad open and clean on his desk, his favorite smooth-flowing pen in his hand, he felt a contented sense that there was nothing more, nothing at all that he could possibly be doing.

7/25/89

But there was always more—a bush, a tall tree, a sweet flower planted outside a neighbor's cabin. . . . Today she was taken with smells, having stood for several minutes near Jim's honeysuckle bush, being taken to the East Coast and back with each breath. As she approached the cliff the air was rich; the evergreens were wet from a nighttime shower and she realized that the smell that surrounded her was the soil of the earth itself. She walked off the path to a tree and squatted down, digging her hand into the wet earth. Yes, this was what she needed this morning—to feel the earth directly. She dug deep, putting a pile of dirt in both hands and brought it to her face. . . . She put her hands deep into the hole and imagined the center of the earth.

. . . Dusk was her favorite time of day. Watching the day grow dark, she grew still and aware. Still it was hard to really catch. Just every few minutes, as she looked up from her book, or stopped watching a cloud, she would notice that it had grown darker right before her eyes. She could gauge the state of her soul by how much this startled and delighted her. The dusk and the stillness brought her inside. Soon she couldn't see out her windows, was blanketed in by the dusk. Her being and awareness encompassed the entire room.

When it came to confronting each of these characters with a trauma, Carolyn chose incest. Within a few days, she began to realize that she had as an adolescent developed a strong persona to mask a terrible truth she had not been able to face. The serendipity of the problem presented and the experience of writing from the imagination allowed her afterward to access her own information and to experience what had been desperately suppressed until then. These are the fictional pieces as they unfolded:

8/14/89

Something was nagging at him this morning. He kept staring out the window listless and without motivation. And he was finally writing his favorite chapter. . . . The sheets sat in front of him, dog-eared from being read in bed last night, his scribblings all over the margins. He hadn't ever really gotten to sleep. He had an urge to tear the whole thing up; then saw an image of himself overwhelmed in his bed by a monstrous brain which encompassed his entire body. It heaved and sighed; it was horrendously ugly and it was him. Good grief. He got up to pace, again, and saw something else. It was his father. He was leaning over him as a little boy with no clothes on. He was only three. His father was pulling on him; he didn't understand. His father was pulling and rubbing and laughing. It hurt and it felt funny. What's this? he thought as he paced the room.

8/7/89

It was in the waking she knew. The first glimmer of light as she opened her eyes and it would be there. As she turned she felt the heaviness, and went to it. Before she opened her eyes, she had visited her sadness, made a place for it.

So this was to be how it was. Another day. All this without thinking, before she had come awake. She opened her eyes. Yes, it was there; it is here, it lives within her, insisting, some days, upon being known.

8/21/89

She is nearing the hard part now. She must do it—remember. She moves to a new sunnier spot, stretching her body. It is mine now. All mine. She speaks to her little self: I'll take care of you. I grew up. I'm big now.

Five years old. Mommy wasn't home and Daddy came, shoved her face down and forced a fist up where she went poo-poo. There are tears, loud cries and wails, she yelled, "Mommy!" and they both knew it was over. She wailed and cried. She bled and Daddy walked away. Daddy didn't love her.

. . . She looked straight at the sun for an instant, feeling the heat on her skin. I'm alive and whole. And I will always have this pain, the wailing, the early knowledge of harshness and evil. A wail comes from deep within her, a bigger knowledge now, of tortuous things humans do to each other. And she feels the sun. The grass grows fresh around her; it tickles her side. She is inconsolable; it will leave, too, this sadness. . . .

Carolyn Flynn's writing is a startling example of two voices, which were thought to be separate and warring, becoming partners. Each, through memory and perception, illuminates part of a story. Two voices that had been divided from each other were now integrated into common understanding.

Pursuing this line of investigation heightened everyone's awareness of the splits within and also helped relieve the internecine warfare that had formerly existed between the different selves. Once the two intrinsic parts of the self appeared, the distinct qualities, values, and experience of each became evident, and it became a given that each had a right to live or that there was a larger self that could accommodate aspects of both.

Stories from the Unknown

Sometimes we tell stories about what we know. And sometimes, as in the stories about solitude, we tell stories about what we want to know. And sometimes the stories are about what we don't know at all. And all these stories teach us.

After attending an artists' colony, I realized I could learn the craft of a writer from watching artists who were not writers, whose craft was totally different from mine. I began to formulate a series of questions regarding other artists.

Imagine an artist whose work and sensibility are entirely different from yours, whose kind of work you have never engaged in yourself. Imagine someone who is both talented and accomplished.

By entering deeply into the life, mind, and psyche of this artist, you can discover how this artist sees the world, approaches her work, and what value and meaning he derives from seeing in this distinct way. In this process, one can actually train oneself to see and hear differently. At first, you may only be trying to understand what a musician notices when she walks through the world. After a while, you will find yourself listening in the street the way a musician listens. Soon the music of the birds or the traffic, the rhythm of language, of wind, or of footsteps will become apparent.

Once I was able to see the bank of a river through the eyes of various painters I loved, my eyes began to focus differently. They took in light the way Monet did or noticed the variation of points and waves as did Van Gogh. Across the bank, I saw the clay cliffs through the eyes of Georgia O'Keeffe; a ribbon of blue below turned like a Möbius strip representing the stream itself. When the colors in the water broke down into a harmonic pattern of squares and rectangles, I was in the world of Mondrian.

Needless to say, this influenced my work dramatically. It was as if these painters allowed me to apprentice with them so that I might begin to paint when I was writing. The exercise taught me to see.

Record the vital statistics of the imagined artist: essential facts, notes about character, reference to family dynamics, an outline of the family tree, an annotated list of important events—even, if so inclined, an astrological description.

Imagine the artist when he was a small child. How would this nascent painter or pianist view the world? What would she be drawn to? What would he see, feel, hear? Describe a moment in childhood when the artist's gift was beginning to express itself, though it might not have been recognized yet. What factors led toward developing the artist's talent?

A child has what Zen Buddhists call "beginner's mind"; he looks at the world freshly. To enter into the child's body when she dances, even before she knows the word *dance,* or when she examines the minute world of ants, or sees the color of bark is to encounter the freshness of experience. Perhaps we have lost the thread of the development of our own relationship to language, but here we can begin as if we are children again, seeing the world, feeling the world freshly, learning languages for the first time.

> *At thirty, this same artist reflects upon her childhood. Now, as a developing artist, she remembers her early experience and can see the beginnings of her maturing work. She makes a bond between what she sees now and what she felt then. Of course, she tells stories about this.*

The hands of the musician, the one who touches the keys or holds the bow, have a different sensitivity from mine, though sometimes it seems to me that words are coming through my fingers. Because of this, I often write by hand in a journal. It is as if the words formed in my mouth are shaped further by their passage through the wrist, through the plane of the palm until they exit from the fingers. Our hands differentiate us from all other creatures, and our particular hands are the way we encounter the world. Even for a writer, the body is the primary instrument.

> *The artist is aware of his hands and acknowledges them. Write this acknowledgment.*

> *The artist is very accomplished. Follow her, invisibly, as she takes a walk. What does she observe? What does she do? How does this activity reveal her creative practice?*

One of my students followed Allen Ginsburg through Boulder, Colorado. "He would walk, then he would sit down on the curb and write, then he would walk again, look in a shop window, get involved in animated conversations, write again. He was so totally curious and totally absorbed it took him a very long time to walk a block."

I asked her why she followed him.

"How else was I going to learn to be a poet?" she answered.

> *Follow the artist through a day, from his awakening to his going to sleep.*

We learn about others by observing them, but we rarely have the opportunity to be in such intimate relationship that we come to know them both from the outside and from the inside. This is the opportunity that the imagination offers us.

> *What does the artist dream? How does he understand the dream? How do you interpret the dream from what you know about him? How does this interpretation accord with the facts and circumstances of his life?*

> *In what does the artist rejoice? How does she express her joy?*

Follow the artist with great attention through the first moments of creating a new work. Trace the process of creation, from the not knowing to the moment when something new and unexpected comes into being.

What does the artist think about? During one day, follow her serious and original thoughts and introspections. Write about them both in the artist's voice and then in an omniscient narrator's voice.

Go to the periphery of the artist's mind. Find the wildest places he can go. Follow him in the leaps he makes to the impossible, invisible, inaudible, outrageous, and forbidden. Imagine that she thinks of herself as someone who always crosses boundaries, who only wants to go where no one has gone before. Go there with her.

Then if you can, go there yourself with your own work.

At some point, it is important to turn the experience around. Now the artist is observing you, asking you all the questions you asked about her. Now they are your thoughts, your dreams that are to be known. She let you into her life with as much intimacy as was possible; now she asks that you open yourself to her.

Describe the very first moment you discovered the magic of language.

Allow the artist to witness your process of creativity.

Allow the artist to follow you through a day.

Imagine that the artist is studying you. Turn all the questions around. The artist becomes the third-person narrator, and you become the subject.

In the course of studying this artist, many of the writers I worked with found unexpected parts of themselves. Karen Gottlieb's piece on an aging painter contrasts significantly with her physical image of herself, yet both these people exist within her. Had she not written this exercise, the inner elderly artist, one of her true sources of creativity, would have remained unseen.

The DUSK series done, the homage to fading light no longer covering the walls, surrounding her in pink and gray, shipped off to the galleries to add more money to a bank account she never touched, she sat for some time watching the dawn. Having done with darkness from light, she wanted an infusion of light from darkness.

Maybe she was secretly checking her vision against inevitability. Maybe testing her courage. She felt the light returning. She felt it in her skin, through her pores. And she felt frivolous like yellow, like midday, like daisies.

The daisies were restless and demanding. They rose, yellow and white inside her like an insurrection, demanding music. They walked her to the radio and demanded hot jazz!

"But I'm seventy-five," she pleaded. "I'm too old to dance like a fool in this pool of yellow. And white. Light."

But yellow was having its way with the light. Yellow was playing havoc with her. And she, a slave to light as she had been a volunteer to darkness, danced with the daisies, as daylight poured through the windows, invaded her now-open doors, and erased soft shadows.

"It's the final cry of life before death," she warned herself. Then, "It must be glaucoma. A moment of blinding clarity and then blackness forever." But only the daisies answered.

"Old woman found dead after dancing with imaginary daisies," the inner reporter she had carried around since adolescence mused, but she continued to dance despite all the voices enraged at this nonsense. "Act your age," they all said in unison, and still she danced, using them as her chorus.

Finally, five days after DUSK had been shipped, she set up an easel in the bathroom. She'd never painted in there before, although, she now realized, the light was extraordinary. She had it built with a floor-to-ceiling window by the tub, and a skylight opened to the sky. She opened the windows and light flooded in.

She stood between the full-length antique mirror and the canvas she'd just stretched, a canvas exactly as tall as the mirror, and she took off her clothes.

There, in the blinding uncompromising light, she studied the body, the skin, the angles, the curves, the flesh that had been hers for seventy-five years. Turning slowly, to catch every shadow, she found herself moving, undulating, her heart beating to the music and light. The music, yellow now, was like honey inside her. Slow, slow, slow, then quick quick quick. Her eyes inside her head were crazy with daisies, daisies falling all over each other, exploding gamy, earthy petals uprooted onto the wooden floor.

Heartbeats later, she began to paint something she had never painted before—a seventy-five-year-old body in various stages of ecstasy, bones, flesh, aging skin, and gray pubic hair streaked with yellow. This series, she decided, she would call JAZZ.

The Shadow Knows

It is odd to think that what we don't know, rather than what we know, can be the very core of story. That the characters within us about whom we know the very least may ultimately provide us with the most energy and liveliness. That often the denied parts of ourselves, our suppressed or disdained stories, are the richest and most rewarding, just as the suppressed and disdained in a culture become the repository of the life force and the elemental.

To be energetic and authentic, a national literature includes dialogues with the despised and thrives on the Dostoyevskis, Baudelaires, Hubert Selbys, and Sylvia Plaths who speak to us from the netherworld. Equally, our own writing wants to be infused with the dark light from *our* underworlds. Time and again, the most energetic writing occurs when someone is willing to acknowledge her fascination with someone utterly "other"—a murderer, a homeless person, a woman bartender in a remote area, a crazy person, a fundamentalist, a battered wife—these are moments when the writer crosses into forbidden territory.

> *Imagine that a mad person is someone who has a story to tell that cannot be told, that each one of us has a story inside of us that we have not been able to tell, that there is a mad or maddened person inside each of us. Find this voice. Write whatever comes to mind. Begin with whatever odd words come up from this voice, which you may never have contacted before. Go down into the dark place to find this creature, the one with the denied vision, the one who has been inarticulate for so long. This mad voice must be heard. Let the creature speak.*

The shadow, the other, is the most unknown aspect of ourselves. We can say it is the part of ourselves whose essence is to be unknowable; it *wants* to be unknown. It is the darkness that is ours, which we cannot escape and which is most difficult to contact. It is the reflection of ourselves that occurs when there is no light. To encounter the shadow, we must be willing to go into the dark, for that is where it lives. If we never move toward it, we run the risk that the shadow will come to us in a meeting that will be furtive and violent. Yet whenever we move toward it, we run the risk of being overwhelmed. In the dark, we often feel as if we *are* the dark. How, then, do we meet the shadow?

The writing we have done to this point has prepared us for this encounter. By conceding that we consider parts of ourselves absolutely foreign and alien, that we abhor, disdain, or deny them, while admitting that these parts, horrific or strange as they may be, are still ourselves, we open to this most exiled part of ourselves. To allow that there is a part of the self that is both stranger and kin to us is to enter into one of the great mysteries of the psyche. And this act, in itself, becomes a peace offering that encourages the shadow to emerge.

The shadow lengthens as day falls. Toward the moment of twilight, it is at its deepest. There is a moment in writing that resembles this twilight. It is the time when the noon light of reason has diminished. At such times, the shadow is likely to respond to a call to manifest itself, for now it can hold its own against the light that would annihilate it altogether and that, therefore, it avoids, refusing to appear, perhaps retreating even further.

Let us try to engage the shadow by considering the following questions, which put the self and the shadow at equal risk and which thus coax the shadow into revealing itself.

The first questions define the territory where the shadow resides. Here we acknowledge that the shadow is a continuum of ourselves, is what we are when we go to the other side, is our other face.

> *List those qualities or attributes in others that you find least like yourself. Let the list develop through spontaneity and curiosity, avoiding judgment. This is a critical moment when the reasoning faculties need to be dispatched while the intuitive is invited to preside.*

> *Be attentive to particulars so as to isolate the specific dynamic between what you fear and what you fear fears you. You will soon find that the notes and list outline a territory, like points on a graph, a shadowy territory that we all share at the border of our isolation. Once you have come to know some of what was formerly unknown, while still aware there is more to be discovered, begin to write a piece that explores this territory of your aversion.*

These are further questions:

> *Is there someone, others, whom you suspect hate you? What are your most intractable prejudices? With what group do you feel least affinity? Who are the people you could not and would not imagine being because they revolt, offend, terrify, enrage you, because they seem beneath you or grotesque?*

> *Under what circumstances would you feel too humiliated to continue living? What horror within yourself would you find unbearable?*

> *Remember a time when you yourself felt hate. Reenter that experience. Write a monologue expressing the thoughts and emotions of the one who hates. What does he or she hate? Why? How do you know you are feeling hate? What distinguishes this response from other possible responses like fear, disdain, dislike? Of course, you can substitute other feelings—dread, disgust, horror—in lieu of hate.*

Each of us responds very differently to such an experience; some of us hate and some of us fear, some of us feel rage and others feel nausea. What we are trying to discover is the emotional barrier we establish between the world, the qualities and experiences that comprise it, and ourselves.

When enough time has elapsed for you to be able to separate yourself from the writing, peruse it to distinguish which responses are based upon moral or ethical principles and which aversions are charged with repugnance, contempt, loathing, revulsion. These latter live in the realm of the shadow.

To bring the shadow from the abstract into the particular, formulate a character by consolidating these aversions; give this person a name, a personality, and a history. As the writing proceeds, allow the character to emerge, even to lead in the revelation of his story. Soon it will seem as if the character has a life of her own. It is important now, as a writer, to honor this development, permitting this fictional momentum to carry you. Allow this not only for the sake of fiction but because the deeper truths are often revealed through the circuitous route of the imagination. In the case of the shadow, which is the opposite of reflection, images can be particularly revealing.

jonny stiletto

yeah. well. ok. so. what you want. what you want you want ta know is what the hell i'm doing here outside. lemme put it to you this way. i am the shadow inside the light. i am the figure lurking in the dark corners of your mind. i am your dark dreams come true. i am the nightmare at the end of your labyrinth. your dreams. your subterranean homesick black and blues. i am your metropolitan death. i am yours. yours. when you scream in ecstasy, i am an inch away. the inch you hold for yourself. when you are sweating and naked, and still your legs, the legs of your mind are still crossed, i am there. i am there blowing hot winds against your thighs, whispering for your all. i am there in the dark recesses, there, where you lose all control. . . .

i have risen like a vampire because you have called me. you have called me to come and reveal your darkest shame. your darkest wet hot shame. i am jonny stiletto and i will slash the wrists of your current life until you are bled dry of all artifice. because you asked. because you begged. begged me not to come, i am here and i am as ready as you are to descend.

tonite, we'll take the A train down. down past the streets of your glamorous aspirations, down past the avenues of your rewritten past, down past the boulevards of your designated future, into the gutter of dreams. the gutter of dreams you dare not speak and i will slash thru the complacency. with you on my back. descending.

i am jonny stiletto. and i have come for you . . . i have come—for you.

—*Karen Gottlieb*

At this point, many possibilities present themselves. The character herself may be thoroughly engaging, and you may wish to focus on who she is and the stories that emerge.

Another approach is to enter into dialogue with this person, allowing intimacy to occur, confidence, revelation, until you know as much as you can about the person—where he lives, what her house looks like, what he eats for lunch, what she thinks, what he fears, knows, what she wants, dreams. . . . Create a fictional context that makes the conversation between the two of you plausible. Tell the story of how you met. Use story to reveal why the two of you are engaged in an exchange or relationship. Be as truthful and forthcoming as you wish the shadow to be.

The Shadow as Cover

Such a direct approach as I have just outlined may be very successful for some, but for others, a more oblique path may be required in order to encounter the shadow. Here is one possibility:

Imagine that your life is threatened; in order to escape the threat, you must create another identity, a false cover. The cover must be perfect, an identity so like yourself and yet so different that you can be perfectly disguised while living the life of this other. As you take on this life, it will seem to be both completely alien and very comfortable and familiar.

Who is the character you become in order to disguise yourself and thereby save your life?

Describe this cover in detail. Validate its effectiveness by comparing the character with yourself. Follow the character through an entire day or week, observing her alone and with others.

Write this character's diary entries.

Here are some questions that might easily become scenes or character descriptions: What does this "other" think when unable to sleep at 3:00 A.M.? What awakens her? What secrets, griefs, insights is she privy to? What did he dream? How does he act? What does he think, remember, or do? What events precipitated this agitation? What are the consequences of these events? What essential part of your self is "covered" by this persona? When we begin to ask such questions, we are creating the framework of story.

You can be assured that if you are scrupulous and kind, the shadow will emerge, and that if you stay with the particulars, fiction will occur. Question, observe, be curious about everything, and accept everything that you see and come to know. Be careful not to make judgments or allow your biases and fears to contaminate or destroy the revelations that occur.

Here is still another fictional approach: when you think that perhaps you know everything, that you know as much about the shadow as you know about yourself— or more—then imagine that this character is your sibling, born from the very same father and mother as yourself. Describe your relationship to your sibling.

"Remember" your early years together; describe a moment when you had great affinity for each other.

When did you begin to part, to pursue such different lives? Tell a story that may reveal the moment of differentiation.

Imagine your mother and father looking at you two children and reminiscing about each, speaking of your similarities and differences. (The purpose of this exercise, as with some of the others, is to examine the territory between the real and the imagined.)

Finally, allow your sibling/other/enemy/cover to look at you. Allow this character to speak in his or her own voice, to create a portrait of you. Who do you become when seen from this perspective? Now, as the "other" has developed a voice, enter into dialogue with him or her. What is it you each want to know?

As you bring this sibling, this other, the shadow into your life—into your family, so to speak—allow your imagination and your life history to merge. Beware of the need to be literal, for this often shrouds deeper knowledge, but on the other hand, don't permit the imagination to distract or distance you from the ways in which the shadow is, in fact, your family, your other, yourself.

This shadow self is not separate from you, not even as separate as a sibling. This is the shadow you cast, the one who is always with you. Examine the portrait of this person, consider the life that he or she is living, from the outside but also from within. Enter into this irony: the one with whom you have created an island of communality and mutual understanding is utterly other; or the one who is utterly other is the one whom you can understand perfectly. Imagine living the other's life.

Lastly, imagine the death of the shadow self. Given the life that he or she led, how does the "other" die? Write a scene describing the death of this character. Write it from the point of view of an omniscient narrator.

Write it again from the point of view of someone else in the room.

Write it from the point of view of the dying shadow self.

Each one of these questions and exercises can lead you deeper into an understanding of yourself, even as each leads you also into story and the imagination. The questions together may form the basis for exploration, or each, individually, may be sufficient to generate characters, dramatic situations, unexpected narratives. These questions can lead you to write a small journal entry or a meditative piece, a play, a short story, or even a novel.

Peter Schmidt, who has become a character in a novel-in-progress, *The Other Hand,* came to me during a writing exercise when I least expected him. He not only had the qualities of a shadow figure but he presented himself as the shadow itself. Here is how he first appeared. Though I have eliminated this section from my novel, this piece is the core from which the novel develops.

There is a man in my bed. It is the middle of the night. He is German. That's not important. What is important is that he is—that is, was—a Nazi.

It is a winter night. All the doors and windows were locked. Locked, yes, of course. And yet, it's true, there is a Nazi, suddenly, in my bed.

He is myself.

Eros doesn't bring us together. We are in bed because this is the house of the dream and we live here together, waking and sleeping. Winter and night have brought to light what casts a shadow in the day. Perhaps, despite the terrible verisimilitude, this is merely a dream and not the unwilling collaboration of two enemies in the arena of soul. If so, I ask it, is it mine or his? Am I a voyeur of his dream or is he observing mine or are we both dreaming one another?

Of all the walls we create or encounter, only one is impenetrable, the one of time. We are held, perfectly contained, within the chamber of our own time, and my life cannot begin until the certainty of his death, the one who preceded me.

The man in my bed lived his life from beginning to end and then he died. Still, he is here now. I find the fact of his body as disturbing as he finds mine. Still, history is such that we can never think of ourselves without thinking of the other; we are irrevocably linked for all time to come. Death, which he relied upon to exterminate me, only links us more closely. Nothing that I can

98

think of can set us free. Perhaps this grotesque reliance upon each other for our identities is a force stronger than the logic of time and the finality of death.

Explain it as you wish, he and I are both here now.

When I finished writing this piece, I was horrified and wanted to rid myself—and later the novel—of this person, but it was not possible. Peter Schmidt was already a dead man. And the novel would have to grapple with his intractable existence.

Whether fictional or organic, the shadow never dies; we always cast a shadow. But how we relate to it and it to us depends on whether it is known. Once known, we have inevitably lost an innocence that can never be recovered. What replaces this innocence, however, is the knowledge of the complexity of our nature, of human nature. Sometimes we are fortunate, and this knowledge elicits a kindness and tolerance in us for others—even, perhaps, for ourselves. In the end, what remains, whether our goal was writing literature or exploring ourselves, is what we can only come to know when we are alone, naked, and the light is behind us.

Finding Other Mysteries in Ourselves

Character is not the only mystery. Sometimes plot is equally mysterious. Sometimes we are as totally engaged by what will happen as by whodunit. So many times we feel as if our life is a consequence of events and circumstances, as if we are not so much the actor as the one acted upon. This was certainly my mood when I wrote:

> *Which of These Forms Have You Taken?*
> This year I have been growing
> down into the tree
> against my will
> making nothing happen.
> Across the woods
> through the bare branch haze
> of bars against the light
> someone is coming with an axe.

I have known this all my life.[4]

Although written as a poem, there is a story being told here. And the mystery of what is going to happen, not the answer, makes the story. Perhaps the ultimate mystery is what happens at the edge of things, when the "lights go out," when nothing as we know it remains. People have always suffered such fears, yet adventurers have based their life explorations on the hope of encountering situations absolutely unfamiliar. Sometimes we go out and seek the unknown and sometimes it enters our lives uninvited. Still, as before, at the very heart of what is completely unknowable is something urgent to be known.

> *The lights go out. Imagine the moment. Things stop. You do not know the cause or the consequences. You cannot leave wherever you are at the moment. Or if you can, you don't know where to go or how to get there. You are in a state of shock. What are your associations, memories, your spiritual, political, and emotional responses?*

> *What has happened? At first you were surprised, but now, knowing what has happened, you acknowledge that this moment, so out of the blue, seems destined, karmic, fated. There is an uncomfortable but perfect fit between this moment and your life, a correspondence between absolute chance and inevitability. Through an inner monologue, describe what is happening and its meaning.*

> *Such a catastrophe brings one to an unavoidable confrontation with death. What is your response to the possibility that you will not emerge alive from this situation?*

> *Because you do not know if you will survive this situation, you begin to speak to your ancestors, to your dead.*

Many things happen during catastrophes. The routine of daily life disappears. What was formerly important becomes meaningless. In a catastrophe, one must confront the necessities: food, warmth, shelter, security, companionship. To face these challenges is to sculpt one's life into a recognizable shape. The knowledge of what is important comes to us, and this knowledge is stark and bare. Under these circumstances, it is difficult to live with illusions about who we are because we quickly become what we do and what we do not do.

> *The catastrophe has occurred. Your few resources, though minimal, are authentic. In this extreme moment, you are pushed toward behavior that you would never have expected from yourself. Perhaps you approve of your actions, perhaps you do not. Tell the story of what occurs, what pushes you, what you do, and how you respond.*

> *The catastrophe continues. It lasts far longer than you expected. You and the others must accommodate, must learn to live accordingly. Other events intervene. There is a new resolution.*

Write the entire story from the beginning, bringing together all the circumstances and responses from the previous writing. As you weave all the elements together, see what new story emerges. Allow yourself to know things you didn't realize or know before.

The airport. I was tired, arriving home from a trip, briskly routine, moving along on a flat escalator/people-conveyer. Then there was a thunderous noise, the conveyer suddenly stopped, and the lights went out. Shadowy crowds, panicked people moved into the corridor, calling out, screaming. Next to me was an elderly woman, her white hair neatly curled, a pale pink cardigan sweater pinned around her shoulders. She moaned that her foot was stuck, she couldn't move. Leaning over to help her wrest her shoe from a crack in the metal floor of the conveyer, I saw her eyes filled with fear.

Hoping for comfort, I sank to the floor of the long metal corridor, which was now fixed, hard, and still. But it was all unyielding right angles, no kind of nest. The metal side felt hard and chill on my back, and the indented strips of the metal floor pinched my knees and legs. The rumble of voices grew louder; the space in between the two metal conveyers was rapidly filling with frightened groups and clusters of people, turned from busy travelers into frightened refugees. Something was wrong, terribly wrong, but no one knew what specific acts would bring rescue and salvation.

People coming from both directions crowded into the metal conveyers and the passageway between them. They screamed and groaned and called out, trying to keep track of one another. "Marcie, Marcie," a high frantic woman's voice trailed into a whine. A man's anxious voice, "Please let me through, let me through, my wife is ahead and I don't want to lose her." The shadows of moving bodies grew thick and layered. Voices—angry, desperate, etched with fear—cut across and compounded one another. It was chaos. A lump of panic rose from my stomach and moved up and into my throat. I had to get out. I had to get out.

I grasped the railing and pulled myself up. More and more shadowy figures were pushing in from both directions. I knew I would soon be trapped. The elderly woman was clinging to the railing on my right, muttering frantically to herself as she was pushed towards me by a large man in a rumpled gray suit. "Get out of my way, get out of my way!" he yelled harshly and pushed the bent and frail woman up against me.

I suddenly saw a way to escape, to gain more space, to break free from the crowd. If I pushed back, hard, I could raise myself over the railing and into the small space between the wall of the room and the side of the metal conveyer. I opened my arms and shoved, hard and determined, knocking the elderly woman to the floor and startling the man in the gray suit, who shrunk back a little. I lunged to the edge, stepped on the bent and shaking back of the elderly woman, and put all my weight on her with one foot while I swung my other leg across and then dropped my body into the free space.

—*Barrie Thorne*

About this piece, Barrie Thorne said, "When I wrote about stepping on the elderly woman's back, I started to laugh, and I [and the class] laughed when I read it. Thinking about it, I laughed all the way down the hill from class. Laughter at voicing the unpermitted. Laughter of the angry self suppressed by the dutiful daughter who always tries to be nice."

The Questions at the Heart of Every Story

At the root of our lives is a question, a series of questions, a quest, some fundamental concerns or obsessions; the mystery, the story, and the meaning of our lives reside there. A story also has a question at the core of it, and the question leads to the mystery within the story. The deeper one goes into the story, the more one learns, the more things are revealed, the deeper the mystery. Perhaps the story has no other function than to ask this question or to deepen the mystery.

When we're not aware of the questions we are asking, of the koans that define our life and work, our writing may not go deep enough. Yet these questions that preoccupy us, which are part of our identity and definition of self, are so difficult to formulate. They are the questions that follow the exertion of all our intelligence and experience. After we know what we know, each one of us remains someone asking a particular set of questions, the one whose life is the means of addressing it.

Failing to honor the persistence of the question, we are in danger of merely solving problems, reducing and trivializing experience through our explanation. Looking to story to solve rather than illuminate life problems, we miss the intricacies and become lost in reductionism. Better that we probe but not solve the mysteries of conflict, of intimacy and distance; power and powerlessness, authority and madness, fate and free will than that we chance diminishing them. There is no solution, for example, to the fate of King Lear or Oedipus; to look for one is to reduce great works of art to the trivialities of pop psychology. Such works speak to the paradoxes and dilemmas of the human condition, even as the questions we ask take us ever more deeply into the eternal enigmas.

I will never know how one world penetrates another or how history resides in contemporary life, but these questions will probably preoccupy me for the rest of my life. Hemingway was entranced with the expression or failure of heroism in ordinary life, while Joseph Campbell wanted to fathom the archetypal nature of heroism itself. Anaïs Nin had unlimited curiosity about the inner life and its manifestations, while John Berger is equally fascinated by the social and political sources and consequences of the way we see. A writer develops a body of work, and we come to recognize the characters and stories she creates, but this does not mean that the writer is repeating herself. Rather the opposite. Over time, the questions the writer is asking become deeper and more penetrating until the questions, not the answers, become his signature. When García Marquez asks who and what is a dictator, the answer is a dramatic meditation that cannot be contained in or reduced to a political treatise. Nor can we make psychological theory out of Marguerite Duras's fictional investigation of the wordless obsessions that direct our lives. Ultimately we are informed, the way only a story can inform, by the questions asked, the directions to which they point, the forms they create about them.

> *Review your work. What do you think about? What are you trying to understand? What obsesses you? What images, symbols, metaphors, dynamics repeat themselves in your work? What core concerns do these reveal?*

> *Write a piece in which you relate this question to your life. Write a story about a character whose essential identity is constructed around this question, a story about a character who does nothing but pursue answers to this question. Exaggerate the pursuit, allow the character to manifest as a fanatic, an obsessive, a seeker, an adventurer in search of the answer.*

> *Sometime after you've finished the story, pick it up and see how it reveals parts of yourself you may never have encountered before.*

Playing with Fiction

There comes a moment when we want to write a story, when the journal entry is not sufficient and when our curiosity about ourselves is satiated. We want something else. Or perhaps it is the creative that wants something else. It wants to make something. It wants something that will stand apart from ourselves.

Here are a series of questions that can take you to a story quite quickly. The task is to do what is asked without spending any more time than is allotted:

> *List three nouns, like knife, egg, moon. [One minute]*

Describe a landscape that has the following qualifications: you yourself have never actually been on this landscape. At the moment you are describing it, no people are on it. [Seven minutes]

A character appears on the landscape, a character you have never written or thought about. Describe the character. [Seven minutes]

Now, finally, add an action. This action must include the three nouns you listed. Combine the landscape, the character, the nouns into an action. [Fifteen minutes]

The rice rose out of the muddy water, endless rows of golden stalks reflecting golden sunlight. From my perch on high, the rice rows swirled in curly shapes, like snail shells the size of mountainsides.

The one-room windowless hut, thatched of golden stalks, took up little space with the wide range of growing food. Its door ajar, its interior dark but for a shaft of golden light, it looked untouched by human hands. A white llama stood nearby, still, with no sign of purpose.

The old woman came out of nowhere, her woven dress a sudden rainbow of color against the golden ground. Her face was wizened, mapped with infinite lines; her small frame moved slowly, draped in color; her head wore a woven scarf, red, yellow, green, blue, orange; her small, frail arms carried a basket as big around as a chair. As I watched, she lifted the basket to her head, and a shaft of golden sunlight struck it like lightning. She dropped one arm free and moved gracefully toward the field, erect and steady, as if carrying nothing more than a feather pillow.

The mountain peak behind her, white-topped with snow, seemed solid and eternal, while the rice fields, delicate and bending in the breeze, appeared to breathe their last breath.

She reached the edge of the field, stopped slowly, remaining erect, and drew a knife from her shawl. It flashed quicksilver in the sunlight, and she began to use it like a trusted friend, swinging in wide strokes, one hand resting gently on the basket, as the golden food began to fall to the earth from which it came. The woman swung out in wide circles, until an indentation appeared in the snail shell. Then she tucked the knife back into its home, gathered the golden shafts, and used one to tie a cinch around the others. With one quick motion, she placed it in the basket, stood up, and began to move toward the hut. Her skirt of color whooshed as she walked, and the sun slipped silently behind the peaks.

She walked past the open door and disappeared into a hole in the mountain. I watched and waited, expecting her return, but the moon rose, a round golden disk on a seamless blue backdrop, and she did not reappear. As the sky turned from blue to black, and the chill wind cut into my bones, I called to her in my soul. The golden rice was hidden from me now, the white llama roamed unseen, and somewhere inside the monster mountain my mother boiled rice.

—*Connie Zweig*

Approaching a Larger Story

The next questions will lead you through the process of coming to know and write a story deeply.

1. *If there were only a few stories in your life that you could tell, which would they be? List the stories. Remember that a story is an event, a consequence. It is a moment in which something is revealed or has an implication. A story occurs in time. It goes from one place to another. Something happens or someone is altered. Something is experienced, and meaning emerges.*

   Eliminate those stories from the list that you have told so many times that they are already fixed in your mind and are unlikely to emerge freshly. Look for a story that has potential for exploration, where there is something new to work with, a story to which you are willing to devote yourself for a significant period of time—a story that has a charge and that has some element of the unknown.

2. *A story exists in a context. These questions help to create the environment of the story. Make notes, lists, quickly jot down images in response to the following questions. Don't write the story yet; simply gather together your associations.*

   Who is the protagonist in the story? What is the point of view?

   What is the overview, the larger picture?

   What is at the root of the story? What is its essence, the underlying dilemma?

   What circumstances, events, moods precede the story? What led up to the situation? What has already affected, impinged on the protagonist?

   What might be some consequences of the story? What is coming?

   What forces are crossing each other? What interference is created? What bridge is made?

3. *Inside every story, there is a smaller story. And inside that is a smaller story. Alongside the story are other stories, oblique to it, partially related to it, parallel stories. For example, there was a moment when each of us felt that we came into our manhood or womanhood. Perhaps it was a sexual moment, the first time a young man was aware of eros or the moment when a young woman began menstruating. Perhaps the story we want to tell is the story of the summer when we came into this awareness. Inside that story is another of one day when this happened. And inside that is the story of an hour, or even a moment, that relates to the larger picture. Similarly, there are other stories that are parallel. Perhaps it is a story our father told about a similar experience in his life or a story we remember about the same circumstances occurring to a girlfriend. These are the kinds of associations we are now trying to gather together.*

Write down some of these smaller stories or parallel stories. You may wish to list them, make notes, or write them out. But at this time, do not belabor the writing process or establish a shape that may prematurely determine the direction of the larger piece.

4. *A person is a momentum. An individual is not frozen but changes from one moment to the next, from one year to another. One reason we often seem strangers to ourselves is that we are always in flux. To know ourselves is to know who we were, but who we are or who we might become is never certain. Needless to say, this is also true for our knowledge of others. The strength of a story depends on our ability to render this mobility of self without losing the focus and coherence of the character.*

Select one or several characters who are part of the story but who are not the protagonist. Write portraits of these characters. Begin with who the character is before, even long before, the event occurs. Write the story of this person as he moves through the event. Then continue the portrait of this person as she emerges on the other side. For this undertaking, focus on character rather than story. Allow the event to remain in the background, to be the environment through which the character develops.

It may well be that what you write here will never appear in the work. But whatever you finally write must be based on a deep knowledge of the characters. Sometimes we hope to know the characters as well as we know ourselves. Sometimes we hope to know them much better than we know ourselves.

Try to write these characters as if you were an omniscient narrator. Allow their portraits to gain a perspective or dimension that you personally may not have.

5. *What is the physical environment in which this story takes place? It would not be the same story if the environment were different. There is an intrinsic relationship between event and place, but we often forget this, as if anything could happen anywhere. Perhaps it is because we are so alienated from nature that we forget how much place matters.*

   Enter the environment of the story you are telling, whether it is a room or a landscape. Enter it as if you are seeing it for the first time, with all the freshness of first awareness. Be sensitive to season, time of day, climate. Be aware of the impact of the environment on all your senses. What do you see, smell, hear, taste, feel?

   Look at the environment from several points of view. First, write it from the objective viewpoint of an omniscient narrator. Next, write from the viewpoints of the characters whose portraits you've already written. One character may notice that a room is shabby while to the other character the surroundings may be comfortable. One may notice the light, the other may notice the temperature.

   Finally, look at the surroundings from the perspective of the protagonist. What does she feel? What does he see? What impact does it have upon her? How does the environment contain and also influence the events?

   When you have allowed yourself to see the place, when you have really allowed yourself to see, muse on the symbolic qualities of the environment. A dark room may be merely unlit, for example, or it may carry and convey an ominous darkness.

   Imagine that the environment is itself a character. Allow it to speak.

6. *There is one more thing we want to know before we write: What is the question that is important to us? What are the questions our life addresses? What questions or question may be at the core of this story? Frame the question carefully. Allow yourself to be someone with a serious question that you are pondering. To have a question is at the core of being an artist, serious and conscious.*

   Now write the story. Bring everything you have written and thought about to bear on the story. You may find that the story is better told by focusing on the peripheries or the associations than by addressing it directly. Or you may find that you want to go to the heart of the situation and use your associations to enhance or enrich the story, as if they were tones or tints rather than the image itself. Or you may find that these associations are for you alone, that they provide the background from which you will write, that they will remain a silent influence but will not appear explicitly in the story.

As you write, remember the mystery at the heart of the story. The deeper you enter a story, the more you will know and the more you won't know. Allow the contradictions to remain. Tread the fine line between enlivening the story with detail, being attentive to specifics, and overwriting. Do not tell us more than we have to know. Trust the intelligence of the reader. Allow us to draw our own conclusions. Write until you yourself reach the place of not knowing.

Now that there have been all these instructions, forget them. Write directly and spontaneously. Let the story lead. Follow it with curiosity and wonder. Try to see the story as if it were occurring for the first time, right now, here on the page.

The Story Grows Up: A Novel Appears

And so we have a story. But perhaps we want more. Let us go through the following series of writing questions and see what emerges:

1. *Make a random list of several titles—ten, perhaps—of novels from your bookshelf or of books that come to mind.*

   Look at these titles as if they were new to you. Select seven of them and imagine that each one is a novel that has been given to you to write. Without thinking of the actual novel, which titles intrigue you?

2. *Choose one of the titles from the seven. Write the first paragraph of that novel as if the title had suddenly come to you and you had to begin the book immediately. Try to write this without thinking, creating within yourself the atmosphere of white heat and inspired urgency.*

   Ebba stood soiled in the corner by the window saturated with sun, stood in the perfect square of pale heat. Her thin blue cotton dress flapped around her bony body in the dusty wind making music on the curves and hollows of her frame. She was waiting for the sound of Bernardo's pickup truck to wind its way up the pink dirt road bordering the serpentine creek that pointed to her house like an old bony finger full of knots and knarks and mystery.

   —Joan Tewksbury, from Ebba, or The Tear, *a novel-in-progress*

3. *With the same intensity, write the last paragraph of the book. Again write without thinking, without stopping. Keep your hand moving.*

   I wonder what advice the Gypsies would give me now that they have moved into the vacant ravine next to our house. Is the answer to this linguistic riddle to be read in tea leaves or ferreted out amidst the smell of cloves and garlic?

I was surprised to see the smoke curling up from their trailer this morning be-cause I didn't hear them arrive last night. Usually they make such a clamor and racket, I want to throw pots and pans at them to shut up. But they crept in on the stealthy side of the moon, and I awakened this morning to the smell of their sausages cooking in onions and grease.

There is an old one this time, an ancient crone if there ever was one, it looks like to me. I wonder if she is going to try to kidnap my children and use them to steal from the neighbors or from the hot-dog stand at the beach.

On second thought, maybe she could give me some advice about the words, read my palm or pen or marbles or something. . . .

—*Maurine Doerken*

4. *Imagine your future death. Without thinking, write down the original titles of seven books that you will write between this moment and your death.*

5. *A very sensitive and astute writer has written your obituary. This person knows your life intimately, has read your journals and correspondence and all public mater-ial, interviews, articles, biographies that have been written about you. She has also spoken with your friends and family, but ultimately, she is interested in your work. She writes an obituary in which she discusses your life in terms of your creative work, focusing on the last seven works of your life. Write the obituary or review of your books. As what you will write about is already implicit in the work you have ac-tually done, in what you have already experienced or written, the reviewer will write of your "last seven books" with reference to what came before.*

It is important to base the review or obituary on solid ground. Look to the past to see what has existed and what is foreshadowed. The more specific you can be, the more convincing the obituary will be. You do not want to write your hopes only; you want to capture the possible. To do this, you must take yourself seriously; this includes making a serious evaluation of your work and life up to this moment.

6. *Imagine that you have and will continue to have a literary friend, one who reads all of your work. You and he have pursued this relationship for many years. He knows what you write, how you write. He knows what preoccupies you and what fascinates you. He knows the dark moments, the periods of despair, of empti-ness, as well as your triumphs. He knows you through your use of language, the rhythms that are yours, the metaphors that emerge from your understanding of the nature of the world. And he understands how all these materials combine to create meaning. Most importantly, he knows the thematic concerns and the meaning of your work.*

One day this friend decides to give you a gift. He writes a long and careful let-
ter describing and analyzing your work.

Write it.

A time comes when self-knowledge is sufficient and the creative hungers to
express itself in form. Remember, the Kabbalah says the *Ein Sof,* the divine, had to
withdraw in order to make room for creation. Now it is time for us to withdraw, to make
room, for the work to emerge.

1. *Again select, at random, one of the original titles of your future work. Imagine*
   that having begun this book, you have a dream that refers to the work. It may be
   a dream that you will put in the book, a dream that belongs to one of your char-
   acters, or it may be a dream given to you by the creative unconscious to guide you
   as you proceed with this large work. When you awaken from this dream, you
   are shaken by its significance and clarity. It affects you profoundly. Write down
   the dream. Think about it. Try to understand it. Write some journal notes about
   the dream and its meaning for the book.

2. *It is another day. You have been thinking about the book constantly. The dream*
   is still fresh in your mind. You are aware of the delight of creative preoccupa-
   tion. This is the day you will begin. You clear your desk. You take a moment of
   quiet and write the first paragraph of the book.

   Read it over. Now write another paragraph that refers to or includes the dream.
   Do not censor, do not think. Simply write. Afterward there will be plenty of time
   to consider what you've written.

3. *Read everything over. Be aware that the seed of what is to come is in the begin-*
   ning, that much of what will develop is already implied in the first sentences.

4. *Write the last paragraphs of the book. Again allow the creative to express itself*
   without inhibition. You have already done much work preparing; now you can
   simply write.

Here are some approaches that, though obvious, may help. Ask yourself: And
then what happened? What led up to it? Throw in a few surprises and diversions. See
what happens when you bring the characters together. Look at what you've written: How
do you know all this? How much of what you know needs to be included? What is implied by what you've written? And finally: And so? And then? Where? And finally?

When I finished my second novel, I was despairing of writing anything else.
I was stymied by all the usual fears—that I had nothing to say, that I had said it all, that
I had no idea where to go or how to get there.

"That's foolish," Anaïs Nin said to me after listening to the litany of my complaints. "It is easy to write a novel. You start with a dream, end with a dream, and then you fill in the middle."

I was a dutiful student. That night, I dreamed about a woman who was flying in her long hair. The next day I began another novel that I called *Flying with a Rock.*

Perhaps it is that simple.

You have the dream, you have the first paragraph and the last. Now just fill in the middle.

The Voice of the Story

There is another aspect altogether of finding our story; this is the aspect of the telling. It is not unusual for people to exchange stories in conversation. The new intimacy of these times is based upon a frequent exchange of private material. But despite this, the story often vanishes after the telling. Or it seems as if the teller herself has vanished with the telling, as if the story inhabited and thereby enlivened the teller, and when the story was finished, the teller, diminished by the confidence, disappeared as well. Still, there is a moment when the writer of stories must become a storyteller, when the discovered tale wants to enter the world. There is a way that our stories may not be complete until they are recorded and, perhaps, not even until they are published, told, or read.

When we've finished writing, we may not be aware of what we've written. That is why we need an audience, an interested and compassionate listener, one who reflects back to us, without judgment, the value of recording our lives. But when the ideal group or perfect listener does not exist for us, we have to enact that person ourselves. If there is no one trustworthy to listen to our work, *we* have to become trustworthy. Ultimately, nothing substitutes for reading the work aloud to ourselves or listening to it on tape, as if we have no idea what we will hear, welcoming what is new, unexpected, and surprising.

There is another, more literary consequence of reading aloud. It gives us the opportunity to examine the rhythms, the music of what we write and to locate what is awkward or inappropriate. I try to read everything aloud whether it is a piece meant to be spoken, a novel, or an essay. As a poet, I cherish words, their sounds and rhythms. And the poet in me does not wish to be exiled when I write prose. The poet knows that language can sing and that prose is enhanced by the music intrinsic to it.

We are trying to discern our own voice, to distinguish it from all the others within us and without, and to learn to be faithful to it. We do this for its own sake and to be able to transmit those other voices that sometimes come through us from other realms. When poet Judith Minty speaks of poems as "given" to her, she is speaking about something far more mysterious than inspiration, about the way in which the writer steps aside to allow something else to occur.

Brenda Peterson recalls that her editor asked her how she got the voice in her novel *River of Light*. "I was very young, twenty-six, and she couldn't believe I could write with a voice of such intensity.

"I told her that it is a voice I borrowed from all those hot Southern tent revival meetings, from those preachers who stand up sweating with a bellows in their belly and say, 'Friends, I used to be lost in sin, let me tell you how lost I was . . .' and then they tell an incredible story, about how their soul was lost and then found, was rescued from obliviousness and nothingness. And everyone in the revival tent gets lost and found, gets healed, by listening to that voice, to the rhythm of it.

"We borrow the voice," Brenda continued, "and we don't have to get self-conscious about it, because it is there for us to use. The voice comes through us to heal the others, and it heals us in the telling."

> "Behold, chillun . . .," he began in a voice trembling, as if stunned by his own memory. "Behold the beastly procession into my ark! The clock strikes midnight down in the town. Nine, ten, eleven . . . and, Lord, what a wailin of wind, a mighty gnashin of teeth and moan of tongues. Up in the rafters a swoopin and flappin of wings, then a siren's shriek cryin out, 'Your blood, the blood of your lives will I require; at the hand of every beast I will require it; and beware, thou man of little faith, for I come like a thief, like a night animal!'"[5]

When the voice appears, we have no choice but to open ourselves to it, though it may feel like a great wind that will overwhelm us or a great wave in which we may drown. When it comes, we know it is not our voice and also that it has been given to us to speak it. It comes through like a chant, like an invocation, incantation, like prophecy, and we are swept along by its rhythm and its insistence. Poets from every culture have prayed to be the mouthpiece, the lyre, the flute of God.

> A woman in a car parked at the edge of the fragrant sage speaks. "I play God," she says to no one at all, "and God plays the chord." There is the sound of a wooden flute, I think.[6]

There is a moment when we choose to allow ourselves to be entered, to allow the breath to enter us, to be inspired. There is a moment when we choose to relinquish ourselves, when we put ourselves in the hands of the story and let it speak. First we must find our own voice and become stalwart in it, and then we have the strength to allow the other voice in alongside it: our own voice with its own particular hum and scent, and then that other voice with its particular rhythm and intensity.

The Story That Must Be Told

Some years ago, I was teaching a men's writing group. Usually the men gathered together during the break to talk sports or politics. But one day, they were telling war stories. Or rather one man was talking about his experiences in World War II, while the others were listening raptly. This speaker was the only one out of the twelve who had been in a war; the other men were desperately curious about this experience, which had eluded them or which they had avoided. I asked the veteran to continue telling the stories, but more formally, in our circle.

He began to recount the usual and familiar tales, moments of bravery, of fear; each was heroic, full of bravado, even nostalgia. He had told these stories a thousand times since 1945. After a while, it became obvious that we were merely being entertained and that the storyteller and the listeners were being deprived of an essential part of the experience—of the truth, actually. But I didn't know where it lay or how to access it.

He continued speaking: "We were in a foxhole . . ."

Through some grace, I asked, "What is a foxhole?"

He looked at me, startled. Was I joking? Was I stupid?

I asked it again, most seriously, "What is a foxhole?"

He looked in my face for a long time. "A foxhole is a place filled with the blood, guts, and shit of all the men who have been in it before you."

There was a profound silence in the room.

Then he continued, "I climbed out of the foxhole and ran to the German tank . . ."

"Wait," I insisted with sudden understanding. "Would you tell this story very, very slowly, slow motion, as if it were a film, frame by frame, seeing everything as you tell it. Tell it in the present tense, as if it were happening now."

He began. He spoke very slowly. He described what was happening, one step at a time. It was as if there were days between each sentence. We went with him at his agonizing pace. He crawled out of the foxhole. He ran, but in slow motion, toward the tank. . . . Then he burst into tears. He wept inconsolably. We all wept with him. There was silence in the room except for the weeping.

When he could speak again, he was very sober. "I never saw this before," he said. "The tanks . . . the brains and blood splattered over them."

"If you had seen this, if you had felt this, when you were living it," I said, "you would not have survived." The only way soldiers survive a war is to become unconscious.

Afterward, the form of the war stories maintains this lack of consciousness. Like "twilight sleep," these stories are designed to keep the soldiers from remembering what they couldn't experience in the moment. Still, the real moment is alive within each of us and must be heard.

Storyteller-director Arthur Strimling was wondering why people tell stories altogether. This is a tale that he told to explain storytelling:

A woman stood up in the story-sharing session that follows each of his performances of *What My Eyes Have Witnessed*, a piece based on Barbara Myerhoff's *Fairfax Tales*. She said that she had followed him from performance to performance without having found the courage, until that moment, to tell the following story:

At the beginning of the war, her uncle had returned to her village in Eastern Europe. He was so well dressed—that is, he was wearing a suit and leather shoes—that she wondered, at first, if he were really a human being. The uncle said he would help the family escape, and her mother packed some food and the few poor belongings they could manage to carry, and they prepared to leave. As they were leaving the courtyard, they heard a tiny baby crying ceaselessly.

"That is an infant that a family has thrown away because they can't care for it anymore," the woman's mother said, having heard such sounds many times before.

"Will you take it?" the uncle asked.

"No," the mother answered, "I have to take care of my own."

That's the end of the story. There is no moral to it. The woman said she had to tell it because it was her mother who made that decision to protect her.

But why did she have to tell it? The story was inside her all these years and had to come out. And now the story is in us. We are also carrying it. This helps her with her burden. When all of us carry it, it will be easier not only for her but also for ourselves.

> *Is there a story that you must tell or write that you have kept secret? Write the story. Write the story, even if it means that you will not allow anyone else to read it. Allow the story to appear on the page. Afterward you can decide how to respond to it.*

In April of 1989, I was privileged to attend a retreat with Zen Master Thich Nhat Hanh and American Vietnam veterans on "Forgiveness and Reconciliation." During the week, we met in small groups. The first task was:

> *Write the story one cannot bear to remember, let alone to record. Afterward tell your story slowly. So slowly that you hear it and feel it. So that you experience it, perhaps for the first time. Tell it first for yourself. Second, so that it will not fester within you. Third, so others will help you bear it.*

The purpose of this exercise was to release the poison and correct the disso-
ciation, disconnection, and repression that were a consequence of that war. It was also
to allow the burden to be shared by the community.

Afterward, it was suggested that a second story be told:

Tell a story, find the story, of how you transformed yourself sufficiently to tell
the first story. Tell this story so you can know and appreciate the developing con-
sciousness within you. Record the story so that it can become a foundation for the
good, the healing, and the joyful to come.

Then there was another set of questions to address:

What is still lethal inside you that wants to be transformed? What do you need
to reconcile within yourself to be at peace? Is there an action you can take to ease
yourself?

In one of the small groups, a vet who had been silent decided to speak. One
of his friends, he said darkly, had been ambushed and killed by the Vietcong. The vet,
beside himself with grief and rage, retaliated. He gave two Vietnamese children poisoned
cookies. Within a moment of doing so, he realized what he had done, but it was too late.
Brokenhearted but impotent to do anything, he watched the two children die.

He had never told this story before. He broke down weeping. Seeing his despair, a Vietnamese Buddhist monk, who had been in Vietnam during the war, stood
up, did a full prostration in front of the weeping veteran, and held him in his arms
until he was calm.

It is not only war stories that are unbearable. Many of us who have not been to the bat-
tlefront have, nevertheless, survived our own private wars and conflagrations. Sometimes
even stories of joy and rare vision seem unspeakable. Sometimes what is most difficult
is granting ourselves the right to tell our story, whatever its content and origin.

The Chilean novelist Ariel Dorfman says that what compels him to write his
story of exile is his fear that the others who are always telling the story of the silenced
ones will not, cannot, tell the true story.

The false story or the formula story diminishes and contracts us. But the real
story, painful as it may be, expands us and opens our heart. Every real story is part of
the construction of self, and every real story adds its dimension and wisdom to the
collective. Ultimately, we are the sum of the stories we've lived and the stories we've
heard. The pied piper who led the children away was a storyteller. Only the children
were wise enough to follow him. It is the child in us who responds to the incantation:
Let me tell you a story. When the true storyteller comes, like the pied piper, to lead us

away from our conventional and restricted existence, let us follow eagerly because something will be revealed and healing will occur.

In *The Magic Orange Tree and Other Haitian Folktales*,[7] Diane Wolkstein, who gathered these tales and is a true storyteller herself, describes the entrance of a storyteller into the marketplace:

> *"Cric?"* the Haitian storyteller calls out when she or he has a story to tell. *"Crac!"* the audience responds *if* they want the storyteller to begin. If they do not respond with *crac!*, the storyteller cannot begin.

"Cric!" means I have something that I want to tell you, and I will tell it to the best of my ability and with all my heart. *"Crac!"* means we will help you tell the story by giving it all our attention and listening as deeply as we can. In this interchange, story is born as a living event.

Part III

The Larger Story: Archetypes, Fairy Tales, and Myths

The more the universe seems incomprehensible,
the more it also seems pointless. . . .
The effort to understand the universe
is one of the very few things
that lifts human life a little above the level of farce
and gives it some of the grace of tragedy.

Steven Weinberg, "The First Three Minutes"

The country beneath
the earth has a green sun
and the rivers flow backwards:
the trees and rocks are the same
as they are here, but shifted.
Those who live there are always hungry;
from them you can learn
wisdom and great power,
if you can descend and return safely.

Margaret Atwood[1]

The Larger Story and the Domain of the Sacred

There is a Lacandon elder whose name is Chan K'in. He is one of the few remaining Mayan Indian teachers who remembers the old stories. He tells us, "The roots of all living things are tied together. When a mighty tree is felled, a star falls from the sky; before you cut down a mahogany you should ask permission of the keeper of the forest, and you should ask permission of the keeper of the star."[2]

This little tale reveals more than is apparent at first. Chan K'in is saying that the trees and the stars are tied to each other as living things and that behind each is an invisible being, a presence outside the human and physical realm. The territory of the keeper of the forest and the keeper of the stars is the sacred. And it is this territory that we are about to enter. A larger story wraps itself about and permeates our little lives and the mundane world. In doing so, it pulls us toward—and sometimes even briefly into—the domain of the sacred.

We can never quite define or identify the territory of the sacred, for we live outside of it, although, paradoxically, it is also ever present. For this reason we often describe the sacred with language that refers to its intangibility. We describe it as radiant, transparent, luminous. We call it blessed and holy. We say it is the realm of seeds, of beginnings, and similarly we say it is the end and the aftermath. We describe it as eternal and infinite. We say it is the abode of the immortals and the gods. And though we fail, always, to capture it completely, it seems that one life task is to move closer to this territory, to understand it, even to live according to it.

It is difficult to enter the sacred. Many stories from many different cultures instruct us that this can occur only when the rivers surrounding paradise or Hades are stilled. But even then, we enter as aliens—not as citizens—without the capacity to understand fully what we see, and, alas, we remember very little when we return.

Physics postulates that there are essential elements that are also essential forces, and the world is composed of their relationships. Behind or within the tree are molecules. And behind or within molecules are atoms. Behind or within the atom, particles. Behind or within the particles are quarks or leptons, fields of energy in a cosmic dance. Behind or within our cultures are individual lives. And behind or within them are stories. Behind these stories are archetypal tales. Behind these tales are strange forces that combine and recombine to reveal and create the world.

We are able to know so little about the sacred realm that we cannot specify it. Whatever one calls it, how one identifies or explains it, finally indicates only that it is a mysterious realm somehow *beyond*—beyond the pedestrian, the human, the terrestrial. A realm beyond, which some believe is sanctified and others find simply inexplicable.

But if there is any agreement on the nature of this realm or of the sacred, it is that it has been approached through and exists in story. By and large, fables, allegories, tales, parables, and myths spring from the attempt to bring the vision of the sacred world into the mundane or to bring us into the sacred and, by doing so, to bind together and revitalize the community. In the beginning, these stories—story itself—were the nonexclusive province of the priests and holy people. Then, as the secular domain began to dominate, story left the sacred arena—even as humans were thrown out of paradise—and became the handmaiden of history and psychology. Soon, with some exceptions, story's intrinsic relationship with the sacred was forgotten, but not its function. Yet even now, when a story we are telling really comes alive or when we have an experience of telling it profoundly, it may be because we can detect the shimmer of a larger story, of the archetypal forms, and of the sacred looming behind it. In these moments, our personal reality coincides with other realities, the world is made whole, and we experience the possibility of transformation through this conjunction with spirit.

Because we are moving into numinous territory, from our personal story to the larger story, a guide can be useful. Chan K'in is such a guide to his people. Like the shaman whose task it is to see into the invisible, to ascend into heaven for wisdom, or cross the terrible boundary into the underworld to retrieve lost souls, he has developed, within his particular cultural context, the spiritual agility and delicate balance that allow him to move between the different worlds. According to Victor Perera, Chan K'in has the "ability to hold a community together through his skill as a storyteller and his authority as the guardian of a cultural tradition descended from the earliest Olmecs and Mayas."[3]

In different cultures, different members are designated for such enterprises. For many Jews and Christians, the rabbi and the priest are the designated mediators between this world and the eternal; they, too, rely on legends, stories, and parables to transmit their teachings. In the *I Ching,* the ancient Chinese book of wisdom, such roles are defined as follows: "Priests are the intermediaries between men and gods; magicians serve as the intermediaries between gods and men. Here we have penetration of the realms of the visible and invisible, whereby it becomes possible for everything to be set right."[4]

Every culture creates the means by which its people can access sacred territory together. But when the time has come for us as individuals to enter into this sacred territory, we may find the passage difficult, if not dangerous. Then we also need someone, a guide, a psychopomp to take us across the threshold.

Sometimes the guide is as mysterious as the psychopomp Hermes, who leads the souls of the dead into the underworld, or as formidable as Virgil, who led Dante into the realms of hell; sometimes she is as wondrous as the appearance of an angel or as disturbing as the odd creature at the crossroads whom we were lucky enough to befriend and thereby earned a gift—the cloak of invisibility, the magic password, the sleeping potion without which we cannot cross over to or survive on the other side. At other times, the unexpected guide is as deceptively innocent as the white rabbit Alice followed down the rabbit hole into the other world. In any case, it is fortunate to have a guide, and if one does not appear, it may be worth our while to put in a request. The guide exercise presented in this chapter helps us to do just that as it takes us from the smaller story of the personal and mundane worlds to the larger story of the sacred.

A Guide Appears

When I began teaching at California Institute for the Arts in 1970, I was already interested in the sources of creativity and the means to access them. But I was concerned with the danger of entering the psyche unprepared and unprotected. This was during the very early seventies when many students were not only fragile—as we all were during the crises of the Vietnam War—but also disoriented by large-scale experimentation with hallucinogens. Consequently, I worried that, in some cases, the explorations of the creative process might overwhelm an already traumatized psyche. Because these students had come to Cal Arts to become artists, I couldn't—wouldn't—ask them to restrain their forays into the creative, but I wanted to develop processes that would protect them when they were working or writing outside the classroom. As a consequence, I developed what I call a guide meditation. Through synchronicity, several people seem to have "invented" the same guide meditation at the same time, always as a means to access the wisdom that exists within.

I will outline the guide meditation in a section to come. First, I wish to tell you my own experience with it, to reveal, at the outset, my own story of innocence or ignorance that was one of my first encounters with story, myth, and the archetypes.

In the writing class in which I proposed the guide meditation, we had just begun to work with different myths. I was so attracted to the myth of Ariadne and Theseus that it never occurred to me to do the meditation myself. I instructed my students in the process I had just invented, and after the students began working with their guides in class, I invoked Ariadne during my own explorations.

One day, I could no longer ignore the nagging feeling that I was cheating. I had not permitted my students to arbitrarily choose a guide. I had maintained that it was absolutely necessary to go through the process, had warned them not to hold preconceptions about the outcome, and I had insisted that they accept whatever guide appeared, no matter how they felt about him or her at the time. Yet I, myself, had violated each of the principles I had so carefully established. Accordingly, I decided to do the guide meditation. Precisely following my own instructions, I sat down to wait for Ariadne to appear in my imagination and to offer me the golden thread.

Some minutes later, I thought I heard metal clanking. Keeping my eyes closed, I warily wrote, "Who is there?"

A silent voice answered, "Athena."

I wrote, "Athena! What are you doing here?" I was quite belligerent, behaving in a manner exactly contrary to the one I had advised for my students. I began writing furiously, "Why are you here? I never think about you. You don't interest me. You never enter my mind." I was outraged but also unnerved, perhaps even afraid. Some figure or voice had entered my imagination without my will. Someone, something, I had never considered or encountered before—and whom I suspected I couldn't control—was occupying my mind.

After a few minutes, I gathered myself together, allowing curiosity and adventure to replace my more than inappropriate indignation. And when this happened, I was humbled by awe, even gratitude. What followed seemed to me to be truly remarkable.

"Why have you come to me?" I asked.

"I have never been mothered," Athena answered.

In an instant, my heart broke. When she was just pregnant, Metis, Athena's mother, was swallowed by Zeus; it had been predicted that she would give birth to a child who was destined to be greater and stronger than he. At the end of nine months, Athena, fully armed and shouting a war cry, leapt from his head. I knew this story quite well but had never realized that it implied that Athena had never been mothered.

In my own life, I had been called to maturity so very early that I had often felt that I had had no mother, that I was the daughter of the great father God, and that I was and would always be a warrior. Now I felt enormous pity for this goddess of war and wisdom.

"Look at this armor," Athena rubbed her hand under the metal at her neck, "see how it chafes me." At the time, I was still fighting in the courts to be reinstated to the community college from which I had been fired, and I was only too aware of how unwieldy, cumbersome, and necessary armor was. I had needed to arm myself against public calumny, and although I had managed it, I wasn't bearing up easily; I hated the armor and felt diminished by resorting to it. I wanted to be able to fight without fighting—as in my imagination an angel might fight without violating her integrity—without rancor, without the slightest stain on my hands, with total sweetness. Athena was speaking directly to my experience in words and images I could not have imagined myself.

But it was when she made a third statement that I was completely undone: "They mocked me when I competed with Helen and Aphrodite for the golden apple. Because I am the goddess of wisdom and because I am the goddess of war, no one, including Paris who was the judge, imagined that I might also be beautiful. It is unbearably lonely to be who I am. Women are not expected to be intelligent. The beauty of intelligent women is rarely recognized."

I don't know if these words were articulations of my inner knowledge or whether they were communications from another world we cannot even imagine. I did know that many women, myself included, were agonized by exactly this situation. During the height of feminism, women who were insisting upon equal education, respect, and power did so at the risk of never, as a consequence, having a private life. Patriarchy does not take well to feminism, and it was quite hard for most men to imagine that an intelligent, powerful, forthright woman could be lovable and sexual as well.

Thus, Athena became my guide and inner companion. I often turned to her when I was troubled. She was often stern in her responses, trying to teach me how to be a warrior. She continued to scoff at me for wanting to fight naked. "Lady Godiva was not going up against an organized and hostile collective," she said, "and her husband had sworn to put out the eyes of anyone who looked at her, let alone injured her. She was neither alone nor unprotected. If you want to be an innocent, don't fight. You cannot overcome enemies by making a magic circle around yourself and stripping down to your core. Innocence does not always inspire compassion; sometimes it inspires rage. And, furthermore, you are not innocent. You are a sophisticated and mature woman. If you need or want to fight, rally your armies, outfit them, and protect yourself appropriately."

The Implication of the Guide

What does it mean when a figure like Athena appears to us? Much has been written about active imagination from a psychological point of view in terms of how such a figure might be constituted within us and what effects, positive and negative, it can have on the psyche. The archetype, we are often warned, can energize us, but it can also possess us, and we must be wary if we hope to avoid being overwhelmed.

But while we are concerned here both with the content of the guide's revelation and its effect upon us, we are first of all concerned with what it means for us to find ourselves in a narrative relationship with a figure from another reality. It almost doesn't matter who comes or what the exalted one says. What does matter is that we are entering into an alliance with an inner figure as if he or she were a living person; the consequences of our relationship may turn out to be as profound as any we've ever had with living family or friends.

We are not speaking here simply about a relationship within the country of the imagination but about a particular kind of relationship with a particular kind of being. Frequently, authors develop a similar relationship with characters, living with them, as it were, day and night for months or years so that when the book is finished, it is as if a death has occurred. Still, it is one thing to be visited by a character, and it is quite another to be "visited" by an archetype, by a mythic figure. When this occurs, we are in the realm of the gods. Because Athena carries both a certain history *and* a certain energy, when one encounters her or others like her, one encounters the ancestors, the particular configurations of the psyche as contained in her story, *and* the divine.

The process of entering the mythic world is not without its dangers. In fact, it was a recognition of these dangers that originally inspired me to design the guide meditation. The guide mediates these dangers, but embarking toward a meeting with a guide takes one into those same turbulent waters for which one is seeking a pilot. There is no solution to this paradox. We cannot find a guide without taking the risk of going toward the guide. When my students questioned my caution, I used to tease them with my own homilies: "Terror is terrifying." "Danger is dangerous." It takes awareness—and perhaps, though I hate to admit it, some measure of years on the planet—to know what these words mean. It wasn't that my students didn't know terror or hadn't ever been in danger; it was that they didn't know how much it might matter to them.

Athena, then, was both the event and the safeguard. She was both my protection and my experience. Because she appeared, I was in the mythic realm, and again because she appeared, I was protected. Particularly if one has neither analyst for the night sea journey, nor priest, nor the steady protection of a contemplative practice, the guide can be a valuable companion when entering the nether realms.

The appearance of a divine or mythic guide can be a staggering and transformative experience if we can, without hubris, recognize the privilege of the visitation. Here, as in many other instances of the exploration of the imagination, it is necessary to proceed both without egotism and without diminishing the experience. Inflation and trivialization are the Scylla and Charybdis of this passage.

Athena astonished me. Her words indicated that we were living the same story, that her appearance was not arbitrary. The appearance of a particular guide has significance because it implies an intersection—something in her story, in who she is, that parallels or illuminates our own story.

When Athena (or any other guide) appears, she brings story with her. In a flash, we see her story and our story together. When our smaller story is overlaid upon the other larger story, a third tale is created that is also ours but that draws to itself all the meanings in both the smaller story and the larger myth. When this happens, it is as if our lives have been catapulted beyond the fourth dimension.

How to Approach the Guide

The guide meditation takes us into a new realm. When we embark on such an inner adventure, it must be with an open mind and heart. It may happen that a guide will not come the first time, that you will have to attempt the meditation several times. Be patient. In time, a guide will appear.

It is difficult to know why the doors open one day and not another or why they open to one person and not another. There are no certain formulas for accessing the imagination; there are only procedures that may or may not be effective for different people at any given time. Too many texts, workshops, and therapists routinize the approach to such an experience, as though the process were as easy and ordinary as following a recipe. But though we can follow such directions, it does not mean that we have encountered the story, myth, or guide on a profound level. Technology, even creative or spiritual technology, can provide modest help, but if overemphasized, it soon becomes another impediment. Something must be left to the mystery. Something in us must be open to that which cannot be contained or prescribed. And as with any creative activity, we may hit a dry spell, which may last for hours, days, or weeks. And then, without any explanation, it rains.

The guide meditation is the beginning of the delicate work we will be doing in the area of the sacred. Before you begin, it is important to address the following questions:

Why you are doing this work now?

Are you ready to encounter the creative?

Are you entering this new realm with appropriate respect?

Are you willing to abide by the laws of the world that you are entering?

Will you be careful not to exploit or devalue the treasures that you discover?

Will you honor the secrets and revelations that you receive?

Our relationship with the other realms must be one of the greatest respect and subtlety. We are not looking to rub Aladdin's magic lamp in order to summon an imprisoned genie, enslaved and diminished, who will satisfy all our wishes. Quite the contrary: we want to be worthy of this relationship. If we follow the teachings in such stories as Aladdin and the Magic Lamp and "The Fisherman's Wife," we will not make imperious commands but will be humble and respectful: "Not my will but thine." And we will attempt to avoid the trap, so specifically delineated in "Rumpelstiltskin" or "The Girl with the Silver Hands," of thoughtlessly offering what we cannot give in order to receive specific favors that ultimately threaten us or those we love. In these realms, it is best to prepare ourselves to meet whatever comes with an open heart.

Patience is very important. Also the willingness to submit to the particular timing of the creative. And finally, restraint: the agreement not to storm the gates of the unconscious or to enter that terrain with the imperialistic intentions of those who remain in the avaricious kingdom of the day realm.

To enter these other worlds we have to be responsible, willing to deport ourselves according to their very particular laws. As James Hillman warns in *Dreams and the Underworld,* one must not enter Hades as Hercules did, with sword in hand. For if we are arrogant or inattentive, we may suffer the loss of what we have gained, like Lot's wife who looked back and was turned to salt or like Orpheus who, looking back, lost Eurydice. And we must remain awake. There are many accounts of those who, like Parsifal, fall asleep and miss finding the Grail.

> Remember the ones who get burned. Their desires cut off from their hearts. Burned by the Prince of Fire who sleeps waiting at the edge of vision. Remember the ones who grasped more than they could contain. Remember the ones who could not stay awake. Remember the ones who get burned.
>
> —*Corey Fischer, Albert Greenberg, and Naomi Newman of A Traveling Jewish Theatre,* Coming from a Great Distance

Spiritual practitioners align themselves with the universe both for their own sakes and for the sake of all sentient beings. The development of consciousness in oneself is of value to the universe. Thus, work on oneself is related to work for others. Awareness of this equation opens the way for a profound meeting between one world and another. Creativity, imagination, and healing coexist in an ecologically balanced moral universe. Perceiving the interrelationship between worlds is an important step in making wholeness out of what has been alienated. All the work we are doing strives to balance what has gone awry and to heal what has been injured through disconnection.

The colonization of the New World by Europeans can be a cautionary metaphor for the way we approach the virgin territory of the inner world. The settlers who came to the United States, like those who arrived in Latin America and Africa, had the opportunity to learn from and coexist with the peoples who were already inhabiting the land. Instead, they virtually exterminated or enslaved the native peoples. Imagine the culture that might have developed if Native American vision had been invited to meld with and inform European understanding. Westerners would have benefited from the indigenous spiritual wisdom that, instead, they did their utmost to destroy and that we now fear cannot be preserved or recovered.

It is better to avoid the inner world than to convert it in the service of one's image of the good and valuable. Left to itself, the inner world or creative exists within us, doing its work in ways we cannot imagine, just as the water in streams hidden under the earth mysteriously nourishes us. Better to leave the water untapped in the earth than to create more deserts through our relentless thirst.

Preparation for the Guide Meditation

Please read the meditation that follows carefully before beginning.

I would like to suggest that you record this guide meditation very slowly (allocating forty-five minutes at the very least) as if you were initiating someone else. Allow enough time for the listener to enter into the experience, for the images to come, and for some moments of silence between each sentence. When you come to the section where you will converse with the guide, be certain to give yourself sufficient time, as much as two or three minutes between questions.

When you have a block of uninterrupted silence available to you—half the time for listening and half the time for writing—listen to the recording with your eyes closed. After you have gone through the experience, write it down in as much detail as possible. Try to write down the experience accurately so that at a later time you will know exactly what happened. If additional insights or images come to you as you write, record them elsewhere so that the memory of the guide meditation is retained purely.

You may wish to record the initial breathing and relaxation section of the meditation separately, to use on other occasions.

None of the meditations or exercises in this book is meant to be inviolate. All of them can be altered. If the language feels odd or uncomfortable to you, find other words. If you wish to go at another pace, do so. If some of the procedures or questions seem inappropriate, eliminate them or substitute others. I have tried to minimize my guidance so that you can fill in the details. Even so, if you feel constricted or overdirected, reformulate the exercise so that you are free to express yourself fully.

Before you begin, consider the following: your purpose is to contact the wisest part of yourself and allow it to coalesce into a mythic or historic figure. Therefore, hold in your mind the expectation that the one who appears will have three essential qualities:

1. He or she is extremely wise and experienced.

2. He or she knows the ways of the mythic and sacred realms.

3. He or she wants to guide you.

When the figure appears, accept whoever comes with respect even if you don't know, or don't think you know, who has appeared or even if you don't like or approve of the figure. Working with the guide, you will have opportunities to learn why he or she appears.

The Guide Meditation

Place yourself in a relaxed and comfortable position. Close your eyes. Begin to breathe slowly and deeply. With each breath, imagine yourself entering deeply, then more deeply, into yourself. As you exhale, imagine yourself releasing the preoccupations and concerns of the day.

When you are relaxed and centered, begin to count down, with several seconds between each beat, into the very core of yourself:

20, go down slowly . . ., 19, into the creative . . ., 18, into the very core of yourself . . ., 17, leave the world and its concerns . . ., 16, relax, release . . ., 15, descend to the place where images live . . ., 14, travel to the innermost part of yourself . . ., 13, allow the wisest part of yourself to emerge . . ., 12, be open to what comes . . ., 11, relinquish your will to the intuitive powers . . ., 10, look forward to what is coming . . ., 9, find safety within yourself . . ., 8, descend even further . . ., 7, yield . . ., 6, drop further into the very heart of wisdom . . ., 5, find the place of stillness . . ., 4, go down into yourself . . ., 3, further down . . ., 2, into the very center of wisdom . . ., 1 . . .

You find yourself in a place of natural beauty and great tranquillity. You are here alone and feel exceedingly safe. Look at your surroundings. Be attentive to every detail. Be aware of each of your senses and what knowledge they bring you. When you have acquainted yourself with your surroundings . . .

Find yourself on an unknown path. It beckons to you and you follow, curious and delighted, observing everything. You feel a sense of hope and anticipate a great adventure.

The path proceeds into the distance. There . . . you see . . . it ends at a cave. Slow down until you feel ready to approach the cave. Reaffirm your desire to meet a guide.

When you are ready, enter the cave. Look around.

Inside the cave, invite an animal to come to you. Do not be afraid. Approach each other. Find a way to bond with the animal.

When you and the animal have entered into a relationship, ask the animal to take you to your guide. Follow the animal wherever it leads.

Soon you will see a figure coming to you from a distance. This figure may be your guide. Approach with an open heart, a willingness to be guided, with anticipation and respect.

When you and the figure are face to face ask:

Are you my guide?

If the figure is not your guide, ask to be taken to your guide.

When you are with the guide, ask the guide the following questions:

What is your name?

Why have you come to me at this time?

What do you require of me in order to be my guide?

What else is required for me to be fully engaged in this process?

Discuss any questions, anxieties, concerns you may have with the guide or anything else that may come up in this meditation.

Make an offering to the guide as a token of your goodwill.

Be open to the possibility that the guide may give you a gift as a sign of his or her presence.

Arrange for another meeting or a means by which you can invoke the guide.

Give thanks.

When you are ready, gradually count yourself back to the day world: . . . 1 . . . 2 . . . and so on to . . . 20.

Awaken.

Write about your experience in detail.

When the Guide Appears

So, the guide has appeared. When all is said and done, nothing quite astonishes us so much as a visitation from another world. Science-fiction depictions of aliens seem tame, wooden, and two-dimensional compared with these awesome revelations from the inner world, these living encounters in the mythic realm.

And if it sometimes happens that a historic rather than a mythic figure appears, perhaps it is because history supersedes the sacred in contemporary life or because the historic can also be charged with otherworldly splendor. Such is the case in the following excerpt:

> *Wild Heart/Corazón Salvaje*[5]
> Neruda, you came to my ear
> one night while I was sleeping,
> in the rolling familiar cadences
> of poetry, your voice too tender
> and too rapid   Though I recognize the
>   rhythms,
> not a single word could I hold onto,
> little fish in swift currents
> they slipped away, one after another
> In the morning, I was abandoned
>
> . . .
>
> Neruda, you came to my ear
> while I was sleeping, reciting your poems
> hour after hour. My hand twitched toward the
>   pen, but
> I could not grasp it.

. . .

I am looking for you
In the sea are many rivers which have no names
The rivers of your body have joined these
waters of many colors and temperaments,
     interweaving
courses of currents, each with its
miraculous succession of fishes and plankton
     and
jeweled ropes of kelp and the pelican hurling
     herself
like a stone out of the sky.

What I would give
once again to be loose in the rhythms,
the unrolling waves of your poem
drowning me, unfastening the floors beneath,
pulling me out to sea, to be

one with the waves and the fountains
raised up and demolished, raised up
and demolished

the waves
miles across and the fountains
inexhaustible.

—*Maia*

If you are not successful in invoking a guide when you first go through the guide meditation, try it another time. Some people have difficulty trusting that a guide will come to them. Others have a different reaction: they find it exceedingly difficult to give up their will to anyone, even a benign and wise inner figure. These feelings are to be respected.

If you find after a few attempts that there is a part of you that is adamantly resistant or afraid of the experience, wait for a time when it may be more appropriate to pursue a guide.

Place yourself in dialogue with the self who resists. Negotiate.

Now try again. This time proceed in segments. Stop to write after you have received the first images. When the territory you have entered has become familiar, proceed with the next part of the guide meditation. Once again, pause, and befriend and record the images before going on. In this way, the geography of the imagination rises slowly and gently into consciousness and the meditation proceeds according to the rhythms of the creative.

Many people are rude, intrusive, and disrespectful of the ways and values of other cultures. Most unfortunately, many individuals approach their inner selves with similar disrespect and insistence. If we can establish reciprocal relationships with our inner figures, we may learn how to relate to people from other cultures. Or, conversely, if we develop intercultural skills, we can apply them to our inner selves. One way or another, we must learn not to invade new territory or to overwhelm the figures who appear to us. If one visits a Navajo person, one waits outside the house until he or she is noticed and invited in. This can serve as a model for approaching a guide.

Make your presence known and then wait. Eventually, a guide will appear to you, presenting himself in his own manner and at her own pace. Sometimes a guide first appears as a shadowy figure or is silent in the face of questions. Allow as much time as both of you need to become acquainted. As we do not know if it is you or the guide who is the shy one, proceed as if it is the guide and not yourself who is wary. It is appropriate to approach a guide with the sensitivity one would bring to the most delicate interactions and to wait, happily, until the guide is ready to make a revelation.

Unless you have contrived the outcome of the meditation, as I did with Ariadne, it is wise to accept whoever comes, no matter how absurd this guide may seem. When Hopalong Cassidy appeared to a friend, he was embarrassed but accepting. After all, he had always known that his imagination wound itself around pop heroes. Ultimately, this playful encounter with Cassidy challenged his cynicism.

Another man was caught between dismay and exasperation when he encountered a guide who claimed that his name was Rambam. Naturally, this sounded silly to him; he felt ridiculed by his imagination. "It could have been Topsy-Turvy, or Humpty-Dumpty," he sputtered. And he was even angrier when I insisted that he trust this communication and explore the identity of Rambam. Because Rambam spoke to him with particular and accurate wisdom, because this figure had a peculiar if uncanny sagacity, he continued to explore his encounters with it, but not without protest. Only when he had accepted the absurdity of his inner life did I tell him, as kindly as I could, that Rambam was, in fact, an appellation for the great Jewish rabbi, philosopher, savant, and physician of the twelfth century, Maimonides. Rambam derives from the initials of his name: Rabbi Moses ben Maimon.

At any point during the meditation, it may not go the way we expect it to. The animal may not appear, or it may be vicious. It may not take us to the guide, or the guide may not appear, may not reveal her name, may not answer questions, may put his own questions to us, may reject us, or any number of other possibilities. The moment we set out on such a quest we are forced—like the protagonist of any one of millions of stories—to deal with circumstances we can't possibly predict. What brings us through— if we come through—is what repeatedly brings the protagonists through: one's wits, innocence, an open heart, the willingness to do what is required, flexibility, generosity of spirit, and wakefulness. These qualities (or, in their absence, the sincere desire for these qualities) seem to protect the hero or heroine, to the extent that one can ever be protected. Still, in the other worlds, just as in this one, nothing can be guaranteed.

Working with the Guide

When working with the guide, remember who the guide is. After a while, we fall into forgetting and merely think of the guide as a wise being. This is not the case; the guide informs us not only by what she says but also by her qualities. Or he may inform us through the details of his particular life or story.

Recently, when I invoked a guide after my life had changed radically, C. G. Jung appeared. It is unfortunately true that I greeted him just as rudely as I had greeted Athena, although I like to think I caught myself more quickly. After several dialogues, it became clear that it was quite different to be guided by Jung than by Athena. He was so much more concerned with the events of my inner life, while Athena helped me to negotiate the public arena. But, further, I was able to clarify several dilemmas by reading Jung's autobiography and applying the details of his life to my own.

After your first meetings with the guide, it is important to see what the guide will tell you about his story, to try to find out whatever you can about the archetype the guide embodies. One can always ask the same questions again:

Why has this particular being come especially to me?

Why at this time?

How does the guide's story clarify my own?

The guide who supports our writing life may also be a companion for our worldly activities, like the imaginary friend from childhood who accompanied so many of us through the difficult first years of making sense of the world.

Just before Q. went into the hospital for cancer surgery, I led her in a guide meditation. A woman in a dramatic and elegant hat appeared, saying she was Mary Ann Evans but refusing to give any more information about herself. Though she wouldn't reveal her identity, she was quite articulate about Q.'s life and assured her that this period of illness would have great value to her as a way of purification. She also encouraged

Q. to be more attentive to her creativity. Q. claimed she had no time, and Mary Ann Evans laughed.

When Q. awakened from surgery, she was startled to find a gift from her sister-in-law by her bed. It was a biography of George Eliot, born Mary Ann Evans. What Mary Ann Evans had had to say to Q., as one woman to another, had had little impact compared with what came from George Eliot. It wasn't only the fact of the novelist's "appearance" that influenced Q., it was the context, the life experience that turned what might have been easy advice or platitudes into serious counsel. Knowing about Eliot's life made the difference.

The Larger Story: Fairy Tale and Myth

Once upon a time . . .

It came to pass in the land of . . .

These are no ordinary words. They are incantations that bring us into another realm. "Once upon a time" means it happened long ago, so very long ago that it was out of time. Being out of time, it was in the eternal and therefore of another world. Once upon a time is happening to the extraordinary beings whose story is being told and is also happening to us, now and always, all at the same time. Once upon a time happens to everyone.

Once upon a time is always now. "There was a king and queen . . ."—they are always ourselves. "And it came to pass that they had to set out . . .," just as we must, "on a journey," which is always waiting for us. When we hear the very first words that introduce a myth, legend, or fairy tale, we become aware immediately that we are not going to be informed so much as taken somewhere. Fairy tales and myths are not only the maps of a journey but the means of transport as well.

When we hear the words *Once upon a time,* something profound happens inside us. We settle down. We give the speaker all our attention. We anticipate the familiar; it will soothe us. And behind what we already know and expect, we anticipate a discovery or revelation that will alter everything.

It is no accident that children traditionally were exposed to fairy tales, myths, and legends before they were told personal stories. And it is not unrelated that contemporary children suffer from serious cultural and spiritual deprivation because they are no longer nurtured with the milk of their mother's imagination. In recent years, fairy tales have been so seriously neglected, gutted, and trivialized that they no longer serve the very important function of introducing the child to the realities of the world, of creating a context through which the child can later organize and understand his or her own experience. Since the larger story is a grid or a scaffold on which to hang all stories and history to come, we deprive our children of meaning when we so virtuously bowdlerize the stories they hear, thereby diminishing their experience.

When the secular seceded from the sacred, the definition of human became limited, and more and more experience became off-limits. It is odd to think of fairy tales and myths as taboo, but in effect that is the consequence when their deeper content is denied. Contact with the larger story is imperative in order to gain wisdom and to restore those parts of ourselves that become amputated in a secular society.

It makes all the difference whether we dismiss story as merely entertainment or distraction for children or we appreciate the hermetic tale that opens us up to wisdom. Just as it makes all the difference if we consider childhood as something to be outgrown rather than a state of mind to be recovered for its recognition of the intuitive, the pure, and the marvelous. But we have to want the intuitive and the marvelous to persist.

Let us imagine for a moment that we, at least, were not deprived. What is it that happens when we hear these stories, which, we remember, are somehow also our stories?

To begin with, it seems simple. We are very young when we hear fairy tales. However old we are in the moment when a fairy tale is told, we are all young. That is, we suspend what we know and listen with a pure and open mind. Like the Fool in the Tarot with a dog nipping at his heels, we are ready to step out, to step off the cliff, to encounter the world.

At first we all want to hear that the princess is very very beautiful, that the stepmother is very very evil, that the king is very brave or very very greedy, that the kingdom is very very vast or very very very very small, so small that our child is no larger than a thumb and sleeps in a walnut shell. No matter how entertaining and innocent the beginning, we soon want to know how scratchy the brambles are, how thoroughly the silver slippers will wear out if they are danced in all night, how far the bereft prince has to wander, how alone the princess is in the tower.

And we want to hear it again and again. We want to hear the Giant say, "Fee fi fo fum, I smell the blood of an Englishman." We want to hear the wolf say, "Little pig, little pig, let me come in," and we must hear the little pig answer again and again, "Not by the hair of my chinny-chin-chin," and the bears exclaim in turn, "Who has been sitting in *my* chair?," and Little Red Riding Hood say, "What big teeth you have, Grandmother," while the wicked queen repeats the dreadful rhyme, "Mirror, mirror, on the wall, who is fairest of them all?" With the storyteller, we repeat the refrains again and again, and that is how we enter the story.

From the first words of a fairy story, we relax—not because we are entertained but because we are in the presence of truthfulness, and this, no matter what the content, is by itself reassuring. Think of the lullaby:

Rockabye baby on the treetop,
When the wind blows the cradle will rock,
When the bough breaks the cradle will fall,
And down will come baby, cradle and all.

Not a happy situation. But at least it is not a lie. Little children and brave and conscious adults like to know the truth. We all want to know what is really coming. And fairy tales, especially, articulate what it is that we, as humans, can expect. So we want to know how very dark the woods are, because we suspect that we will have to face how very very dark the dark is. We want to be told how very very high the mountain is because the story implies that we, too, will have to climb it. We want to know how loving and how cruel adults can be, how treacherous and protective authority is, how dangerous and how miraculous are strangers, and how reliable or tricky can be the kingdom of nature and the animal world. And we want to know that despite the illusion of ordinary and secular life, magic and enchantment exist in all their ambiguity, their negative and positive forms. And finally we must hear how very very deep the sleep is, just as we learn that we are still very much asleep. And we believe that when the prince comes or the glass coffin is jostled, we will awaken because, more than anything, we want to be awake.

We begin with fairy tales, the small stories of animals, orphans, witches, wizards, wise men, wise women, queens and princes, and commoners and pretenders, but soon, as we proceed toward myth, other elements enter and we cannot tell if these characters are human or not. The little animals we read about give way to creatures of other dimensions. We cannot know if the birds are just birds, if those eponymous six swans or twelve ravens are the lost brothers, as those stories indicate, or are aspects of creativity or the Holy Spirit itself. We cannot tell whether the goat we are reading about might be Pan, whether the coyote is Coyote who will beguile us, or whether the beast in the Minoan labyrinth is an animal, a man, or a god. We do not know whether the lovers in the Song of Songs are ordinary folk, King Solomon and his lady, or whether the verses constitute the love talk between God and the people. Finally, we are at the other side of a mystery not so much straining to see the magic in the figure of Demeter, Kwan Yin, Buddha, Christ, or Krishna but rather the opposite, straining to perceive the human or animal manifestation of the god.

We know as we listen that we must listen to more than the story because more than the story is afoot. And though what we hear or read may often seem frightening, there is a way in which we can hear it without being afraid. From the moment the story begins, we are in sacred time, which means time set apart, outside the ordinary world, time in which we cannot come to harm.

The larger story is a communication from another world in symbolic language, and the smaller stories we live and tell are enhanced by their relationship to it.

In the presence of the larger story, objects, events, creatures, people, the elements are rescued from the banality and reduction of everyday life and resonate with other qualities. They become more than themselves, which is to say, they become fully themselves.

So the prince is *The Prince,* the woods are *The Woods,* the dark is *The Dark.* Each child, each adult, who listens to such a story understands, no matter how faintly, that her life can also be redeemed by the revelation that when she is lost, she is *Lost,* and when he is cold, he is *Cold,* that she is the waif who is really the princess and he the coward who is really the prince. In the larger story, the feather becomes a magic wand, our dog can devour the universe, the old sparrow who lands on our stoop is the emissary of the good witch, the trees bend down and hide us in their branches, and willy-nilly, the world is permeated with the luminous presence of the divine. Thus, the larger story allows us to penetrate the veil that normally obscures our perceptions and reduces our lives to a single dimension. Story confronts the conventions of realism and materialism, which diminish meaning and deny us a large part of our rightful lives by insisting on the rectitude of limitation.

"Oh," you say, "that's just a fairy tale you're telling me, just an old wives' tale." Exactly. And so, even as we denigrate the story, we cannot help but connect it to those who traditionally were associated with the numinous, the magical, and the divine.

Stories That Connect the Worlds

In the last chapter, we looked at the smaller story, the way events and moments in our lives cluster together to create meaning that we call "story." If we are aware of story, we can also be aware that the stories we are living out resemble archetypal tales, which we live out simultaneously. It is as if we are living several lives at once. We might say that this realization allows us to take the straw of our lives and spin it into gold.

"Spinning straw into gold" is not just a pretty phrase or an image from a fanciful tale but is a real activity. The moment we are cognizant of its meaning, we are alive in the story of Rumpelstiltskin, and we enter the occult reality of the daughter initiated by the trickster demigod into the mysteries; we are able to suffer the dangers and glories of turning dross into wonder.

Up to this point, individuation has been an essentially personal affair of making a self out of the scattered, sometimes broken, always in disarray pieces of our individual lives. But myth and fairy tale, which reside between the sacred and the historic, expand our understanding of self by integrating the personal into the universal. By allowing us to speak, as fairy tales do, with the ancestors, to speak in the voice of the ancestors, to walk with the wise ones, to participate in their stories on all levels, to dialogue, through myth, with the gods, these tales allow us to become one with all of them.

The self is the plumb line through all the worlds. Perhaps this can stand for a working definition of the self toward which we are aspiring as we strive to heal ourselves and to save our lives. The self is the single point, the meeting place of the individual, the integration of all the levels—biological, psychological, intellectual, historical, cultural, and spiritual. The self is the moment when the greater story rests in us and all the stories become one.

One of the most important pieces Barbara Myerhoff wrote on the process for the elderly of creating identity was on "bricolage." Herein she speaks of the survival technique of the old people who, unlike ourselves, are always too aware that they are shattered and disintegrated on all fronts:

> The culture they had invented to meet their present circumstances in old age was bricolage in the best sense—an assortment of symbols, memories, and rituals, blending in a highly ecumenical spirit; they used something from all layers of their history: Old World, Yiddish, Jewish, modern, American, Californian, secular, and sacred. They knew that improvisation and invention were essential, but like all people they needed to convince themselves that these solutions were proper, authentic, believable, and occasionally traditional. Their need for such persuasions, and for being visible, coincided with their naturally performative bent, resulting in a highly dramatic self-presentational culture that was extroverted and often touched with a frenzy of desperation.[6]

If story is the glue through which both individuals and cultures cohere, the larger stories heal the pervasive division between this world and the other, between earth and sacred space. We are all part of the larger stories, and the larger stories are happening in us. The several worlds penetrate each other, and if we didn't exist, there would be no territory in which the myths and tales could come to life. When we put all our stories together, a larger story appears. And it is through this tale, this archetypal grid, that we finally come to know ourselves.

Fairy tale, like myth, takes us to the other realm and to the gods. And like myth, it initiates us, leads us through the journey of discovery, individuation, and transformation. In fact, transformation is one of the leitmotivs of fairy tales. The metamorphosis of the frog into a prince, the prince into a donkey and back again, the brothers who become swans and ravens, like the Beast who is transformed through Beauty's love, are the means by which we come to understand the complex process of change that the psyche undergoes as it develops and struggles with enchantment and with good and evil. Still, the tasks and challenges of fairy tale are not necessarily as stringent as those of myth, which postulates the difference between the human realm and the divine and sometimes offers a bridge between the two. Fairy tale is far more psychological and teaches us how to live in the human realm. Myth refers to the drama of the soul and is, therefore, enacted in the realm of the divine. Ironically, while the mythic path is universal, it may not be for everyone, but the fairy tale can be.

> *Remember a time in your childhood when you entered the world of imagination through fairy tales and myths. What intrigued you about those tales? After hearing such stories, what did you make up? Pretend? Dream?*

> *Reenter your childhood. Imagine yourself as a very young person alive to wonder and fantasy and wanting to hear a story. Tell yourself the wondrous tale that the child in you would like to hear. Don't be inhibited. Let the magic flow. Write or record a marvelous tale, including all those elements that would have made your eyes round with amazement and delight when you were young.*

Fairy Tales as Teaching Stories

Fairy tales articulate the shady regions of the demigods—witches, sorcerers, enchanters, magicians, giants, elves, ogres, trolls, fairies—where the human, animal, and spirit worlds intertwine. Fairy tales inhabit the liminal world between the human and the extraordinary, inviting us into the realm of the marvelous but instructing us in its dangers as well. Fairy tales advise us about the murky areas of our own psyches and surroundings as well as the hazards of the magical world. Whether we are considering the twelve dancing princesses and the thrall of the underworld, or Cinderella and the need to be attentive to the laws of the realm, or Rumpelstiltskin and the aftermath of ignoring pledges we've given, these stories are as adamant about the perils of the extraordinary as they are about the glories.

However treacherous these realms may be, it is not the intent of fairy tales or myths to warn us away, though that has been one way in which they have been misused. The intent is not to cut us off from this part of our lives, any more than it would be reasonable to cut us off from life itself; the intent is to teach us the ethics of the realm of the psyche and to transmit the means to negotiate it. Thus, these larger stories repeat certain warnings, particularly against hubris and boasting, against making promises—no matter how desperate—that can't be kept, and against being inattentive. If one avoids these dangerous shoals, one avoids the greatest dangers of the inner world.

Despite their link to the magical, fairy tales also serve a more prosaic function. They educate children about the realities of ordinary life. Fairy tales can be teaching stories without being moral tales. They tell you what to protect yourself from and sometimes how to do it, but they do not tell you what to be. They carefully instruct us in an area that we have certainly forgotten: the ecology that exists both in the outer and the inner worlds. Through them we learn, as in "The Fisherman and His Wife," that when one meets a creature, one treats it well. Or that when one meets someone at the crossroads, as in the African tale, "The Old Woman with Sores," one is attentive and respectful. Fairy tales instruct through showing the relationships between the characters and events.

In "Hansel and Gretel" we learn much from how the relationship between the brother and the sister differs from the relationship of the father and stepmother to the children. "Hansel and Gretel," like so many tales, is also a story about hunger and the terrible threat it poses to the bonds of community: the hunger of the family, the birds, the stepmother, the children lost in the woods, and the hunger of the witch. In this way, the story instructs us in the dynamics of society—the pressures that decimate it and the qualities that bind it together.

"Hansel and Gretel" is also, like so many stories, an investigation of enchantment. What does it mean to be enchanted? To be caught in a spell? A thrall? Enchantment itself may be one of the obsessions of fairy tales. What does it mean to be asleep? To be turned into something else—a frog, a donkey, a bird, an ancient hag? What does it mean to wear out one's shoes dancing every night? To be caught in circumstances one cannot escape? To be bound by fate? By other powers? Other realities?

In their concern with enchantment, fairy tales enter directly into the darkest areas of our psyche. And here we must be careful not to be literal. It is not the old woman at the corner asking for alms who is going to put a curse on us or strike us with the evil eye. The danger of our own enchantment, unconsciousness, obsession comes directly from within ourselves.

Remember a moment when you were enchanted. What enchanted you? How were you vulnerable to the enchantment? How were you freed?

Arachne's Dilemma
I am caught in a web of misery,
Being both the spider and the fly:
the devouring and the devoured.

Eating myself from the inside

            out.

This is deceptive.
It shows no signs,
there are no visible teeth marks
on my body. No
half-eaten fingers.

But my soul is
riddled with holes
like antique lace.

　　　—*Cathleen Rountree*

Entering the Tale

Every story has meaning for us. Although our lives do not follow the scenario of every fairy tale, in one way or another we can find affinity with most of them: we fall asleep, are enchanted by an ogre, are endangered by the stepmother; we are locked in a tower or are sent to do impossible deeds by the king; we are devoured by the wolf, mate with the demon lover, and long for the prince to awaken us. Each story is ours, though some stories are more ours than others. And while one story may always seem pertinent to our lives, others may have greater meaning at one time than another. And perhaps it is true that each of us is living out one story in particular, though which one it is we may not know now—or even at the end of our lives. Still, it is interesting to search for the story that our life is following at this time.

Close your eyes. Remember a fairy tale that was told to you when you were a child or that has been prominent in your imagination recently. Do not become lost between choices. Take the story that insists itself. Let the story decide that it wants to be known at this time.

For this exercise, any story that comes to mind will do. At different times in our lives, different stories—or the same story told from a different angle, a different perspective, in a different character's voice—will yield different insights.

This first time, write the story in the first person from the protagonist's point of view: "Once upon a time when I . . ." Tell the story in minute detail as if it were happening to you now. Emphasize the moments, actions, feelings that seem most significant to you.

As you write, remember that fairy tale always speaks about innocence. It is addressed to the child in us who knows nothing and therefore needs to go into the world. When you begin the story, remember your own innocence and write from the place where you know nothing.

What we want is to enter the story. Take the barest outline of the story, live with it long enough, even several weeks, to know it well and to fill it out with the material of your imagination.

It is our task to describe the woods where Hansel and Gretel are lost, to familiarize ourselves with lostness. We enter deeply enough into their lives to intuit what they feel, to articulate the specifics of their despair or hope. Then, using our own lives, we discern the circumstances that brought them to the woods, the path they (we) will take to and away from the witch. It is for us to discover what Hansel thinks and feels when he is in the cage and how Gretel gains the means to defeat the witch.

After you have written this story at length, rewrite the story in ten sentences. We first expanded it to know it in detail; now we reduce it to its essence.

Afterward, identify the moments that seem most moving or intense for you.

The many moments and images in fairy tales reveal the dilemmas of our lives. There are Hansel and Gretel alone in the woods, the birds have eaten the bread crumbs, and the moon rising in the wilderness illuminates no sure path; the way home is forever blocked. In that moment, one knows that poverty—economic limitation, meanness of spirit, emotional destitution—has triumphed. The brother and sister realize, as each one of us must at some time, that they are utterly on their own. There is the Goose Girl passing through the gate of the city under the severed head of her magic horse, the gift of her Queen Mother; the horse speaks, "If your mother could see you now, how her heart would break." There is Sleeping Beauty. She falls into unconsciousness, and a deep sleep from which no one can awaken by will falls like a pall over the entire kingdom. Or there is Jack, full of youthful enthusiasm and naïveté, climbing the beanstalk to the mysterious and dangerous kingdom. Fairy tales are constructed of such redolent moments. This is the reason these tales still survive.

Select one very small moment in the story. Write about it as if it happened to you.

What is its larger meaning?

A fairy tale is an essential story of initiation. By the time we've become acquainted with many fairy tales, the innocent one in us has been led through the mires and pitfalls of the macrocosm of the larger world and the microcosm of our psyches, and we are prepared for a complex and realistic relationship to life.

Far from being simple, these tales incorporate many levels of meaning. "Sleeping Beauty," for example, can be read as a warning that we must not neglect the arcane powers, personified in the thirteenth fairy, or as a warning of the pervasiveness of both individual and collective unconsciousness. It speaks to the dangers inherent in innocence and isolation as well as the precariousness of paradise, and describing the trials of both the sleeper and the awakener, it guides us through a process of awakening. It is a profound tale that is as accurate in its rendering of external reality as it is of inner reality and process. And while the story as a whole serves to inform us deeply, providing moral instruction for living in the world, the individual moments, if allowed to resonate within us, provide even deeper insight into those essential levels of reality that are too often ignored or dismissed—as the thirteenth fairy is in the story—much to our detriment.

One way of understanding "Sleeping Beauty" is as a metastory describing the consequences of ignoring what is peripheral, disdained, or alien to us. For these are the qualities of the thirteenth fairy—the one who is feared because she is old, ugly, and cranky, the one who lives at the edge of the kingdom and who, therefore, is overlooked for the celebration of the birth of the princess. But the failure to receive an invitation does not exclude her. To the contrary, she arrives after everyone else has arrived, enraged and murderous, not because this is her nature but because she has been neglected. At this point, there is almost nothing that can be done to mitigate her wrath. And if the price, finally, of this indifference is not death but "only" interminable unconsciousness, it is small comfort. For if the prince doesn't come, if no one breaks his or her way through the impenetrable brambles that surround unconsciousness, the innocent princess and her courtiers will continue in their sleep unto death.

Because a social context that would validate these tales no longer exists, their psychological and cultural impact upon us as children is reduced, and consequently, we are often driven to living them out again as adults. However, in our maturity, it is more difficult to enter into the living imagination that is accessible to the child. The rational aspect of our culture insists that this knowledge can be acquired intellectually through the communication of ideas. Unfortunately, this is not true. What fairy tales teach is encoded in emotional and imaginative experience, and it is to this that we must return.

Entering into the fairy tale, allowing ourselves to live within it, is one way we can compensate for this enormous deprivation. But not being children, play—that is, imaginative involvement—is no longer easy for us, and we must attend to it more closely. To enter the experience empathetically is what we are after here. But because each fairy tale is an entire universe, we can only gain what it has to offer by breaking it down into its components and experiencing each of them as deeply and particularly as we can.

One way to do this is to examine the physical landscape, the environment, the "props" of the story. The glass slipper, the pumpkin, and the rat of the Cinderella story are not arbitrary, nor is the bodice that the Wicked Queen sells to Snow White, nor the chicken bone that Hansel sticks through the bars to confuse the Wicked Witch. These details, which are the ones that children would naturally pay attention to but that we might ignore, contribute to the central meaning of the story. We have a sense of this when we come across a different version of the story. Emotionally, we want the slipper to be glass, not Lucite, and Cinderella to call for help at the tree, not at a crypt, where her mother is buried.

Examine the props and landscape of the fairy tale you are considering. Put them together. What story do they evoke by their very nature? By their relationship to each other? What story, for example, could you create from a tree on a grave, a pumpkin, a rat, some field mice, a sooty fireplace, and a glass slipper?

The stories are wise, but to gain their wisdom, we must look at each detail and delve into the very core moments. Fairy tales can beguile us, entertain us, amuse us, but that is not their essential function. What is lost in the contemporary sanitized versions are the individual teachings that go directly to the core of human life. The task is to find the moment in the story that fascinates you and then enter it without preconceived notions.

Perhaps this is the best way to do this:

Imagine that the story is a sketch that you will develop. Write the story very slowly, stopping at any place where you feel a charge or intensity. Then begin to expand that moment as if it were a story in itself. Here are several questions you can ask yourself at this juncture to help you delve more deeply. Needless to say, you will be able to think of other questions on your own.

What issues does this story raise? What is the nature of this moment? If this moment were the core of the story, what would develop from it? What else is to be said? What is implied that has not been articulated? What future events are implied by the story? What preceded the story? What is its social and political context? What does it reveal about the nature of society? What feelings are associated with this event? What disturbs you? What is this story, this moment, really about? If this moment were your only story, what would it reveal about your life? About the world?

These questions can be asked of any story. They are not answered in the fairy tale per se, but answers can be deduced from the border where we and the story conjoin. When we ask these questions, we engage with the story on a profound level. For example, what was Donkeyskin's experience living in the forest for a year? What did Snow White learn when she was unconscious? (This question is a variation on a more mythic question: What did Lazarus learn while he was dead?) What does Cinderella's father feel about his daughter's situation? Why was the Frog Prince enchanted? What underlies the fisherman's wife's hunger? Why does Rumpelstiltskin want a child? And so forth.

We ask these questions not to engage in intellectual exercises but to inspire writing pieces. Imagine the stories that might arise from the following titles: "Snow White's Nightmare"; "The Witch Who Ate Children"; "The Community That Fell Asleep"; "The Last Dream of Beauty's Beast"; "The Giant's Wife Meets Jack"; "The Old Age of Rapunzel"; and so on.

Another way to approach the tale is to tell it from the point of view of someone or something other than the protagonist. We are not always the hero of the story—nor are we at all times the hero of our own lives. Sometimes the resonance of the story depends upon another perspective.

Yeah! OK. So. I'm the wolf. Typecast. If there's a guy and a girl you know who is supposed to be the wolf. So I'm supposed to be lurking between the trees, waiting for her, as if I have nothing else to do in my life. And when I see her I'm supposed to put the make on her. Right? Yeah. So here I come, mouth open and dripping. Lust, right? Hunger, right? And she has this little basket full of goodies which are supposed to be for her grandmother. Give me a break! And she's so innocent, she doesn't know a thing, not even what's in her basket, like it's a big secret from g-d.

You want to know who's the innocent one? Let me tell you . . . it's not the girl. Not today. Not in 1990. The truth is she's sneaking up the path with a telescopic sight on her stun gun looking for the last remaining wolves in the forest and the cookies she's baked have eau de amnesia in them so the moment some poor creature who can't run fast enough is caught in the crosshairs of her vision, she shoots him on the spot, fills him with sweet things so he forgets his life and drags him home naked for her pleasure. And when he protests that he has other things to do, she gives him a bitter rap—she *did* learn from her grandmother—on resistence, hating women, fearing intimacy, and not wanting to make a commitment while she's got her hands on *my* thigh.

So if you think it's ok to hang out in the woods and enjoy the breezes, you got another guess coming. Oh, Little Red Riding Hood, what big teeth you have!

—*Mack Braverman*

Tell the tale from another point of view—the one that seems to speak to you most pointedly or the one to which you have the most aversion. Or tell it several times from several points of view. It is not necessary to tell it from the perspective of the hero or heroine—even the pumpkin and the glass slipper in "Cinderella" have something surprising and unpredictable to say. If you are a woman, tell the tale as if you are Hansel lost with your sister Gretel in the woods; if you are a man, take Gretel's point of view. Tell the tale as if you are the stepmother in Snow White, or are Bluebeard, or Rumpelstiltskin, or the king who wants gold spun from straw, the prince coming through the brambles to awaken Sleeping Beauty, or the Giant's wife in "Jack and the Beanstalk."

In one workshop, a participant asked the following questions about Rapunzel:

Why did the wife want the radishes? What is the nature of her desire? What did the husband see when he went into the garden? Why does the witch want a child?

These questions about the story led him to these about himself:

What desires in myself have I failed to face? What would it mean to scale the tower? To live alone in the tower? To let down my golden hair?

After he listed these questions, he began to tell the story from the husband's point of view. Within minutes, he was overwhelmed by the pregnant wife's craving for radishes and his need to satisfy her desire. She wanted the radishes. He wanted her to have anything she needed. He needed her to have anything she desired. His desire was to provide for her everything and anything that was necessary. The man described his wife sitting in a rocking chair craving the forbidden radishes on the other side of the wall in the witch's garden. More than anything else, he wanted her to have those radishes. As he wrote, the radishes regained their original magic, for his desire blended with the wife's desire, all symbolized by the radishes. The writer came to see that the Rapunzel story was a later variation on the biblical story of the Fall. The radishes, like the forbidden fruit in the Garden of Eden, offered the wife—and thus him—everything. At the core of the story and the myth are the same elements: the garden, prohibition, desire, temptation. Through this understanding, the fairy tale gained new life. Each one of its elements resonated with new meaning. After he read his piece aloud, everyone in the class wanted to:

Write about want, need, and desire.

When the man read his story, he said, "I love this woman who wants radishes. She does nothing. She has no activity. She is pure desire, desire in its purest form. To me, this is eros."

Through this retelling, the man's previously submerged relationship to his own needs and desires was awakened. For most of us, need, want, and desire are experienced as negative qualities in our essentially puritanical society, though they are the means through which our animal nature protects us and our emotional and intellectual nature develops. Where would we be if Eve had not desired the apple? When need, want, and desire are acknowledged, they form the very core of our humanity; suppressed, they become the nucleus of our neurosis.

Through this experience, the man learned that he had suppressed a passel of needs and desires that he was later able to acknowledge. But more important than this, he was reconnected to the experience of desiring and to the nature of need.

Fundamental to all fairy tales is the theme of innocence transformed—not only innocence per se but also innocence in the face of something. Little Red Riding Hood's innocence is in the face of wildness, wilderness. Jack is originally innocent of the mercantile ways of the world. His dreaminess overcomes any practical knowledge he might have acquired. Of course, Jack also has that essential innocence that in myth and story is sometimes symbolized by virginity and that is basic to seeing the mysteries. One question that fairy tales often address is how to transform innocence without losing one's purity of heart. Various versions of the Cinderella story speak to this. In some, the stepmother and sisters are severely punished; in others, they are forgiven and brought to the castle. This speaks not only to the relationship of crime to punishment but more subtly to the nature of Cinderella's spirit.

What is the nature of the innocence in the story you are considering?

Having identified the innocence that is the subject of your story, can you find a similar innocence within yourself? Using the details of the story as a guide, write a story in which you are the innocent one in your own life.

Perhaps you, like the fairy-tale character, have transformed this innocence. Or it may be that you are still somewhere within the story, confronting whatever you must face before the moment of transformation.

At night in late spring, I listen to the croaking of the frogs. By early summer, they disappear and I miss their song. Then I look forward to the winter rains and their return.

It happened once by a swimming pool at a neighbor's house. There was a frog. It was the summer I was six. And her housekeeper, who spoke another language, managed to catch it and bring it to me. We were kneeling down on the grass and I was just opening my hands when my mother swooped down upon us, snatched up the frog before I could and threw it, just like the princess had, over the fence into the street where it was smashed on the asphalt.

No prince appeared. But it took me a long time to give up my innocence about the wild things, to give up longing for the prince or the golden balls he could provide. It's the frog I want now. And I would offer a thousand golden balls to the pond for the sake of it.

—*Riena Schulman*

Imagine that the fairy tale you have chosen is your story—not your entire story, but the story that you are living now. Imagine that it is both the story you are living out in the world and the story that is living within you, that is living you. Imagine that the fairy tale describes the dynamics between different aspects of yourself. For example, it may be that you, like Rapunzel, are coming out into the world from an enforced seclusion, and it may also be that there is a sealed garden within yourself.

What theme in the fairy tale is most relevant to your life now? Betrayal? Enchantment? Setting out to seek your fortune? Freeing the prisoner from the castle? Bringing back the treasure to the king?

Write the story of your life as you are living it now, allowing the fairy tale to inform the story, to add direction, to create a context, provide a shape. Like the proverbial hero of fairy tales, allow adventure to entice you, danger to excite you, challenge to motivate you.

Use contemporary language and images. Let the fairy tale help you focus on the conflicts and issues in your life now.

In fairy tales, the knight sets out full of purpose but without knowing where he is going. He provides us with a model to imitate. If we imagine that we know exactly where we are going, what we want to get, and how to get it, we will fail at the essential task—to enter the unknown through contact with the creative daimon. Seeing the therapeutic possibilities of fairy tale—for example, elucidating a traumatic relationship with a parent or the nature of long-ignored sibling rivalry—it is possible to be overcome by preconceived ideas of what we wish to "accomplish," notions about how we want to be or what we want to become. In doing so, we can lose what we are seeking by failing to recognize the creative or by "falling asleep" at the moment of vision. The creative is shy and often unwilling to reveal herself to the knight who thinks he knows exactly what he is seeking. We must proceed, therefore, like the king who insists that the glass slipper be fitted on everyone, no matter how sooty she appears or how unlikely a candidate she seems. Then, and only then, when the parts or partners that have been disdained or sullied are restored to their rightful place, can the divine marriage take place so that the world is made whole and we, too, are healed.

Fairy Tale as Our Story

After working with specific fairy tales, you may feel the inclination to write one of your own.

Focus upon a moment in your life that you do not fully understand. Tell it as if it were a fairy tale.

This is the beginning of a story that Linda Neal wrote in response to just such an assignment:

The Girl with the Compass

Once there was a beautiful young maiden who wanted children, but she had been taught that learning was more important than loving, for her future would be determined by knowledge. Her mother was in a land far away and her father was dedicated to the life of the mind. Because her mother had been banished, her father didn't know what to do with this beautiful young girl who was left in his charge. As she grew up, he began to wonder how he could help her with the passage into womanhood. So, he gave her two gifts that he thought would be important to her success in the world. He gave her a compass so she would never lose her direction. He told her that if she held it in her hand, it would serve her well but that she must never drop it or she would get lost if she ventured out among the big rocks outside the village. The second gift was a quiver full of arrows to carry on her back as she went into the world. He told her they would fly through the air once she learned how to shoot them, and she would learn that skill from the bow master in the next village. But her father regretted that he had no bow to give her nor did he know how to make one. So, he warned her that she must be very careful on the path to meet the bowman and use the compass so that she would reach the man safely.

Armed with these gifts and challenges, she proceeded on her way into the world of the rocks. She had a compass and three arrows, and she skipped along on the road to the neighboring village. When she got tired, she rested under a willow by the side of a creek. As she sat there under the tree, she began a little chant:

I have my compass.

I have three arrows.

I am happy to the marrow.

She dozed off singing her song, unaware of the old hag who had lived by the river for many years. . . .

Though this tale set out to follow the known circumstances of Linda's life, she did not immediately understand the symbolism of the three arrows, the bow master, and the old hag. As she worked with the story, she began to see elements that had been absent from her more conventional understanding of her life. Further, seeing her life as a story being lived, rather than as a melee of disconnected events, made a great difference to her. And although she found that the convention of the tale required a happy ending, she did not take this to mean that everything would work out for the best but rather that in writing the story and bringing the elements together, she would find a measure of wholeness in her life. For that is what " And they lived happily ever after" ultimately means.

The Worlds of Myth

Fairy tale brings a larger dimension to our lives, but myth takes us beyond ourselves. Sometimes we can see the myth hovering behind the fairy tale, and its presence takes us just that much further. Behind the story of Rapunzel confined to the tower in the witch's garden because of her mother's desire for radishes is the shadow of the myth of the Garden of Eden. The goose that lays the golden egg in "Jack and the Beanstalk" may relate to Hathor, the Egyptian goddess, in her goose form. The twelve dancing princesses may be developments of the Greek Horae who performed the Dances of the Hours or the Egyptian Ladies of the Hour who each ruled a time of the night and protected the solar boat of Ra in the underworld.[7] And perhaps the twelve brothers are the signs of the zodiac or the apostles—we don't know. Behind the fearsome figure of the thirteenth fairy in "Sleeping Beauty," we may see the awesome figures of the Furies if we look carefully enough.

Just as myths hover in the shadows of fairy tales, so do they hover behind our own experiences, offering an archetypal grid through which we can transform our lives. When we enter the myth, we enter a place where history and culture combine with the sacred in a union so powerful that it persuades us to leave our smaller selves behind. In myth, the power itself, the gods themselves are present, whether openly or in disguise. When we enter myth, the experience is more than having the archetype enter us—sometimes it is even as if we ourselves enter the gods. The territory of myth extends from psychology to cosmology, from the nature of the atoms of our psyche to the origins and significance of the celestial bodies, from the individual to the entire universe itself. Story organizes the events of our personal lives into meaning, and myth builds upon this, fusing the individual story with the collective one. If story is a means by which we construct our lives, myth is an important agency through which we create culture. And just as individuals have an inner necessity to tell stories, cultures have the same intrinsic need to create myths.

But myth takes us even further. Myth serves to incorporate us into the larger story of the gods. Through the smaller stories, we weave together the diverse aspects of our lives, plumb the depths of our psyches, and place ourselves in society. But through myth we come to understand the greater meanings that play upon us and connect us to the universe itself. Some myths, like that of the World Tree or of Jacob's ladder, speak precisely to the means by which the gods enter the world and the ways in which humans can descend into the underworld or ascend to the heavens for the sake of knowledge or vision. In Jacob's vision of the ladder to heaven, the literal transit from earth to heaven is also a metaphysical statement regarding the spiritual ladder bridging the human and the divine. Myth becomes the connection between our ordinary world and a greater reality. Jack climbing the beanstalk to the realm of the giants is another version of this basic myth, reduced in its fairy-tale aspect from a description of the realm of the gods to a description of the realm of the demigods.

Myth postulates the difference between the human realm and the divine and the difficulty of "storming heaven," offering the opportunity to reach toward the divine by living it, by following the stations. Of course, great suffering and duress are implied, for this process that myth articulates is nothing less than a radical transformation: Psyche begins as a vain and innocent girl but ends up as a god. She begins as a girl, is devastated, restored, and ends up as Soul. Prometheus steals fire from the gods, suffers for his actions, but transforms the world. Adam and Eve lose their innocence and acquire knowledge without which they would scarcely be human except in form. These are the weightiest and most extreme journeys to soul.

The World Tree, with its roots in the underworld and its branches in the heavens, is a portrait of the relationship of the worlds to each other and the process of passing from one to another. The beanstalk, the ladder, the *axis mundi,* the cross, the grove of the goddess, the tree of life, the tree of the knowledge of good and evil in the garden, and the kabbalistic Tree of Life are variations on this fundamental teaching. These are also metastories, myths about myth itself, where myth *is* the other world, the other side of our mind, both psyche and cosmos.

In Edward Albee's play, *Tiny Alice,* a fire breaks out in the upper story of a dollhouse just as it breaks out in the upper story of the larger house within which the dollhouse sits. In this image, Albee refers to the simultaneity of experience, the coexistence of different realms—"as above, so below." If a myth does not refer both to the realm of the gods and to that of our own lives, or if it is does not speak both about the world and about our psyches, it is not a myth.

What we will never know about myth is whether it is a story that we, as individuals or a culture, are writing or whether it is a story that we are "receiving," or both. Just as we will never know with what is called scientific certainty whether the sacred is a domain that we designate or that is revealed. Perhaps, then, it is appropriate to recognize the Roman god, Janus, god of the door and the gate, as the god of myth as he looks both ways with his two faces.

Ecstatic and mystery religions are built upon myths that describe the interpenetration of the various realms; often, as in the myths of Orpheus, Persephone, and Isis, the individual is invited, even enjoined, to live out the story of the gods, once or continually, in order to gain wisdom, insight, or compassion. But even monotheistic religions such as Christianity, which sharply differentiate between the human and the divine realms, occasionally invite the individual to enact the *imitatio dei,* to follow in the footsteps of Christ, executing the substance, if not the form, of the stations of the cross.

Though the stories of the gods are often cast, for the sake of our comprehension, in human terms, the deeper meanings loom on their horizon. The physical occurrences of the Big Bang, the flood, the parting of the Red Sea by a meteor, the history of the Trojan War, of the Israelites, the Babylonians, the Egyptians, recast by the cultural imagination, become occasions for the metaphysical. This means that myth ultimately describes the world as it is, without distinction, one dimension coexisting within the other. Whatever other meanings—ethical, cosmological, cultural, national, or historic—are encoded in the story, the essence of myth is to illuminate the relationships and interrelationships among the gods, individuals, and society.

The curse that Apollo levies upon Cassandra—that, for refusing to bed with him, she will prophesy the future accurately without ever being believed—is not a little tale of male lust and female shyness but a profound story of the consequences of refusing the god. Actaeon torn to pieces by his dogs after coming upon Artemis bathing in the woods, Semele burning to ash at the sight of Zeus, Jehovah appearing to Moses as a burning bush—these events speak to the psychic consequences of looking directly at the divine.

Because the soul in ancient times was often associated with the feminine—Psyche, for example—rather than with the masculine, the one pursued or devastated by the god is frequently personified as a woman. As mythic culture was subsumed by history with its more secular face, these symbolic relationships were literalized, gutted of their meaning, even reversed. As a consequence, the feminine, originally honored by her association with soul, was increasingly trivialized and oppressed.

In Western culture, we suffer from an ambivalent relationship to myth because of the gulf between the exoteric, typically patriarchal interpretations imposed on these stories for the sake of social regulation and the less familiar esoteric meanings that are profound spiritual teachings. The best way to approach myth is through the poetic imagination, ignoring the distortions of the more literal interpretations in order to pursue the symbolic content.

If Psyche represents soul, so do the Israelites in the story of the Exodus from Egypt. This narrative chronicles the literal and spiritual venture of a people out of oppression while it simultaneously describes the individual struggle that we all experience in order to exit the narrow place into the geography of faith. Ultimately the history upon which the myth is based is subordinate to the greater meaning: the narrative description of the eternal and infinite, the ever-present and the continuous. The Haggadah, read at Passover, asserts that we are always leaving Egypt for the Promised Land, that what happened to our foreparents is happening to us now. Leaving Egypt becomes a condition of the psyche that everyone passes through, not just once but again and again. The seder is an opportunity to live, through the retelling of the story, the coexistence of historic, cultural, and psychic experience.

In some mythic actions or rituals, like the mass, the literal, historic world falls away almost completely as we are transported to the reality of the sacred universe. Myth postulates the sacred as a real place—as, in fact, the *most* real world.

When the mythic story is extended, as in the life of Christ or the story of Psyche and Eros, we glean its essential structure, the eternal scaffolding within a changing context or narrative. Then we know we are in the presence of extraordinary, as opposed to ordinary, reality.

While contemporary culture is preoccupied with the historic literalism of myth and fairy tale, it eschews the deeper imaginal reality. When we hear "The animals spoke," we translate it: "It was as if the animals spoke," "It seemed the animals spoke," or "They imagined the animals spoke." We can no longer imagine a time when humans and animals communicated. When we read that the great goddess Demeter declared perpetual winter after her daughter Persephone disappeared, we dismiss this symbolic rendering of archetypal grief by reducing it to a primitive explanation of the seasons. On the other hand, when fundamentalists, Jewish, Christian, or scientific, read that Sodom and Gomorrah were destroyed or that the Israelites spent forty years in the desert, they resort to text and archaeology to find evidence for the material event. In each case, the literal obfuscates the point. The historic occasion doesn't disprove the existence of the sacred, but it doesn't verify its existence either. Too often only what science validates is given credence. This narrows experience to certain external aspects of the day world. In the face of this limitation, the other worlds disappear.

The shamans who speak with animals and trees, the ones who can see the gods in the hills, the poets and inner explorers who talk with Athena or Saint Francis, the aborigines who sing the world into existence, the ones who enter the occult meanings of the wanderings in the spiritual desert inhabit these other—and very real—worlds their entire lives.

> *Once there was a time when you knew these worlds. Do you remember? Invoke your guide to help you enter or re-enter another reality. Imagining your guide beside you, write of the descent into another world where you may find yourself with the ant people or the bird people or other creatures with whom you would like to commune. See if you can imagine them deeply enough for both your languages to merge into one.*

The overwhelming pressure from Western civilization is to disdain everything but the rational. Those who are fortunate enough not to be affected by our prohibitions on thought and psyche live *within and according to* myths that describe and express a most complex understanding of the universe. They are thus brought into profound and personal communication with nature and the cosmos while simultaneously being guided into their own psyches.

It is myth also that differentiates among the sacred realms and the different approaches to them. The underworld, the realm of soul making, is the site of the chthonic creative forces. One descends to the underworld in order to gain wisdom through encountering the dead and the most primal powers. This mythic descent into the underworld can be undertaken consciously for the sake of healing, magic, and soul making. However, this journey is, more often than not, perilous. In its course, the ego or self is decimated, and consequently, one is never certain that one will return or be reconstituted. Still, this passage is required for all visionaries, and many, like the shaman, risk returning there again and again for the sake of curing individuals or in order to restore and sustain their people.

However, to be raised up into the heavens is a most rare event. Few, if any, can practice this feat, which is a gift of the gods rather than an ordeal to be undertaken voluntarily. And while the descent and return from the underworld have a cyclical quality, the ascent into the heavens is often permanent, as in the countless figures who, like Andromeda, are placed among the stars. Because the return is so rare, the legend of the return of the Messiah has particular resonance for us. Of the four rabbis who were shown the splendors of heaven, legend tells that only one returned sane and whole. For human beings, it is more difficult to survive heaven than it is to survive Hades.

Creation Myths

The first story that myths tell is that of creation. Almost every culture has a creation myth, and many of these, as far flung as the Hopi and the Hebrew, resemble each other. In this century, the story of origins that physics tells in its language has an uncanny relationship to the story told in Genesis. How can this be? Because stories are transferred from one culture to another? Because these are a true retelling of the beginning? Because they are encoded in our genes? Because they are renderings of a common mystical understanding? Whatever the resemblances or differences across the cultures, the need to tell the story, physical and metaphysical, of "The Beginning" seems universal.

Invoke your guide. Ask your guide to tell you a creation story.

Afterward, ask yourself:

How do you imagine the beginning of the physical universe? Is your understanding reflected in the story just told? How would you explain the origins of the universe to a child?

What greater story emerges as you fuse the physical with the metaphysical?

In the following excerpt from a poem, I was reaching to understand the way spiritual truth is encoded in a physical event. Seemingly speaking about the literal genesis of planet earth, the poem simultaneously speaks about mystical knowledge. In the blend of the two, our understanding of the meaning and predicament of life on earth is greatly increased. In this poem, as in the story of Genesis—which like the Christ story is one of the spirit incarnating—there is an attempt to explore the great mystery of the descent of spirit into matter.

> Spirit wraps itself about a mote of dust, a speck of green in the endless sky, then falls wet and dark into the rivers and the hungry clay. So it repeats itself—not history, but creation.

> In the beginning was fire and the rain came later. Rain came out of the fire from the very breast of light. Then the light continued, falling, wrapping itself about the leaves, gleaming on the dark feathers, glittering in the fur. And the rain followed it to make a bed for everything which burns.

—*from "The Descent of Rain"*[8]

Perhaps there is another way to approach the creation. Perhaps you know more about it than you think.

> *Describe a moment when you created something, when you created something out of nothing. Place this incident under the microscope of your awareness so that you can discern the minute progressions that occurred until something came into being and you found that it was good.*

> *What story would you tell if you beheld everything that you have made, blessed it, and saw that it was good?*

This piece by Gary Frankford focuses upon that moment just before creation when one can be overwhelmed by what seems like an infinity of inertia. It is as if Gary stopped time here and expanded that tiny moment, just before putting his feet in the fire. Then having brought something to life—finally—he becomes aware, in the next instant, of the paradox that death has also just been born.

> The cells of my body crave the old slowness. I dread beginning work. Each day the same thing. Dread. All I have is what I did yesterday, what is left of it, that is. How to begin again? The question itself is grief. Why, every day that same question? It is all collapsing. What an ache.

> Stop. I stop and catch my breath. Sit down. I am being strapped into an executioner's chair. Can you imagine that in that situation at that moment one could say, "Excuse me, I'm feeling a little uncomfortable." This sense of

155

beginning something. Beginning what? Death? Is that a beginning? That's the whole point isn't it: nothingness, beginnings, the feet finally in the fire. It was inevitable wasn't it? I've never had to think that thought before. Probably a lot of thoughts I'll have to think now. It's painful. I feel the straining against—against the memory of the old tenderness in the Garden. Now what? I've got to go. Finally. Thank you, God, for nothing.

—*Gary Frankford*

The nature of creativity is not only the purview of the scientist but the constant preoccupation of the writer, as well as of anyone fascinated with human nature. For creativity is the most mysterious quality of the human, and it has the strongest affinity with the divine. The process we are engaged in here is dual: to learn the way of creativity and to discover it within ourselves.

When you bring together the three perspectives—mythic, physical, and personal—what is revealed about the nature of creativity itself? Perhaps you might begin writing about the physical world, about the Big Bang, the appearance of the first molecules or of living creatures on the planet. How does the scientific story echo mythic stories you have heard? Is there an analogue in Genesis or the Navajo creation story, Diné Bahane', or other origin myths you may know?

Reread the exercise you just wrote on creativity, on the moment when something came out of nothing. Does it relate to the scientific perspective? Or remember other moments of creativity—inventing a tool, conceiving a child, giving birth, sculpting, solving a problem. Do you see a pattern, a relationship between the three categories of creation? How do the three inform each other?

The Myth of the Garden

The first time that I, as a teacher, worked actively with myth was in 1971. We began with the story of the Garden, with Adam and Eve. I do not remember now how or why we entered into this arena, but I do remember that I wanted to begin with the first story of Judeo-Christian culture. The students proceeded through the story, breaking it down into its elements. Their task was to:

Write a monologue in the voice of each of the mythic characters in turn: Adam, Eve, the angel, the snake, the tree, God.

What astonished us the very first time we read these monologues was that the pieces were almost heroically unconventional. More than twenty years later, I remember the electricity in the room as the first woman read Eve's rage at being condemned for her desire for wisdom. Equally dynamic was a young man's piece about Adam's timorousness and conformity to authority. We felt as if we were a conspiracy of heretics speaking our truth to each other for the first time. I had had no literary expectations for myself from this exercise, but the verbalization of the hidden or forbidden was exciting to me, and I couldn't get those voices out of my mind for days. Released from a prison within myself, they were determined to speak ceaselessly, compensating for years of silence. Until that moment, I had had no idea I was interested in Adam and Eve; in retrospect, this was the first inkling I had of what I now call my theological imagination.

Nothing awakens creative energy so much as the opening of a closed door. Afterward, the images rush out pell-mell and without cease. Sometimes it is difficult to weather the storm of this outpouring, but in the end, despite the turmoil, something more than worthwhile is manifested.

This section from the end of my first published book, *Skin: Shadows/Silence*, originated with that writing exercise:

> Come into the garden. There are two trees which we will make ours. This is an act of rebellion. No . . . This is an act of war.
>
> This is the second time. I do not seduce you with youth or beauty or innocence alone. I do not invoke the serpent as panderer. We are our own messengers. We come to each other with desire and consciousness and with full knowing.
>
> I do not seduce with youth or beauty or innocence. This is the garden again. There is nothing living here. The sun is boiling up black to illuminate the charred wood of two trees. We are of those trees. I cannot distinguish the gnarls on our bodies from those grotesque burls.
>
> We are the oldest living things. I do not seduce you with youth or with beauty or with innocence. We come to each other in age and in pain. Our gifts are not perishable, are not fleeting. Everything in us which can die is already dead. . . .
>
> Our bodies are the only government.
>
> Your breath is sweet with apples. Our groins are white as apples. I take you again and again into the white center sequestered between my legs where we engage in the battle of apples. You enter me. I grow about you. . . .
>
> Praise be the one who offers us apples.[9]

Writing the piece, I had not known how much this myth had affected me or that I violently disagreed with the orthodox religious view. But this piece was the beginning of what has become a lifelong preoccupation with midrash—a retelling or reinterpretation of biblical material.

The apple was never intended for Eve. Eve plotted with the snake. She wanted to give Adam a piece of her flesh, a sliver of her bone to bear within him. She wanted to fill the hollow in his side with her own body. When she came to him with apple on her tongue, she prayed that he would not be able to resist her. . . .

Eve says, it was because of the lamb. It was that god gave the lambs to Abel. It was that Abel was the best beloved, the favorite and that is why he was given the slaughter.

It was that god came to Abel, his mouth bloody like a wolf—the first teacher— and the grease and smell of burned flesh upon his tongue. His mouth already full of death. God came to Abel in such robes. And they were lovers.

—*"Eve Awake"*[10]

For a woman to engage in midrash, an activity always reserved for men, was terrifying and elating, similar perhaps to Eve's eating of the apple. In order to confront the myth, we have to amplify ourselves. It was not only passion that I felt, though there was plenty of that, but it was the exhilaration that came from my unwillingness to modify what I was seeing. It came from the determination to stand behind something terrible and truthful. Now I understood what it meant to be courageous in one's writing, and afterward I was committed to that path.

While we may not connect with one fairy tale or another because they are closer to the psychological and, therefore, the particular, myth, by its nature, speaks universally. It is not as certain that each of us will identify strongly with the dilemmas in the story of Cinderella; however, all of us born into Western culture live out the story of the Garden in one way or another. Individual fairy tales may or may not affect our lives, but I believe that every myth resonates for each of us.

In the following pages, we will examine several myths in order to gain the skill needed to examine any myth you wish on your own.

Ariadne and Theseus

Some time after we worked on the myth of Adam and Eve, the class engaged with the myth of Ariadne and Theseus.

Because Athens had to pay tribute to Crete, Theseus, the successor to the throne, volunteered for the team going to Crete to dance the bulls. There, Ariadne, priestess of the moon and dissident daughter of King Minos, befriended him and held the thread guiding him in his descent into the labyrinth. At the moment that Theseus killed the imprisoned and voracious half-man, half-bull Minotaur—progeny of the queen priestess Pasiphaë and the god Poseidon in his white bull aspect—an earthquake devastated the palace of Knossos, marking the end of the Minoan civilization. Ariadne and Theseus escaped the island. Theseus returned to Athens, inaugurating a new age in Greek history, while Ariadne remained on the island of Naxos to marry the great god Dionysus.

In this class, which combined writing with performance, we were considering the moment when Theseus descends into the labyrinth. For the purposes of the exercise, the group divided into pairs; each couple then spent time with each other developing trust. On the day of the enactment, each was to bring a ball of yarn or thread to class.

California Institute for the Arts, situated on a hill, is built on many different levels with numerous corridors leading off each other. One could say that the school was designed as a labyrinth and is, therefore, the ideal environment to experiment with this myth.

After some introductory remarks, several people set off to find their own labyrinth and Minotaur, having placed the other end of the thread in the hand of their "Ariadne." I stayed behind with the Ariadnes. The ones holding the thread tried to make themselves psychically available to the ones going forth, protecting them in their mind, communicating their alertness and presence through a code of little tugs on the rope. One of the men in the class, particularly tall and stalwart, a veteran of the navy, had brought a thick hawser to use as his thread. He carried it rather proudly, winding it masterfully about his shoulder. The boat that it was designed to moor must have been of a substantial size.

After a while, we were aware that the tugs on the thick hawser had stopped. The rope was still taut, but when Ariadne pulled, even yanked at it, there was no response. We waited. She tugged again. Nothing. We waited. After some time with no change, I went to see what had happened, assuming some minor mishap such as the rope becoming jammed in a swinging door. I followed the rope and came upon this Theseus white and shaking in a stairwell.

"What is it?" I asked him.

"I don't know," he answered, trembling.

"What do you think?"

"Don't you understand?" he said. "I don't know."

"Do you want to go on?"

"Where?" he asked.

"To wherever it might be."

"It's right here," he said, not at all eased by my presence.

"What is here?"

"I don't know. That's the point. That's what's here. What I don't know is here, right here. And there's nothing to be done. It can't be killed. It just is—I don't know."

"And . . ."

"And . . ." He couldn't really speak, and my questions were not helping. In his silence, I heard the unutterable words, "I'm terrified."

We stood together in the stairwell. There was nothing, no one around us.

"Don't you understand?" he said. "I don't know." He didn't want to go on. He had found his Minotaur.

I put my hand on his arm and, after a while, led him back from the abyss that had opened at his feet in this most ordinary place. Later, he said, nothing in the navy had ever frightened him so much. For weeks, he didn't bring in any of his own writing and avoided the exercises in class when he didn't skip class entirely. Essentially, he avoided us as much as he could without losing class credit. Then one day he came to see me in my office. "Now I can write," he said, "maybe not today or this week, but from this time on. I always thought I'd seen a lot in my life, even though I'm young, so I didn't know I didn't have anything to say until that moment on the stairs. Now I can write, because for the first time, something has happened to me." He had walked straight ahead into the unknown, the unknowable living myth.

The myth does indeed take us into the unknown and the dark. There is something there that draws us and that we fear. And we have no idea what it will finally turn out to be. As the myth tells it, we have to go into the labyrinth alone. But Ariadne, who knows the way, does remain on the outside guiding us with a golden thread. It comforts me to think that there is such a thread in the imagination, that there can be guidance, that someone or something will lead me back.

Myths are beguiling and confusing. First, they appear to be mere stories, fantastic ones at that. Second, they are so resonant psychologically. Third, they often have historic antecedents, and this does seem to reduce their mystical qualities. We have found the city of Troy, the palaces of Agamemnon and Knossos, the evidence of the flood that the book of Genesis records. So how can myth be anything but a remnant of a historic incident?

What are myths then? Whence do they appear? And what do they mean?

The myth of Ariadne and Theseus, like so many others, has historic validity. The ruins at Knossos are exceptional evidence of the quality and content of Minoan life. Yet while the myth accurately chronicles this life—the origin of the bullfight, the practices of a cattle-centered culture, the conflict with Athens, the rise and fall of Crete, of matriarchy, of the goddess—it cannot be limited to this analysis. In addition to disclosing the life, the thought, and the beliefs of ancient Crete, this myth speaks to us about the intricacies of our own psyches and about the sacred life. Theseus's pursuit of the Minotaur is a map for a descent into the underworld and the labyrinth of the unconscious. Whatever it reveals of history is narrow compared to the experience of living the myth and learning firsthand about the repeated and necessary confrontations with the monster who may be the god, about the conflicts between the secular and the sacred and between the rational world and the wondrous universe.

Unless we enter the mythic realms, unless we open ourselves up to the realities within and without ourselves, we are not really alive, not really human, are only part of ourselves, like a person with one eye who has lost a dimension, or the sailors who lived in a flat world and never ventured too far because they were literally afraid of falling off the edge into nothingness or sailing into a sea of monsters. Perhaps nothingness *was* at the edge of the world, but of another kind: it was and is the place of the eternal, of the underworld, its monsters and demigods, the glories of the inner world, psyche, and vision. In other words, while the literal is reassuring, it is in conflict with the province of the imagination, the ability to see and work with the invisible, to talk with and about the gods.

> *Imagine a thread. The thread is given to you. You do not know where you are going or how you will come back except that you will follow the thread. Write yourself along the way into the labyrinth. Describe your labyrinth. Who is holding the thread? What do you expect to find? What do you fear you will find? What do you find?*

> *Rewrite this experience from the point of view of Ariadne, the one holding the thread.*

The Golden Thread

It unwinds in his hands, slipping shiny between his fingers as he moves cautiously into the darkness. She waits in bright light just outside the entrance, the sun warming her back. She peers into the darkness. Sweat collects between her shoulders and seeps from her armpits. Her hand clutches tightly to the end of the thread, and she strains to hear his fading footsteps.

He is gone, moving into a darkness she'll never know, and the thread is stretched between them. Fiercely she clutches the unraveling end, anxious, waiting. Will he return to her, will he love her? Will he take her away, now that she has committed this crime of disobedience? Her future is unwinding away from her, and she can only wait, holding the flimsy shiny thread, waiting, sweating in the hot sunlight.

The thread tightens, goes slack, snakes along the ground at her feet as it disappears into the labyrinth. It is all she has, a single strand, and she can only wait.

To follow him would be a double suicide—together, with the thread rolled up in a tidy skein between them, they would be lost in the darkness. If she left and ran for help, his tug on the loosened thread could pull it into the abyss along with him. He would be lost, and she would be left alone without him, surviving only to face the wrath of a kingly father who has been disobeyed.

Her choice has been made, so she waits in the bright fierce sun and wonders, "What now? What next? What have I done? How can I move from this spot?"

She winds the thread between her fingers, cutting into the soft white skin till lines of blood accentuate each knuckle. The thread pulls, goes slack, pulls again. She cannot tell if he still moves away from her, or if—his task fulfilled, the great bull finally slain—he moves toward her again.

What if he never comes back? How long must she wait, not knowing if there will ever be another tug on that tiny web that ties them together, that slender shiny thread that's wrapped so tightly around her pounding heart?

—*Judy Welles*

Write in the voice of whatever you find in the center of the labyrinth. Who or what is your Minotaur? How did it get there? Why have you two come together? How does it see you?

What do you do when the two of you confront each other? What happens on your return?

The story of Ariadne and Theseus entering the labyrinth is also a metamyth, a myth about the process of living the myth, about how it leads one to confront the unknown in order to be transformed. Myth, more than any other kind of story, resonates with the necessity of inner journeys. This is true whether one is considering the life of the Buddha, the stations of the cross, the passage of the Israelites out of Egypt across the Red Sea and into the forty years of desert wandering, or the ordeals of Psyche and Eros.

One way or another, myth not only enlightens but shows the way. Myth is a map that articulates the journey. Myth is always about enlightenment and always extends the same possibility to those willing to live it. And myth goes one step further: it implies that, willing or not, we are all confronted again and again in our lives with the circumstances of the myth. Like it or not, aware or unconscious, we will at one time or another be challenged to disconnect from our allegiance to the material world, be lost in the desert, will wander confused and bereaved until we fulfill the requirements of the gods. We will all be broken, will all be crucified, and, we hope, will all be offered the possibility of resurrection. Perhaps the mythic path is a condition of human life, our choice being whether to have it inflicted upon us or whether to live it consciously.

Stories That the Tarot Can Unlock

I remember the moment when psychologist Jane Alexander Stewart and I laid down the twenty-two oversized cards of the Major Arcana of the Tarot, saying to those who had assembled with us, "These are the stations of the journey." Suddenly, we were both in sacred space and in story.

There are many stories about the origin of the Tarot, and this one, probably apocryphal, is too good not to be repeated: the Tarot was created when the Christians burned the books and razed the greatest library of them all in Alexandria. Mystics, philosophers, and savants from everywhere in the known world gathered together, fearing that all knowledge was about to be lost. In order to preserve wisdom through the dark times, they encoded everything they knew in the Tarot deck, hoping that those who came afterward would be able to decipher the hermetic images.

While we may not be able to decode the occult wisdom of the universe from the cards, we may be able to use the cards to help us through the equally complex process of coming to understand who we are and how we might proceed. Meditating on the images in each card can release a flood of personal associations, images, and arcane knowledge about our own lives and character—and, just as importantly, it can inspire stories.

Contemplating the Major Arcana, one can discern a pattern equivalent to the development of the psyche. The first part of the deck, including the cards of the Empress, the Emperor, the Hierophant, the Chariot, and the Lovers, articulates the individual's relationship to the day world, to parents, authority, power, action, relationship. The second part of the deck, which includes Death, the Hermit, the Hanged Man, the Tower, the Star, and the Sun, raises issues regarding solitude, reversals, destruction, shattering—in other words, regarding descent, return, and transformation. These later cards refer more specifically to the ordeals and triumphs of the development of the inner life.

By contemplating the order of the cards—how one state of mind leads to another—and by meditating on each of the cards individually, we can discover a great deal about human life and about our own story. And because the steps are so clearly outlined in the sequence of the twenty-two cards, the Tarot provides a beginning practice for breaking myths down to their components.

The Fool

The Fool is the first card. It represents the self as the innocent, as having what the Zen master Suzuki Roshi called "beginner's mind." In traditional imagery, the Fool is represented as a young person dressed in motley, holding a flower, with a small dog nipping at his heel as he virtually steps off a cliff. The Fool is the one who steps out, who, unrestrained by caution, is energetic in pursuing life.

Here are some writing questions that Jane Stewart and I developed in order to elicit the Fool in each of us. These questions are not only appropriate for work with the Tarot but, like the work with the guide, provide an introduction to any mythic pursuit.

List the five most foolish things you have ever done in your life.

In detail, write the story of the very most foolish thing you've ever done.

After you have agonized over the story, write a piece revealing how this was the wisest thing you ever did.

Unless we can see the wisdom and meaning of our errors and foolishness, can see the useful consequences of our impetuous and spontaneous behavior, we will live only the narrowest vision of ourselves. What is foolish often seems foolish only to our conservative and cautious natures, for without foolishness, we would not explore or develop. While we are often restrained from foolishness by others who have ideas about who we should be and how we should behave, these attitudes do not necessarily accord with our own deeper wisdom. So it is important to discover the particular nature of our foolish side and to honor it as well as we can.

The great comedians have always played with the duality of foolishness and wisdom. The fools in Hamlet and Lear are actually the wise ones who see deeply into the nature of life. In the Celtic tradition, the master poet-shaman, the Ollam, played the fool to the king, being equal to him before the law.[11] These early Irish poets, like Siberian shamans, wore cloaks of bird feathers and through ritual and trance retrieved lost souls and conducted their audiences on journeys to the other world. They had custody of all the original tales, they committed the history of the tribe to memory, and they recited these tales on auspicious occasions. A single mistake could cost them their life. Finally, it was their duty to keep the king honest through their foolery. Their praise sustained the king, while their satire could overthrow him.

Charlie Chaplin's characters play the fool but only because they are the wise ones. Chaplin is a model of one who gave voice and image to disdained parts of the self and society. He was willing to honor the tramp, the innocent one, the weakling, the spurned one inside himself, and he did it with great tenderness and affection. Ultimately, his portraits give us great comfort. It is possible to get such comfort from ourselves if we allow the fool to emerge.

> *Find an image of the fool that delights you. Imagine yourself as this character. Find the courage to enact the character to the extreme. Find the fool's voice. Find a situation in which this fool can flourish. Write exuberantly, wildly, immoderately. Be a fool on the page. Step off the cliff.*

Step off the cliff. That's the clue. Writing depends upon stepping off the cliff. We praise the little flower, in the imagery on the Tarot card, for taking our attention, for revealing its secret and all secrets to us, as it does in the Buddha Flower Sermon. And then we praise the little dog, whoever or whatever it is—a gadfly, the muse, the messenger of the gods, Cerberus guarding the entrance to the underworld—for biting us on the ankle just in time, so that we lose our balance and go off into empty space, knowing that we will come down elsewhere, and knowing also that we will come down hard.

The Cliff-Jumping Club

You were nothing each time you jumped. And then you landed and reconstituted yourself. It was amazing how little it hurt. Or, how easy it was to bear. The reconstruction, the thud of the muscles jammed into the earth, joints bent tight and then standing slowly and taking a few steps, gingerly, and smiling. She had done it. Passed through nothingness, through the pitch and yaw of an instant, hung in space, descending, and landed. At the top you were something. You were fear. Staring down. Fear staring at itself, and then you jumped and passed through nothingness, and at the bottom you reconstituted and became courage.

The cliff-jumping club used mainly abandoned construction sites on hills. She could not remember how it became a club, who or what led them to formulate the rules. The cost of admission. This hill was on the edge of the line. The line was invisible but everyone knew it was there.

Billy Morales crossed the line. Billy Morales followed the club to the cliff, hung out, hung back, wanted in, didn't say so, didn't not say so. Came closer and closer until she knew. Everyone knew. He wanted in and he would jump.

How do you know who it is who raises the price, ups the cost of admission? How does she know it was not she who added the codicil? Billy, had not merely to jump to get in, he had to run off the cliff. How to remember who governed or in what shape consensus came? Billy must run. Where others paused and squatted. Fear staring at itself. Billy must run. That was the deal. They all concurred.

And Billy blinking slightly in the strong light, dark skinned, broken English. Billy blinking at the condition, saying nothing, turning and facing the cliff, willing his legs forward into a slow run. He never even looked at what he was going over. He wanted to be in the club so bad. His legs pumped forward, like pistons driving him inevitably over the edge and then for that instant, hanging out in space before he began the arch of his descent, his legs still pumping just like he was running on air.

She was at the bottom watching him in that moment of time. The sun was behind him. He was black, his legs moving slowly, determined, through the air, his body propelled out further than she had ever gone. Billy jumped into nothingness. She had never seen it so clearly, the passage into nothingness. The air opened and took him. He was nothing, treading the path of nothing that had opened at his feet, left solid ground running. He had willed it but not chosen it, running into the air. She saw the light breaking behind his body. He was a kind of sun then. The rays darted thin as fine gold needles from the dark center of Billy's falling body.

She saw his passage into nothingness and knew as he began his slow descent that he would never get in, never reconstitute at the bottom as one of them. She had a strange feeling like falling on land. And all the children fell together then, each in his own space falling away, falling while the sun shone through Billy and there was no courage at the bottom.

—*Marsha de la O*

Story Questions for the Tarot

To enter the Tarot is to enter the archetypal world and to discover the elemental mythic forces that have been affecting us. For those who have lived their lives as if they were only affected by what can been seen, heard, felt, and verified, it is wonderfully unnerving to identify the invisible forces that have been forming and informing us all along.

The following questions can be applied to each one of the cards in the Major Arcana. They are designed to elicit the influence and impact of the archetypal forces.

Who is the Empress? (The maternal? The matriarchal? The ruling feminine?) How does the Empress manifest in your outer life? In your inner life? How have you played the Empress, and how has the Empress affected you? Who has carried the archetypal energy of the Empress in your life? When have you carried it? What is or has been required of you to survive in the domain that the Empress rules?

Take each of the Tarot cards in the Major Arcana. Meditate on each in turn, writing down the questions that the images provoke. Then answer them in the mode of the essayist or the fiction writer.

The Tarot is not only about character and archetype, it is also about story—stories that we know and stories that we don't know. Hungry for a new story, one can:

Select three to five cards at random from a carefully shuffled deck—here you may include the Minor Arcana. Align the cards in sequence. Study the images. Choose another card to represent the protagonist. Write the story that emerges from their narrative relationship.

Here is a final cautionary word from Jane Stewart regarding this work with the Tarot: "Remember that this is designed both for your illumination *and* delight."

Following the Map

The archetypal situation and the mythic realm hover around the perimeters of story. Even at the edges of the most prosaic situations, myth shines, like a corona of light emerging from an eclipse.

Living in terms of myth not only redeems our lives at the end but helps us along the way as we encounter the difficult and unexpected. The mythic story helps us particularly when we are suffering, though living the myth may also shatter us before we are made whole. There is no journey without myth, but also there is no journey without some measure of suffering.

Once when I was in great despair, my friend Corey Fischer, of the Traveling Jewish Theatre, turned to me and said, "Oh, yes, I know how you feel. You're in the desert." This statement led me to discovering how to work with myth.

As soon as he spoke, I knew that I was, indeed, in the desert. I was in dryness. My spirit was parched. I was surrounded by barrenness. I was besieged by the very particular phantoms, devils, and invisible torturers who reside in the arid wastelands.

When Corey located me in the desert, I felt what Edmund Wilson called "the shock of recognition." From then on, I was able to gain perspective; I was no longer in despair because I knew the myth behind it. I knew that one stayed in the desert a long time, the symbolic equivalent of forty years or forty days depending on whether one was remembering the story of Moses or of Christ. And though I didn't aggrandize myself by identifying with either of these mythic figures, I was able to examine each of their paths to see how I might learn from their ordeals. Their stories became blueprints that could be followed as necessary. I investigated desert stories, desert myths for clues as to how to proceed.

I knew, for example, that some of the Israelites made it over to the "Promised Land"—every word of the story began to resonate for me with symbolic content—but many did not. The Israelites were kept waiting in the desert until a new generation was born that was uncontaminated by the past life. I knew by this that I had to give up much from my former life before I could begin a new one. I remembered the anger that had prevented Moses from entering "the land of milk and honey," the land of fulfillment and peace. From this, I learned that I had to be careful, to watch out for anger, impatience, and despotism. I knew that I must not "strike the rock" or its equivalent unless I was willing to stay in the desert—in my emptiness and despair—forever. I had to endure thirst. I had to remember that I had been given "manna" before and that I had to divest myself of the influence and impact of *Mitzra-yim* (Egypt), which means the narrow place.

According to the Christ story, I understood the desert as the place where one's faith is tested, where one is tempted, is led astray spiritually. These signposts were very helpful. Suddenly, there was a road through the desert where there had been no road before. If I was careful, I might come to the end of the dry time.

I began to write. I imagined myself in the desert, then developed a story of a woman who was lost there. Questions came to me, and I was respectful of them even though—or especially because—I had no idea where they were leading. I wrote them down, mused over them, imagined scenarios that might answer them. I tried to answer the questions by writing little stories or vignettes.

I kept what desert myths I knew in my mind, musing on them as if they were koans. I allowed myself to fantasize archetypal characters. I asked what might be considered archetypal questions:

How is a woman confined in the desert different from a man confined in the desert? Who are the gods of the desert, what are the forces and energies I must deal with? Who and what needs to be honored here? Does a woman come to the desert as Moses did because she has been given a task to do? Or is she, like Moses's sister Miriam, exiled there like a leper? Or does she, like Christ, come there to confront her demons and deepest self? Why was I in the desert? Had I been taken prisoner there like Joseph? Or had I come there deliberately? Was I on retreat or an outcast? Was I alone or was I with others?

These questions and others persisted for a long time. Then circumstances intervened—or so it seemed. A friend asked me the meaning and origin of my name. I began to think of the story of Dinah, my namesake, Jacob's daughter—a myth I hadn't thought about before. I imagined her in the desert. This fascinated me.

Eventually, I began pursuing Dinah's story exclusively. She filled my imagination until I was no longer content just to think about her. Then, I took myself to the actual desert. In that moment, I began enacting in life what I already perceived was being enacted in my imagination—the voluntary immersion in the desert of body and spirit.

What is the story and meaning of your name? How has the story of your name affected you? Are you living out its story?

I traveled to Israel, to Sinai where Moses had spent forty years, to the Mount of Temptation where Christ had wrestled with Satan, and to Shechem (or Nablus) where Dinah had been born. I thought, "This is where my psyche was formed; this is the geography of my ancestors."

Perhaps you already know your inner landscape, the piece of land that speaks to you as if you belong to it. Or perhaps you locate your story in a particular geography because of an unexplainable affinity with it. Identify the geography of your imagination. What story or stories might you be living out because of this affinity?

If you had to locate yourself on a landscape at this moment, what would be the geographic equivalent of your state of mind? What story emerges from this location?

Standing among the stones in the hot sand, I felt a hidden part of my psyche unfold. I began to understand why I, who had been born by the sea in Brooklyn, was living so happily in the dry hills of California and why I presumed I could call this landscape my own.

Then I heard a voice speaking inside of me. I recorded what it said:

My name is Dinah. It is a desert name. . . . Do you know about names?. . . A name is alive, has a life far longer than a life. It persists in its own form, drags itself through the centuries. . . . Once I did not exist, but afterwards Dinah exists for all time.[12]

Now I was determined to find out what the desert meant to me, to me as a woman, a contemporary woman, a contemporary American Jewish woman. I struggled with this question for nine years. In the course of questioning, I was able to leave the inner desert, or perhaps it is more accurate to say I learned to see the desert. I found the life force there, its nuances, varieties of vegetation, its animal life, its night sky.

To find my story, I had begun with myth because there is a time when one is grateful for the map and follows it rigorously. But afterward, having acquired more confidence, one goes off the road, explores, wants to find one's own way. As much as I might have been following the route of the Israelites to reassure myself during a dark time, I was also trying to find my own story and where it differentiated itself from the collective tale.

Though we can say that the resurgence of creativity within me was like the coming of rain, we can also say that it was like the appearance of stars in the desert sky or the startling brilliance of desert light. The desert took on another aspect. Myth is not simple; it offers the possibility of seeing things in complex ways.

Soon I was so completely absorbed in the writing project that I didn't notice the desert conditions anymore. Having claimed the desert image in a new way, I lived as if it were mine. The book that developed out of the first questions and the questions that followed the questions is called *What Dinah Thought*. And this is the first paragraph:

> My name is Dinah. It is a desert name. My father was Jacob and I was his only daughter, the only soft flesh, the only breasts to bud from his leathery hands. Who would have thought that he could have a daughter, but it was in his old age when his limbs were also beginning to soften as if they had been chewed, as hide is, by the teeth of time. Because I am a woman, I was not taught to kill. To everything that happened, until now, I have only been a witness.[13]

From the moment Corey Fischer "found" me in the desert until the time I finished writing *What Dinah Thought*, I felt as if I were being guided along a path. Perhaps what we think of as receiving or being given a sign is simply the ability to recognize the occurrences of story as one lives one's life with awareness.

Our Lives as Myths

To see our lives as myths, we have to extract the archetypal events from the particularity of daily life. To some extent, this is the opposite activity from writing our story. In the latter instance, we need all the details in order to make the story ours. In this case, we have to find the mythic scaffolding, the universals, behind the specifics.

> *Tell your story as if it were a myth. Begin with a mythic phrase to stimulate the mythic imagination: "And it came to pass that . . ." or "It is told that . . ." Tell the story in as few sentences as possible, writing no more than a page. The myth appears in the bareness; it is like a skeleton. It needs no adornment to be recognized for what it is.*

A knowledge of myths does help to locate the equivalent moments in your life and also to find the larger stories that your life may resemble. For example, if you, like many people these days, have had a child late in life, you may find yourself writing in a mythic voice: "And it came to pass that a son was born to X and Y in their old age after they had despaired of having a child." This in turn would take you to the story of Abraham and Sara. From there you might write your story in accordance with that biblical text, identifying other elements common to both your story and that tale. ·

One of the best ways of identifying such moments is to consider the dramatic events with which fairy tales, myths, and legends are usually concerned and then extrapolate from them. The story of Hansel and Gretel speaks about being lost and devoured, the myth of Psyche and Eros speaks about betrayal and ordeal. The Exodus story from the Old Testament is concerned with purification. Many other themes underlie these stories; identifying them will help you identify the essential themes in your own life.

What themes underlie your life?

When you have identified the major themes or significant moments in your own story, select a myth that seems to be analogous. Tell the myth as if it were a contemporary story and you were the protagonist, modifying the myth through the details of your life.

Then tell your own story with the myth behind it. (The difference here is a matter of emphasis. In the first exercise, the myth is central and modified by your life. In this exercise, your story is central, modified by the myth.)

Through working these two exercises, and going back and forth between personal history and myth, you will develop a story and characters that are perfect amalgams of them both.

This new story can then be explored and developed. At the same time that you are writing about yourself, you will be writing about someone you don't know at all. A character, much like the Minotaur or Chiron, half human, half other—perhaps animal or god—develops from this synthesis of personal story and myth. You can follow plot or character, or you can let this new story lead you where it will toward the depths of the imaginal world. Perhaps a poem will develop, a journal entry, a story, or a novel. Film often takes this approach: *The Fisher King, Jesus of Montreal, He Who Must Die, Man Facing Southeast, Black Orpheus,* and Kurosawa's masterpiece *Ran,* which elevates Shakespeare's *King Lear* to the level of myth, are examples.

All the elements are here for you and everything is possible.

Writing Your Myth

Myths, tales, and legends are so rich that one can work with the material for months. In *The Hero's Journey,* Joseph Campbell identified some of the stages through which the hero passes during his journey. Many of these appear in a different order and in different combinations in myths. Here are some of the elements that you will find as you investigate the myth's basic structure: the call; setting out; becoming lost; encountering nature; purifying oneself; sacrifice; making an offering; encountering a stranger or an animal; posing a riddle or answering one; being tested; enduring an ordeal; crossing an impossible barrier; overcoming an enemy; descent into the underworld; finding what one is seeking; epiphany; transformation; blessing; bringing back something; return.

> *Take each of the elements in turn. How has each one figured in your life? Over time, write a story regarding each one of them. Then bring the different parts together. All these elements, taken together, comprise a metamyth: the archetypal journey of transformation. Combining them, you will have structured your own myth, and you may also have laid the foundation for a larger work.*

There is another way to work. It is to begin with a myth itself.

> *Find a myth that engages you or choose one at random. Any myth will do. All myths are appropriate for this work.*

> *Analyze the myth. Break it down into its components.*

Keeping this framework in the back of your mind, consider its story deeply. What particular issues does it address?

> *Formulate a series of questions that the myth inspires, questions that take you more deeply or broadly into the material. Answer the questions through images, fantasies, dreams, and events.*

It is always fruitful to ask the following questions, too:

> *How is this myth alive today in our century? How is the mythic story transformed by being translated into contemporary circumstances?*

Even as the myth reveals our personal stories and lives, so, too, does its presence illuminate history. The movement to settle the United States was sustained by the faith that the new world was the New Canaan. In a gross distortion of myth, Hitler's megalomania was sustained by his belief that he was re-enacting the Parsifal legend. The conquest of Latin America occurred, in part, because the Aztecs associated Cortez with their returning god, Quetzalcoatl. (This latter story is at the core of Hart Crane's brilliant poem, "The Bridge.") In our own time, the women's movement is partially inspired by the belief in the return of the Goddess.

When Jean Katz approached Judith, the biblical hero, she found herself writing a most dramatic, heretical, and passionate piece. Unnerved but undaunted, she remained with the material as it developed. In her piece, archetype and individual blend to reveal something of the nature and ways of woman, devotion, and war. Though Jean has chosen to write through another character, Aviva, rather than directly about herself, this doesn't diminish—rather, in this case, it enhances—the power of the work. If interested, Jean could easily illuminate the parts of Aviva that are also Jean.

Jean's piece emerged from the following writing suggestion:

> *Go to the periphery of the mind of the mythic character. Imagine that this character has set herself a task that is prohibited and impossible. Go to the farthest point from the conventional into the invisible, inaudible, forbidden. Go there with art, with the mind itself as part of the creative process.*

Judith—A Dance Midrash

Aviva is planning a dance. An orphan of the Holocaust, at age forty-five, she has become a prominent dancer and choreographer. This dance will be the culmination of her career, the choreography they have all been awaiting from her. It must be totally contemporary, yet rooted in ancient tradition. A breakthrough. A statement. A new view of what is possible in dance. A statement in art about the twentieth century. So, she moves. Turning and swaying, she begins to see the dance in visual and kinesthetic imagery. Images of sex. Images of violence. Images of rape. Images of murder. A dance about murder in a moment of sex. A dance about Judith and Holofernes. A dance about Judith and Hitler. That's it. A statement about women's power. A statement about a brave woman and a murderous tyrant. Biblical history and modern history in one dance.

"Judith will enter the stage wearing a somber black suit, black sturdy oxfords, and a black simple fedora hat such as the menopausal matrons of Munich wear. She will carry an umbrella in one hand and a shopping bag in the other. She will be surrounded by people dressed in the black and gray pajamas of concentration camp inmates. The backdrop will be barbed wire. A gate will have a sign over it saying, 'Arbeit Macht Frei.' Six men and six women will dance frantically around the stage while Judith moves serenely among them, calming them, exhorting them, reproving them.

"Suddenly, she drops to a cushion at the right side of the stage. She removes the oxfords, pulls a pair of gold, jeweled sandals out of the shopping bag, and straps them on her feet. She removes the hat and lets her raven black wavy hair fall to her waist. She removes the black suit to reveal a slender body dressed in diaphanous veils with jewels outlining the seams. She drapes a colorful robe around her, bound at the waist with a gold girdle. Next she dons a huge mask, much like Chinese dancers wear. It is painted to show the face of a woman of great beauty.

"She selects one woman from the twelve dancers and covers her with a pastel robe. She puts a simple mask on her head.

"They wave good-bye to the other dancers and dance across the stage as though taking a long journey.

"Twelve Nazi officers dance onto the stage. They surround the women, reaching for them lewdly, then fall back. Again they surround them and lead them to a tall dancer in a Nazi officer's uniform with a huge, grotesque mask on his head. The face resembles Hitler. The face resembles a Chinese monster. He wears a Nazi officer's hat atop the mask. The stage set is like an Assyrian desert camp.

"All the dancers fall back. Only Judith and Holofernes/Hitler remain on the stage. They circle each other warily. She removes her robe. She begins to dance seductively, undulating like a Greek belly dancer. He begins to dance seductively, an eight-inch erection protruding from his tights like a dancer in a Bruegel painting. She offers him wine. He takes it, drinks it, then tosses the cup away.

"He takes her hand, as though to lead her to the cushions at the side of the stage. Suddenly, he lunges at her, forcefully pushing her down on the cushions. He lies upon her, his buttocks moving up and down, up and down, faster and faster. In the moment of his climax, in the moment of the final spasm, Judith draws a knife out of the garter on her thigh. Her left hand embraces his shoulder. With her right hand she beheads him.

"The Holofernes/Hitler head rolls on the floor, spurting blood across the stage. The blood spreads in a pool around the head. Judith shoves his heavy, inert body off of her. It rolls onto the floor into the blood. She rises slowly, very slowly, and dances round and round the body, examining it closely. She dips her finger into the blood, touching a drop to each of her ear lobes. She dips again and rouges her cheeks with it. She dips again and paints her fingernails and toenails with the blood. She makes a circle around her navel and touches a drop to each nipple.

"Judith crosses the stage to find a burlap bag. She dances across the stage, waving the bag like a victory banner. She stoops to pick up the head with both hands and thrusts it into the sack. Her aide appears, picks up Judith's colorful robe, and drapes it around her. In a sweeping movement, Judith tosses the burlap sack containing Holofernes/Hitler's head over her shoulder. She dances off the stage with her head high, her chest forward, a gleam in her eye and strutting steps.

"The set changes back to the barbed wire of the concentration camps. The eleven dancers in prison garments lie about, dispirited. Judith and her aide reappear, dancing proudly across the stage. As they reach the gate with the sign 'Arbeit Macht Frei' Judith removes the Holofernes/Hitler head from the sack. She places it on the sentry post beside the gate. The eleven dancers rise. They approach it in awe, reaching, withdrawing, returning, standing taller, taller till they surround Judith, hoist her on their shoulders, and dance joyfully in a circle.

"Judith slips down as they continue to dance. She removes the golden sandals and puts back on the sturdy black oxfords. She removes her mask and puts it in the shopping bag. She twists her hair into a bun and covers it with the somber black fedora hat. She pulls the black skirt over her veils and puts the black tailored suit jacket over her jeweled brassiere with the blood-dotted nipples. She picks up her shopping bag and her umbrella and walks quietly off the stage."

Aviva imagines the audience gasping in stunned silence, followed by thunderous applause. She ponders how to stage the dance, how to handle the beheading. She can't really murder a partner every night. Or can she? There must be some mask designer who will know how to do it. That German choreographer, Pina Bausch—she knows how. Call her. Check with her. How literal should she make the rape scene? Is there a male dancer who can do it every night on stage? Auditions will tell. Aviva continues to visualize the sets, part ancient Assyrian and Judaean camps, part Nazi bunkers and concentration camps. Aviva decides that she will dance Judith herself. No one else carries such a fierce rage under such a placid demeanor. It will be her ultimate triumph.

—*Jean Katz*

The structure of myth exists in the mind and needs only to be tapped. This piece not only elaborates the story of the biblical Judith but leaps to the prepatriarchal myth of the Dying or Corn God, whom the queen sacrificed each year for the sake of the community. It is the subtle shadow of this myth at the end that gives the piece its final eerie quality. Without an underpinning of myth, it would be difficult to incorporate, so smoothly, the four separate time zones in one action: The Assyrian/Judaean period, the concentration camp period, the contemporary time of Aviva, and finally the even more ancient period of the Dying God. Ironically, it is the shadow of the latter myth that lends a horrific credence to Aviva's seemingly casual and chilling question: Can she murder her partner every night?

To work with myth requires study and attention. One has to be willing to enter the story and bear its consequences. Even in Jean's piece, despite the centrality of Judith, the overriding focus is on the story, or rather on the structure that supports the story. It is the structure of the myth—here the conflict between the weak and the strong, or the relationship between sexuality and death, between death and redemption, between dance and life—that is most essential to the piece. Again, the exploration of the myth does not provide an answer but rather is the means by which the elements and tensions within a situation, and their eternal qualities, can be examined and made known.

Odysseus

Each myth is a treasure house of wisdom regarding the world and psyche. But the way to the treasure is difficult and intricate. And often when it seems that one has found everything there is, another level of the myth will be revealed, another room of jewels and gold. This was our experience when Jane Stewart and I began to think about the hero, Odysseus. We were interested in his journey of transformation because it was so clearly marked by a variety of adventures and mishaps over the ten years when he was trying to return home to Ithaca and his wife Penelope after the battle of Troy.

It was some weeks after we had begun working that Jane said, "The journey of Odysseus is the journey of the masculine's search for the inner feminine." She was as startled by her own words as I was. Suddenly the myth had become transparent, and a paradox lay at the heart of it. For it is paradoxical that Odysseus, the hero's hero, champion of the Greek army, should follow his ten years in battle with ten years of encountering the feminine.

With two exceptions, all of Odysseus's encounters as he struggles to return to Ithaca are related to the feminine. In preparation for his reconciliation with his wife Penelope, Odysseus undergoes an intense rite of passage as he encounters and is thrust into relationship with the spectrum of the feminine—the goddess Athena, his mother in Hades, the nymph Calypso, the monsters Scylla and Charybdis, the great witch Circe, the innocent Nausica. The wise Penelope had been ruling the kingdom in his absence and had, accordingly, balanced the feminine with the lessons of the masculine. But the crafty Odysseus had only intensified the masculine during ten years at war and was no longer Penelope's fit companion. For the Greeks, balance was one of the highest virtues, and they understood, as few societies have since, the necessity to balance the feminine and the masculine.

You are Odysseus. Having been battling for a decade, you are disconnected from the feminine. Now you are returning home. What have you forgotten? With

*whom have you lost contact? What relationships must be restored? What do you
need in order to be reintegrated into society?*

*You are Circe (or Calypso, or Odysseus's mother in Hades), and Odysseus comes
to you. How do you see this man? What does he want of you? What do you want
and gain from this encounter?*

Everyone, man or woman, knows what it is to be distracted by worldly bat-
tles, to be taken over by the values and necessities of the combative situation. Then
there comes a time when we must return home to ourselves. Because of the preceding
duress, we may not feel fit to enter the emotional and ethical world we once knew. In
these cases, each of us needs to find our way home.

*Imagine (or remember) a journey that has taken you far from yourself. Where
did you go? What compelled you to leave? What do you need to do to come home?*

I was once told a story about a Vietnam veteran overcome by the beauty and
physical thrill of dropping napalm while high on LSD. "How," he had asked in an-
guish, "can any experience compare with that intensity? And how can I return to what
is considered a normal life?"

The man was searching to reconcile himself with quieter modes, less aggressive ways, with more organic rhythms. Some of the qualities he longed for were associated in his mind with the feminine. Whether you are a man or a woman, the need to
know the feminine—within and without—is great. For the feminine, which by its nature is sometimes hidden, has also been violently closeted by patriarchal forces. The feminine that may occasionally choose to don a diaphanous veil does not want to be
required to wear the chadoor. Yet in more ways than one, the modern world has imposed the chadoor on the feminine within each of us.

The Eleusinian Mysteries

The Eleusinian Mysteries were performed in Greece for two thousand years until their
suppression in A.D. 396. From a contemporary viewpoint, these mysteries were profound rites of transformation through which one immortalized the soul in this life
and in the other. According to Pindar, "thrice blessed are those who have seen these mysteries and descended into Hades. They know the end of life and the beginning."

These mysteries, the religious rites of the great goddess Demeter, taught the participants the occult secrets of the reconciliation of opposites: life and death, upper and
lower, masculine and feminine, body and spirit, mortal and god. Through a carefully

orchestrated descent into and out of Hades, the initiates experienced the ultimate realization of "living the myth."

As in other mystery religions, including early Christianity, it was believed that an individual could enter into the mythic story, live out the myth, and thus be transformed. Myth operates in two ways. First, one's own personal story is structured upon mythic reality. Second, myth is a drama one can choose to enact. Here we are talking about far more than writing a mythic tale or writing ourselves into it. Writing is a part of it, but the larger experience is living the myth itself, empathetically, for the purpose of soul making.

In the Eleusinian Mysteries, the initiates, called the mystai, enacted a rigorous nine-day ritual while walking from Athens to Eleusis. Through a series of rituals, meditations, and dramatizations, they enacted the mythic story of the triple goddess: the crone Hecate, the mother Demeter, and the daughter Persephone who was abducted by Hades, the god of the underworld. The narrative focuses both upon Demeter's grieving response to her daughter's disappearance and on Persephone's transformation in the underworld from a nameless girl, called the Kore, to the Dark Queen. During the holiest moment of the mysteries, in the sanctuary of the temple at Eleusis after much ceremony, ordeal, theater, sacrifice, purification, and prayer, the mystai were blessed with the epiphany of the goddess Persephone herself.

So profound was the Greek belief in the personal enactment and experience of this story that it was said that one needed to experience the mysteries only once to be assured of immortality in this world and the next.

In 1981 and again in 1991, in Greece, theater director Steven Kent and I led a group of "mystai" in the reenactment of the Eleusinian Mysteries, which to our knowledge had not occurred in fifteen hundred years.

We went to the sacred sites. We did the rituals. And we entered the story. We entered history and myth and thereby discovered that these characters and stories were our own.

It would take an entire section, if not a separate book, to outline the entire workshop. But the next exercise outlines the nine stations of the mysteries. At Delphi, the site of the Pythia, the great oracle, we spent the day, silent and fasting, reviewing the myth's nine stages.

> Like those who went with us to Greece, you can find these states of descent and return—for each of us is familiar with them—within yourself, can see how you have lived the myth in your own life, and then write about it:
>
> I am abducted [to Hades].
>
> I am separated [from the mother].

I am grieving [for the daughter].

I am in the dark.

I am barren.

I embrace death.

I am fertile.

I am reunited [with different parts of myself].

There is light.

Here are some excerpts from the journal kept by Marina Olivier:

I Am Abducted. The white horses came for me. Distraction was the white mare and fantasy the stallion.

I Am Barren. There are times I don't want a child or anything alive to come from me. There are times when breathing overwhelms me and when love is a scourge. There are times I hate everything green and curse the water.

I Embrace Death. I have always wanted this lover.

I Am Fertile. I pick dry grasses and silver dollars, listen for the rasp of the two black seeds against the silver petals. I am fertile; even these dry flowers seed within me.

There Is Light. Even though the sun is 93,000,000 miles away.

I remember the day at Delphi very well. The night before, during the death ritual, my candle, out of thirty-six others, was the only one which burned down altogether. It was difficult to ignore what might be a terrible omen. Sitting in silence, in the afternoon, under a bower of flowering vines, I felt my face shrivel as if I were an old hag. Hecate is here, I thought. I heard a cackle in my mind: "You will never write again," the crone snickered. "You will never again have a lover. You will live your life in sickness, suffering, and pain. What do you decide?" I felt myself crumble with despair and disappointment. My face was so twisted, I was reduced to one of the ancients. I could feel the advent of sickness and slowing into death. I struggled with these dire predictions for more than a half hour. Then, I don't know from what source, I heard myself reply, "I accept whatever comes. I want the whole ball game. I will stay here until my rightful end." Then I heard wild laughter within, and the strong voice of the hag: "We were only testing you. You will have a long and productive life."

Here are excerpts from a piece I wrote when we returned from Greece. I believe it reveals the intersections between the personal life and myth:

> We seek a vision, and when it comes we're walking up and down wondering when we'll have hot water to wash our hair, pretending this is our ordinary life. We ask, "Is this it? Is this . . .? It?" Uncertainty is our companion. The vision is transparent, we can put our hands right through it.
>
> We've come to do the mysteries, find ourselves in Greece. Some mornings, our rooms open to an air shaft plunging down endlessly to the dark; the sour humors rise up from a murky source. Other evenings, outside the windows, the light plays on the Acropolis across the way. Perspective shifts. We're tired, events wear us down. We sleep restlessly, awaken too early when the fruit market opens on the street below. We can't speak the language, the guide fails to arrive, the bus is late, our suitcases are delayed, then very heavy as we carry them blocks and blocks. This is how our grandmothers came to America, with all their possessions on their backs and everything falling away. Surrounded by strangers, we say we're alone and abandoned. Our watches must be corrected, our journals bog down, the daily life persists, insists. We are irritable and quarrel, complain the sheets are rough, keep us awake at night. We are outraged, petulant, dependent. Only the very old do not complain. They know why we are here.
>
> . . . This is the crossroads. This center is Hecate's, is sacred. The offering must be garbage, so we bring Her the decaying pieces of life. At Her age, she knows the full value of what has been used. The suppressed mysteries are of the three: the one who loses, the hag, and the innocent one. These are the rites of Demeter. We are afraid our hearts will open, as they must, to her grief. We are each the Kore, the daughter, the simple one. Our suitcases are tagged but we have forgotten our names.
>
> We find the map but do not know how to travel. We know the myth is our life, but how do we follow it, barefoot, in these times? We try to step onto the sacred road, but the highway covers it. Whatever world we travel has obstacles; the map splits into the four directions and we cannot yet manage all roads at once. Paths open to the underworld; we are divided; each of us falls down.
>
> . . . This is Crete. We've crossed the Aegean in the dark. Our hands are sticky with figs from the tree marking the entrance to this underworld. Dark waters swirl about us, the spray bathing our faces, and we are not surprised to find

ourselves crying. Who is this ferryman? Why does this three-headed dog have myriad eyes?

Mystai means secret or hidden, closed like the eyes, or a flower folded in on itself. We are called mystai, initiates, we fold in and enter the dark. . . . The enacted drama is our life and we go down, down the rope of our psyches into the secret parts of ourselves. Persephone pulls us down, just as Hades abducted her. It is time to marry the god of our own ineffable dark. Perhaps we do not know the way out.

. . . We say, as it was said, "We have purified ourselves. We have sacrificed. We have imbibed the sacred drink." The youngest among us is thirteen; there was always a child to lead them. The oldest is eighty-five. We have gone into the sea, we have leapt the bulls and danced like Zorba on the sands. We have given up what is most dear and sacrificed what is most loved. From everyone, something is taken away. Then we take it all back into our bodies, eating with gusto, this holy food.

. . . The light leaps off the water. Apollo, the sun, has not killed the earth snake. It crawls up through our spines, becomes light. The old poet woman seer says, "I have been waiting to come here all my life."[14]

There is one more story I would like to tell. After Steven Kent and I had planned the workshop, we meditated. During the meditation, I heard an inner voice say, "When you are in Greece, you will see a hill covered with olive trees and behind it the sea, and then you will know what you cannot yet know."

All the time I was in Greece, I expected to find the hill everywhere. But I could not find it. I gave up on the way to our last destination, because Delphi is inland. It had been my imagination, I told myself. Then as the bus climbed the hill to the ancient ruins, I saw, to my astonishment, a hill of olive trees with the Gulf of Corinth behind it. And then I knew that the gods exist and myth is the tale they tell.

The Entrance and Return

The larger story addresses the most profound issues, brings together and reconciles all the worlds. Psyche creating itself, entering the labyrinth of the inner world, confronting good and evil, sexuality, encountering the lost feminine, and reconciling the opposites, life and death, light and dark, male and female, upper world and underworld, barrenness and creativity—these are the essential focuses of the Eleusinian

Mysteries, and they are the quintessential concerns of the larger story. To participate in these quests requires, as the stories tell us, a certain grace, courage, and determination. How we enter the world of the larger story and return from it is a story in itself:

> *Return*
> When you go
> to the dark place
> you must come back
> singing
> the note inscribed
> on your palm
> the song written
> on your hand
> the way trees
> grow about the
> shape of wind.[15]

Part IV

Writing as a
Spiritual Practice

At last the notes of his flute come in,
and I cannot stop him from dancing around on the floor.

The Kabir Book, *translated by Robert Bly*

For a dream image to work in life,
it must, like a mystery,
be experienced as fully real.

James Hillman, Dreams and the Underworld

He suggested I pray to the Muse
get down on my knees and pray
right there in the corner and he
said he meant it literally.

W. S. Merwin, "Berryman"

The Path and the Practice

Recently I was struggling with writing a particularly difficult passage in a novel. However hard I tried, the writing remained abstract and ponderous. Frustrated beyond endurance, I strode out of my studio into the hills, gesticulating wildly. "Listen," I yelled into the air when I felt I was safely distanced from anyone who might overhear me, "we're materialists down here, we like form, shape, and color."

As there was no answer, I listened to the silence for a long time. Then I began again, "I'll make you a deal. I'll record whatever you dictate, but let me edit it a little to conform with earthly conventions. I admit, it will lose some of its meaning, but on the other hand, we'll understand it better. Whatever you send will be so much more effective if enclosed in specific images and a story we never expected. When you send a story, we listen. That's how we are. Stories are like a body. We can touch them and they touch us. Stories touch the very heart of us."

In my cranky manner, I was addressing the muse.

The muse is like the angel one sometimes meets on a path while seeking wisdom, peace, and compassion. Buddhism, Christianity, Judaism, Native American religion, and paganism are all paths; each, in its very own way, takes one to the same depths and summits. Creativity is also such a path, writing is one of its practices, and the muse with her sweet breath or fiery torch stands in the dark place and lights our way.

If I could have the muse of my choice, she would be Doña Clara de Erazu, the Spanish nun of the seventeenth century who gave up the habit to become a Mexican bandit and swordswoman. She was especially good with railway robbery. The silver that Spain was wrenching from the mountains of north-western Mexico, she put in her pocket and spent freely in the cantinas. She dressed as a man, was finally arrested in Peru, and deported to Spain for a trial. The Pope pardoned her, and the Cardinal gave her several thousand pesos as an allowance. She traveled back to Mexico and up to Xochimilco where I first met her on a train. I was a passenger. She was robbing the train and invited me to join her. I said, "What is there in it for me?"

She answered, "Freedom, absolute freedom to write what you are called upon to write. You will have to learn swordsmanship, how to ride a horse, jump trains, and let silver run like water between your fingers, keep late hours, drink well without falling asleep, pray in the cantina, and dance in the cathedral."

—*Regina O'Melveny*

Being on a path is often likened to fording a difficult river or climbing a mountain. Moses went up the mountain, and so do many seekers. There are sacred mountains everywhere; Mount Fuji, Mount Sinai, Mount Parnassus, and Mount Graham *(Dzil nchaa si an)* are some of them. After the ordeal of climbing the mountain, one hopes to receive some wisdom and teachings to bring back for oneself and others, just as Moses received "two tablets of testimony, tablets of stone, written with the finger of God."[1] I am not suggesting that the path of the creative should or can replace other spiritual disciplines; I am only saying that it, too, has a series of practices and is a way to complement and amplify one's spiritual life.

Maintaining a spiritual practice is an ordeal like climbing a mountain, and it demands the same of us: commitment, discipline, endurance, focus, and awareness. There at the top is the sky and, perhaps, the large vision, but ultimately the meaning is in the climbing, in the "angels" who accompany us, and in the specific rituals and activities that take us to the summit and sustain us along the way, both going up and coming down.

There is a fundamental difference between the creative practice and other spiritual disciplines. Following the creative is a path, but it is not a known path. It has to be carved out by each individual practitioner. There is a practice, but its particular rituals are mysterious and unique, and again each practitioner must discover them for herself. There is the need for a spiritual lineage, but there is no lineage per se. There is the need for teachings, but they have to be discovered for oneself, and the teachers have not been ordained and do not present themselves; they also must be sought out and enlisted in the process. There have been others who have gone before, but what they discovered cannot be translated or passed on; one only knows they went before. And some were lost and some were not, and the pitfalls need to be discovered and the markers placed again and the territory mapped anew. And the gods? The gods also must be recognized before they can be invoked, honored, praised, beseeched, and loved. And then each practitioner must discover his own prayers, sacrifices, offerings, rituals—everything has to be invented from the beginning. And so, as in the mystery religions, one travels with one's eyes closed, utterly alone, into the unknown.

Of course, not every writer looks at creativity as a spiritual discipline, and indeed, not every person or artist is interested in such a practice. But for those who are, writing becomes another kind of activity altogether, and its effect depends not upon the product—the finished piece—or on the consequences—accomplishment, recognition, remuneration—but upon the process with which the written word is pursued.

We are not angels. We live in the world; our activities do not always transpire in the sacred, but when they do, the most mundane action is transformed. A ritual meal nourishes us differently than does our daily supper, for the ritual meal primarily feeds our souls; we eat every day to nourish our bodies, and then we partake of the Sabbath meal in order to experience agape. Writing practice is both the same and different from what we do on a daily basis; though we may write each day, we can also set aside time to approach the word differently, refreshing ourselves in the process. When writing for the world, we are concerned with finishing a manuscript. When writing as a practice, the word becomes the means to access another world.

The path of creativity can be as rigorous as any other path and contains many of the same practices and teachings. Just as enlightenment cannot really be the goal of a spiritual practice, for the very desire for enlightenment stands in its own way, so the desire to write a great book, be prestigiously published, or make the best-seller list cannot be the focus when writing as a spiritual practice. Whenever these goals predominate, they interfere with the quality of the work. Thus, it is best, when possible, not to indulge them.

The writing path, like any other path, requires us to shed our hopes and illusions. Understanding and vision cannot be fully cultivated until the ego, the will, or the worldly self defers to other ways of being and knowing. "Abandon all hope, ye who enter here" are the words that mark the entrance to hell. But this warning can also be read as an instruction for those willing to undergo the ordeal that may lead to enlightenment. For it is only after we abandon hope and illusion, after the ego with its fantasies, needs, and constructions has been stripped away, that we may see clearly—and that shimmer of things as they are is sometimes called paradise.

Paradox and contradiction mark this path. For though we are speaking of this activity as an ordeal and likening it to climbing the most forbidding mountain, the climb is, often as not, accomplished by the simple act of being still and attentive, focusing on the word and the perception, cultivating awareness, all in order to be relentlessly present. In this way, the practitioner fosters spiritual awareness exactly as she refines her craft.

The approach can be both simple and careful. We try to come to the desk as to an altar. We take the phone off the hook. We may light a candle or bring in a flower, just as one readies the temple before prayer. The door is closed or the windows are opened. Each of these small activities focuses our awareness on what we are about to undertake. The moment of entrance into the sacred world is negotiated slowly. Each word is taken in as a holy object for which one is grateful. Its meanings are not apparent; it opens itself gradually, the lotus of many secrets, or burns with the sacred fire.

Pursued in this manner, through the practiced willingness to see and then to believe what we see, the creative can bridge the gap between the inner and the public worlds, between daily life and the world of spirit. And if, then, our small heart opens—opens to others, to the natural world, to wonder and awe—then the vision, the work of art, the image, the poem may appear in that flash of light, that moment of *kensho,* or in the still, small voice of the heart of the universe itself coming to meet us.

The Muse

To imagine the muse is to bring the muse into form. Every activity of the creative process requires that we bring spirit into form, that we create a vessel—ourselves or a work of art—that can hold the spirit.

Lover or demon, invited or feared, the muse can transmit the energy that enlivens our work. In Greek mythology, the nine daughters of the great god Zeus and Mnemosyne (memory) were the Muses, the inspiring goddesses who presided over poetry, history, music, theater, hymns, religious dance, and astronomy. In today's language, the muse is the guardian angel or the daimon of creativity.

Imagine your muse, female or male. Invoke the muse. Call the muse to you.

The Muse
She first came to me in the winter, when the air was a cold breath held by the earth for days at a time. . . . As I tested the current and sounded, she was one of the first things to surface, a woman adapted to the enormous pressures of the deep. . . . My back felt like a latent history, my spine a lineage which ran the length of my trunk from the womb to the head. This line was a matriarchal one, with each vertebra being a mother, the vertebrae stacked like so many pelvic bones holding the legacy of the central nerve. When I saw her supine form rising, she moved into vague recollection as if she were traveling the span of my backbone.

She was a large naked woman of bread with three breasts. She shifted, bulged, then became my grandmother who smelled faintly of rancid butter. . . . Then she lapsed back into Bread Woman again, strangely familiar. . . . A friend brought me a book of bread art, and there she was, a Frascati Easter bread, a woman with three breasts swelling over her bodice, arms on hips, wearing a broad skirt with a name written on it. When I looked closer, I saw that the name was my own, Gina.

. . . In the dream my grandmother carried an axe. . . . My grandmother cut off the tips of my fingers. . . . I ran to the library but she followed me. Then she cut off my fingers to the first joint. I hid in a restaurant, but she cut off my fingers down to the second joint. I ran. She cut them off to the third joint. I was frantic. The last time she cut off my hands. I held up the two stumps of my arms. . . .

My hands were gone. . . . I did not understand the sacrifice. I had wanted some kind of mastery over the Bread Woman. And now she had exacted this sacrifice from me. I hadn't counted on losing my hands, my ability to manage things, manipulate, maneuver, manus—hand. . . . I remembered my grandmother, Margarita, fingering the beads of the rosary. *Ave Maria, Madre di Dio. Ave Maria, Grazia Plena.* The church of Santa Maria in Cosmedin has an enormous stone mask which, according to legend, bites off the hand of anyone who does not tell the truth. It is called *La Bocca della Verita*, the mouth of truth. The mouth of the underworld. *Lago D'Averno.*

I put my hands in the stone mouth. When they were severed, I saw I did not know what was true. I had told only partial truths, lived a partial life, without hands. I was unable to praise. The truth Bread Woman demanded had little to do with intent and honesty. She wanted me whole.

There were times I had refused to see, when I observed and did not embrace. When I did not see the way the bottlebrush tree flames with bloom at certain times of the year. When I refused to get down on my knees to pray. When I spoke of her, Bread Woman, as if she were a fiction and not the living presence who came to me at all hours, whose absence opened a deep loneliness under everything I did. When I drank wine without first pouring some upon the earth. When I watched the moon rise and set without acknowledging her pull on me. When I consumed life without recognition of what was sacrificed and what was given.

. . . The Etruscans, an ancient people who lived in the region where my grandmother was born, believed the liver was oracular. In animal sacrifices each lobe was dedicated to a particular god or goddess and provided divination of personal and state matters. In return, the Etruscans brought fruit and honey to the spirits of the underworld. Their cities were planned around a center, the mundus, a meeting place for the world of the living and the world of the dead.

. . . I pressed my hands to my belly, the stomach, the liver, the intestines, the womb. Here was the mundus of my body. What gifts did I receive, what offerings did I bring, what dead had I neglected? What could I bring to Bread Woman to answer her hunger? She had been hungry for thousands of years, since the last dark-eyed Etruscan woman placed a honey cake in the earth. She was hungry even though my grandmother and her mother and generations of mothers made bread in her image. The three-breasted bread woman baked for Easter was covered from the waist down. She was made with her fullness and sensuality obscured.

I want to learn to make bread. I want to learn to make prayer.

I ask Bread Woman to teach me prayer.

—*Regina O'Melveny, "Bread Woman"*

The muse is both a deity and a messenger, is the one who makes demands and brings the gift, is the one who inspires the work of art. The muse demands dedication, and our service to her requires discipline. Dedication, discipline, devotion—these are the bases of writing as a spiritual practice.

Remember moments of devotion, efforts that required discipline, aspirations that required dedication. How did you act in the face of these requirements? How have you brought these same qualities to your writing or other work? Imagine yourself as a priest or priestess approaching your creative work.

Like any other deity, the muse urges us toward service for the world, just as she strips the world and its concerns from us. For it is surely not only for our own sakes that the gods are willing to appear to us and breathe their holy fire into our work. The muse, when she appears, takes us out of our little life and thrusts us into the world.

Under the tutelage of the muse, we go into the world naked, but that is what the creative requires, for how else can we see what we must, be sensitive to what exists, and also present our work in a truthful manner? Anyone who interacts with us in this manner is one whom we can recognize as our muse.

Beginning the Practice

Here we began with the muse, but we can begin anywhere: simply breathing and accepting inspiration are, ultimately, variations on the same theme. The life force enters us, sustains us, and we send it out again to sustain others. Breathing and inspiration are the basic processes that maintain the world. So we breathe in. So we allow the muse in. We take in that larger life. We breathe in the spirit, breathe out the word. Practice breathing. Practice connection. Practice inspiration.

And after this beginning? We begin again. Like the Zen concept of beginner's mind, the creative always requires beginning and beginning again. Freshness. Innocence. Emptiness. We breathe. We accept the inspiration. We pray to the muse. As Berryman told it to Merwin, "Get down on your knees and pray." Each day the same and each day, therefore, new.

> Now every morning, I get down on my knees to the muse, the goddess, Bread Woman in all her aspects. I ask for clarity and emptiness, so that I can be open to my deepest feelings and to her voice in my work and my daily life. In the evening, I light candles, arrange flowers in her honor. I praise the abundance and joy of Bread Woman, the painful and terrifying wisdom of Skull Woman, and the guidance of my grandmother spirit. My hands grow back with each gesture I make toward the sacred, with each work of art or writing, with each motion toward those I love.

> —*Regina O'Melveny, "Bread Woman"*

One quickly learns that it is expedient to honor the gods of place, to pay homage wherever we find ourselves to whatever gods reside there. When we have identified the territory that we wish to enter, we must honor the muse who governs it.

Sometimes the muse appears and we recognize her. Sometimes we call her name. We invoke her. We bring the spirit down from the high places. We look for the words that are right, for the names that are fitting, for the call that we hope will not be refused.

> *Write the invocation of the muse. Imagine that you are shouting it into the wind. If you can, go outside and call the muse to you. What offering will you make to the divinity so that it will enter you?*

The Quiet Moment

Not everyone wants to speak to the muse. For some, inspiration comes through quiet moments. Silence can be inspiring. A tree can be inspiring. Or we may be inspired by something we read, by something someone has said or done. Inspiration may not come from the outside at all—it may be the consequence of our ability to open an inner door. So we may begin by:

Lighting a candle

Or opening a journal to a blank page

Or writing down a dream as if it were a holy text

Or meditating on a theme or an object, hoping to see what has not been seen before

Or speculating, as the Kabbalists did, on the permutations—perm, mutate, mute, tame, mare, pet, perpetuations, perturbations, perpetrations—of a word, until deeper meanings are revealed

Or querying oneself on a subject, again and again and again, refining the question more and more rigorously, until you have set your knowledge, conventional values, and habits aside so that you can know more, know deeply and freshly.

One can make a ritual out of opening the door. Your ritual may be as simple as clearing the desk each morning or opening the window and breathing in the morning or night air before approaching the work. This ritual of preparation, the repetition of a satisfying activity, is the drumroll that proclaims and simultaneously welcomes the miraculous.

When we have found a way to open the door, then we do it again and again. And each day, then, will be a beginning.

About meditation it is said, when sitting, simply sit, simply breathe. Then, when writing, simply write, allow the word. After sitting one sometimes studies the teachings, just as after simply writing one may study the work that has been done. But in the beginning, open the door, write, and accept what comes.

Meditate for a few minutes until you are calm. Write for the same length of time. Meditate again. Write again. Meditate again. Write again. Let the silence refresh you. Allow the silence to enter the piece. Discover what can emerge from this emptiness.

Gratitude

Meditation is not far from prayer; prayer, praise, and gratitude are interconnected. Sometimes we write out of rage or pain, desperate to reveal an injustice, to awaken the world, or to express the agony of our lives or of others. But joy, as private as pain, also wants expression. Joy and appreciation can be the angels that open the door for the creative to enter.

One of Michael Ortiz Hill's favorite meditations is to:

> *List ten gratitudes that relate to incidents or moments from the day. These can set the mood for the writing that follows, or they may be transformed into praises, poems, vignettes, little stories.*

These gratitudes, written as small pieces, can capture the freshness of the moment. They ask us to be present in the event as we write. As frequently happens, important events, whether large or small, can be subsumed in the preoccupations of the day. It is too easy to give thanks absentmindedly. Every one of us has taken part in a ritual or service that was performed by rote; this is a deadly experience, and in writing, such remove reeks immediately of disconnection, routine, and duty. Good writing insists on vitality, and the reader knows immediately if we are present or not.

Beauty

Beauty is at the heart of spiritual practice and is inseparable from writing and creativity. Our own word *beauty*, from the Latin *bellus*, is ultimately connected to *benus* (Venus!) *bonus*, meaning "good," from which the word *beatitude* also develops. Hence the beautiful, the beneficial, and the blessed are etymologically linked.[2] For the Greeks, beauty and harmony were sacred revelations; beauty was always present when the gods were honored. Similarly, beauty is the Navajo designation for an alliance with the spirits and nature. Beauty, or *Tepheret*, is the very heart of the kabbalistic Tree of Life, the place where spirit and form meet, the site of the connection between the divine and the earthly.

Contemporary culture often denigrates beauty, considers it effete and shallow. This is because beauty is misunderstood. It is exactly this misunderstanding that underlies our cultural reading of the myth of Psyche and Eros in which Aphrodite, the goddess of love and beauty, is accused of jealousy and petulance and is thus trivialized.

At the conclusion of the myth, Aphrodite effectively initiates Psyche by giving her three tasks to complete. The third is to descend into the underworld to bring back the secret of beauty. This is the most difficult task and ultimately the most dangerous. Psyche completes the task but, unable to keep from opening the box that contains the secret, falls into a swoon. It is then that Eros feels pity for her and asks the gods to make her one of the immortals.

A deeper reading of the myth instructs us in the danger of confusing Psyche's earlier and innocent—that is, undeveloped—beauty with the beauty that the goddess Aphrodite represents and that is also carried by Persephone, queen of the underworld. In this reading, the myth is a warning against being dazzled by bathing beauties, movie stars, fashion, and the like while being blind to beauty itself and its divine aspects. Too often we opt for the decorative or the superficial, avoiding the beauty that Keats associated with truth—the terrible beauty, the terrifying beauty that strips us naked by its presence.

One can make a serious practice of perceiving beauty wherever it exists. With a certain awareness and concentration, we can open ourselves to the presence of beauty, and in such cases, it rarely remains on the surface or is conventional. Divine beauty often appears where one would not normally expect it—in the twisted, lined, and naked, in the unadorned, uncultivated, odd, and humble, as well as in the most perfect oratorios or the most elegant and refined prose.

> *Find a natural object—a twig, an old bone, a pebble—that is quite ordinary in appearance. Look at it for a long period of time. Do whatever you can to allow yourself to see the object for what it is. Focus your awareness on the object. Try to remove yourself and your judgments from the activity. Do whatever you can to bring yourself to see the object as beautiful. Focus on its beauty. Then allow yourself to see it as ordinary again. Alternate your awareness. Finally, allow yourself to see it as unbearably, awesomely beautiful.*

> *Write about what was required, what occurred to allow you to see the beauty. When you saw the beauty, what did you see? What made it beautiful? What happened when its beauty faded? Where does the beauty lie? What constitutes it?*

We have all been struck by the beauty of something we would have ordinarily ignored. For me, the world is transformed into a place of holy beauty by variations in light: the astonishment of falling light; light illuminating a rusted shovel; light falling on fallen petals; the wild mustard flowers gleaming in the setting sun as they catch the light; a patch of foxtails against a weathered fence, suddenly illuminated and brought to life a half hour before sunset.

When I tried to fathom the quality of beauty, I realized it was a disclosure of the thing in itself. There are moments when an object, a person, a living creature is utterly present and naked, is utterly itself, and this startling moment can only be called beauty. This presents a dilemma: Is the tree showing itself to me, or am I allowing myself to see?

And this nakedness, this presence of the thing in itself, this unmodified confrontation with reality, does far more than please the senses. This presence of beauty heals. When we are desperate, we take ourselves to the sea, or the mountains, or the stars, in the hope that we will heal in their presence. It is not only nature we are seeking but beauty. And then we understand something incomprehensible—that nature and beauty coexist. Sometimes a painting or a poem will stir us in the same way. Why? Surely it is not simply the pleasant relationship of color, shape, and rhythm that affects us so overwhelmingly. Surely it is something else, something as powerful as stark uncovered reality—that is, something as searing as the presence of the gods themselves.

Therefore, the pursuit of beauty, our devotion to it, is a spiritual act. And it is honorable to strive to incorporate beauty into one's work. This is not only homage to the divine, it is communion with the divine itself.

The body descending into spirit, as in Psyche's descent to the underworld, or the spirit descending into the body, as in the god's incarnations—these are images of spiritual events. The mystical teachings of Judaism, Christianity, paganism, and Tibetan Buddhism describe the constant movement of divinity into matter and matter into spirit. It may seem like an odd consequence, but the love of the gods leads inevitably to the love of form, of the body, because the divine always expresses itself through matter.

This is the way Barbara Lipscomb recorded the next writing exercise:

> *Choose a moment*
> *a vision*
> *a scene*
> *from your life*
> *of utter beauty.*
> *Enter it,*
> *simply.*
> *Bring beauty*
> *to beauty.*

Compassion and Metaphor

There is a place of heartbreak toward which the creative process ultimately draws us, a place where we understand our glory and failure, our hope and desperation, the beauty and the suffering, and from this understanding some miracle of acceptance and identity occurs. Sometimes it comes from falling in love with an image or with a character we barely understood a moment before or from watching what was flat and impenetrable round into a world. Sometimes it comes from the appearance within us of ideas, feelings, selves that we disdain or fear yet still must accept as ourselves. These moments, if we allow them, if we struggle for the words to hold or reveal them, these moments when the intellectual struggle is one with the heart struggling to see and accept, bring us to compassion.

Compassion is the way the heart perceives the identity of all things. Metaphor is the writer's path toward that same understanding, is the braid that ties all things to each other. Metaphor can be more than figurative language; it can be the mystery itself. To pursue metaphor is to search out that net of Indra, the divine revelation of intrinsic relationships and connections.

Through compassion we become half of metaphor: we are the one who is identified with all things. Without compassion, we will never know anyone or anything, not even our own story. Too much judgment, too many ideas and attitudes will stand in the way of the fundamental principle that we are similar to, connected with, and part of everything else. And without knowing and respecting our own story, we are disconnected and alienated in the world, without the ability to know or respect anyone else's story either. Therefore, without our own story, without compassion, we will lack fundamental understanding of the world, even about cells, trees, atoms, and stars. But if we pursue metaphor itself far enough, if we stop and contemplate the connection we have found between the wind and song, between night and grief, between our lives and all life, then compassion is inevitable with its sweet rain of kindness and tender feelings.

> Look at what is disjointed, awry, alienated. Find something that reconnects what is severed. Find the metaphor that unites the sundered. How is this similar to what you yourself have experienced? What occurs when you see these things as they are, without judgment and with an open heart?

The Ecstatic Dance

Writing can be a form of prayer and a means to enter the sacred world. In the ecstatic moment, it is difficult to know if the vision is coming toward one or if one is moving toward the vision, but one way or another, the barriers between the worlds dissolve and one is united with the radiant emptiness. To have this experience is not necessarily to become conscious, but it may be a step toward it, just as consciousness may also induce such states of gratitude and understanding.

In Chile, in 1972, under the Popular Unity Government of Allende, it rained torrentially for the days preceding the holiday on September 18. Though it was the end of my visit to that country, I was relieved by the rain. Times were very tense, a political coup was threatening, and I thought the rain would keep people indoors. But by the afternoon of the eighteenth, the rain had diminished, and despite the political tension, makeshift kiosks were speedily erected to house small musical bands and sell food and drink as the people began gathering in the parks and empty lots to celebrate their precarious freedom. Like others, I soon found myself dancing the *queca,* awkwardly pulling one boot out of the mud as the other sank in past my ankle.

"It's good that it is storming," I had said earlier to Ariel Dorfman. "There won't be as many incidents of terrorism or attempted assassinations."

"No," he had said. "It is not good. The people have to dance."

Be aflame. Burn. Shine. Fall in love with the spirit. Put on gospel, liturgical, or Sufi music, let your words rip. Turn on the tape recorder, and hold nothing back. Wail on the page. Walk up and down singing the words that appear on your tongue. Do automatic talking at the top of your lungs to the music you love. Whisper your love of the gods to the page. Weep. Shout. Speak aloud while you dance. Take off your clothes and intone poems. Chant, rhyme, and sing your own song. Say what you've never said aloud. Speak to the plants. Enjoin the birds to answer you. Confront everything you hate. Praise everything you love. Keep talking. Make poems. Keep it going. Another five minutes. Let yourself be carried away. Open all the doors and windows in your body. Let the words pour down like a torrent. Let it rain and rain. Get down on your knees and pray aloud.

Why dance the praise? So the words can be formed in the motion of the body. So the spirit emerges from the very cauldron, the heat and fire of the self. For the reason that some writers always use a pen for various drafts, rather than a machine, the better to feel the physical intimacy of the event of writing. The words *strophe* and *antistrophe* from Greek drama originate with the steps of the actor back and forth on the stage; the rhythm, the feet of the lines developed from that pacing. The walking and the talking are one action. The word that is forged in the mind and body at once, so it emerges from the two of them at once—this word is whole.

Zorba danced on the beach after the death of his son because dancing on sand is so difficult and only that crucible of praise could hold his grief.

There are times, even broken times, when the writer must still dance because, without that dance, the world can never be whole and the word, also, will remain broken.

Asking the Big Questions

After my husband and I returned from the pilgrimage to the death camps, we had two very different approaches to the experience. Michael, who is a contemplative, applied himself to erasing any vestige of story that he had carried back with him. He was afraid that he would misuse the experience by inadvertently co-opting it for the story or for the sake of the drama. He was afraid that this profound experience might become base currency for an exchange between himself and others. And so he cultivated silence and tried to empty himself of the experience—or, more accurately, tried also to empty the experience of himself.

My approach was the opposite. I had to find the story and its meaning. My approach was that of query. I knew the story did not lie in the chronological order of the events, which could easily be told, but in some other order or arrangement of personal experience and history to be discovered. On my return, I had to enter into the experience once again until something was revealed. For me, it was essential to bring something back, as the hero brings something back from his journey with which to heal the community. Without that story, my journey would have seemed self-indulgent.

Ultimately, each of us found a way to deal with the experience that we hope had integrity. It may be that for each new event, one searches for a way once again; we cannot assume that there is one way that is always right for each of us. It may well be that if I make such a trip again, I will return in silence, but this time, it was not possible.

For an entire year, I struggled in my journal with my reluctance to write about the experience. The issue was not literary so much as ethical and perhaps spiritual. Then I began to list all the questions that had preoccupied me from the onset and that remained in my mind: questions regarding the nature of evil, the sources of cruelty, the responses of victims, the means of endurance, as well as questions regarding forgiveness, the responsibility of the witness, my obligation to the event of the Holocaust, to my own experience, and to my different communities. As the questions developed and refined themselves, they became the core of the novel, *The Other Hand,* which I am currently writing.

The mode I used after the experience and while writing the novel is no different than the mode that I have used in writing this book: I ask questions. And the questions have questions. I use the questions to take me deeper into the matter, to take me to an understanding or insight I would not reach without that incessant and insistent querying. After a while, I learn to discern the questions that actually sustain my habits of thought and those that challenge them. At the root, it seems to me, my life is devoted to answering the same questions, which appear again and again in different forms. As the physicist John Wheeler said, "reality is defined by the questions we put to it."

What questions do you pose to yourself? What questions would inform the work you are doing? What questions follow from these? What intuitions do you have? What is driving you? What fascinates and obsesses you? What is your particular understanding? What is being revealed to you? What puzzles you?

What questions might you ask of yourself and of your work?

And the question we have been asking again and again and must continue to ask:

What is it you have been given to say?

There is a popular story about Gertrude Stein's death. Respecting her great genius, her enormous intelligence, a friend asked her a last question: "Gertrude, what is the answer?" To which Stein answered in her manner, "What is the question?"

Lineage and Teachings

The teacher is as important to the writer as the muse. But each of us has to find his or her own teachers. There needs to be a lineage, and we need to create it for ourselves.

When I was first learning my craft, I "trained" under Virginia Woolf and Samuel Beckett. I gave myself a subject and tried to write about it as they might have written, imitating their sentences. Soon I perceived that it was impossible to separate the form from the content. The shape of the sentence reflected the shape of their minds. And so, entering their forms, I entered their worldviews as well. In this way, they became my teachers.

The teachings we receive are implicit in the lineage we claim. In other spiritual disciplines, the teachings are explicit and are passed directly through the line of masters to us, thereby binding us to them. This cannot be the same for the writer; she must choose her lineage, invent the very world from which she wishes to learn.

List all of those people, living or dead, personally known by you or not, who have been important to you in terms of your creative life. Then examine the list, arranging the names in the order in which they have affected you.

What is your history of influence and development? What are the qualities these people have in common? How, together, have they impacted you? Who is formed through associating with these teachers? What specific heritage emerges from this line? What might be the concerns and focuses of the work that emerges from this line or tradition? Write a short autobiography that addresses these questions.

Consider those writers who have influenced you through their lives rather than their writing. How did they approach their work? What disciplines did they employ? What are they teaching you about the practice of writing? About focus? Devotion? Discipline?

Some writers take to the cafés, Colette was locked into her study from the outside, while Tennessee Williams was said to have locked himself into his study each day with a bottle of booze. Some write as did Dickens, in the living room within the hubbub. Others, like Rilke, need absolute solitude. Some schedule retreats, some write every day. Some go to the desk as if to a nine-to-five job, some write on weekends or in the middle of the night or during the hours of dawn, while for others the poems arrive while they walk the land in the evening.

When I was young, determined to learn to be a writer, I decided that there was an affinity between walking and writing. My father, who was a writer, disdained the bus, always walking from our house to the train station, but he was not seeking exercise. So from the time I was eight, meandering each day along the peninsula of Sea Gate, which was my neighborhood, I practiced walking like a writer, imagining what a writer might observe and think about. As I grew older, the walks became longer, and night after night, despite rain or snow, I passed by the lighthouse, poked about the debris of the beached hospital ship in the bay, and stopped on the jetty to feel the ocean spray.

Perhaps I did learn how to be a writer from those walks, as well as beginning the practice of solitude that has been just as essential to my work.

Find a lonely walk. Take it for several days before you begin to write.

When I listed writers who had influenced me some years ago, I discovered a self I hadn't known before I saw the names: Pablo Neruda, Anaïs Nin, D. H. Lawrence, Virginia Woolf, Samuel Beckett, the Greek tragedians, Fyodor Dostoyevski, Herman Melville, Nathaniel Hawthorne, Gertrude Stein, William Faulkner, T. S. Eliot, Doris Lessing, Hart Crane, Julio Cortázar, Carlos Fuentes, Miguel Angel Asturias, Herman Hesse, Ernest Hemingway.

Since then, this writer has relinquished some of her teachers and taken on others. Today the list would also include Rumi, Kabir, Marguerite Duras, John Berger, Gary Snyder, Nadine Gordimer, Wendell Berry, and Jean Giono. As I become older, my concerns are different, and I look to different influences. Recently, when speculating on how I became who I am, I remembered books that had mattered to me when I was a child, particularly the *Burgess Books of Animals, The Swiss Family Robinson,* and *Robinson Crusoe.* Now I understand that the woman who has spent so much of her adult life thinking about society, politics, and sexuality has returned to the concerns of the little girl who loved animals, trees, and land.

I think of all of these writers as my teachers, as part of my lineage. This one has taught me about the light and this one about the dark. This one takes me to ecstasy, and that one teaches stillness and solitude. This one is street smart, shows me the ropes, while this one tracks bear, tills the land, and teaches me the names of birds.

Such a list can intimidate us, but that is no reason to avoid making it. Every writer needs support, a context and a creative community in which to work. And awesome as may be the work of the writers who have influenced you, they were also ordinary people, struggling with the same issues—finances, time, distraction, blocks, discouragement, lack of confidence—and still they lived their lives and their work appeared. This knowledge supports us even as it supported them.

The search for a teacher is serious and arduous. When the teacher appears, we are grateful, for our lives, work, and souls are about to be deeply influenced. A spiritual practitioner may have traveled very far, may literally have climbed the mountain in search of the teacher. It sometimes happens that he then studies with this person for most of his life. For the writer, the search for a comparable living teacher is more difficult, and sometimes she cannot be found. Then we must proceed another way.

> *From the list you have made of people important to your creative life, choose the person who most challenges and interests you, who has the most to teach you. Learn what you can about this person's work and life, and contemplate it. Then step into that person's reality to see how he or she sees, feel as he or she feels, understand what he or she understands.*

Choose the teacher as carefully as you would choose a guide for a spiritual practice. Be certain that his or her life and work have authenticity, that you trust this person. Sometimes someone comes to us with a certain charisma that we find difficult to resist, but he or she may not be able to offer what we need for our development.

Earlier in this book, I suggested that one accept whatever guide comes. Here I suggest caution. I believe we should choose the teacher as carefully as the teacher chooses the student.

Joseph MacKenzie had been writing about Jack Kerouac when, halfway through his piece, he made himself a note, "I want to meet Opal Whiteley as soon as possible.

"I was alone, I didn't really like beer that much, and this was the woods—my land—not his city." He left Kerouac for the young girl who, born in 1897, began keeping remarkable diaries when she was six. The first excerpts from her childhood diary were published in the *Atlantic Monthly* in March of 1920.[3]

> It was time to perform my end-of-year ritual, inspecting the woods to make sure everything was scheduled for winter. I needed to know that the ice was forming on the edges of the pond, that the leaves were turning from green to red-orange and gold and that the bears and squirrels were preparing for the

winter snows that would carpet everything without further notice. . . . I got what I needed from Opal Whiteley—to realize my innocence, creativity, and potential.

—*Joseph MacKenzie*

Incorporating the Teacher into Our Lives

What follows is a series of questions designed to help you establish a relationship with your teacher. Once confirmed by the imagination, the reality of this connection will also take hold in the heart. In a spiritual practice, a teacher is an ongoing companion. Even when we are separated from the teacher or the teacher dies, the teacher is still with us, and we carry the sense of his presence in our mind and heart. Each day, when one begins one's practice, the presence of the teacher can be felt, for that person becomes the conduit through which teachings and rituals are passed to us in an enlivened form.

> *Imagine that you have had an intimate and intense relationship with your chosen teacher for at least three months. Beginning with a time in your life when the creative connection would have had the most significance for you, write about your relationship with each other. Focus on your desire to have a teacher who can transmit the secrets of creativity and support you in your creative work. Tell the entire story of your connection and the phases through which it developed. Be generous with detail.*

Write the story of your first meeting.

There was a time when I wanted a teacher. I needed to take a leap with my writing, and I couldn't do it alone. I wanted excellence and knew it required effort and dedication to achieve it. I needed a model and an example who would encourage me. Once I determined to open my heart to the task, it was clear that I wanted Neruda to be my teacher. Like anyone else, I was embarrassed to ask for such a gift, even though he was dead. I didn't want to impose upon his spirit, and I hardly believed that I was worthy of his trust or attention. Tentatively, I began to write small pieces about Neruda, fabricating a relationship with him. I felt foolish. But I continued. Ultimately, it became a series of prose poems. But that is not the core of what transpired.

This week I was given the book *Pablo Neruda: Absence and Presence,*[4] which consists of photographs of Neruda's three homes accompanied by excerpts from his poems. There he was, my dear friend. I studied the book as if I had finally been able to enter the home of someone beloved whom I had known for such a long time.

I had imagined conversation. Surely, he was one of the great talkers. I needed that talk. After all, I had come to him so frightened, a dumb, teenage girl with shaking hands, essentially insecure about language. Moses, who is in my lineage, put coals in his mouth and stuttered afterwards, while I imagined that doves flew out of Pablo's mouth whenever he spoke. *Palomas. Palomas blancas* quivering wings. Words like startled feathers. *Un nido* of burning sentences.

I imagined long literary evenings, odes intoned to the beat of the *charanga,* gossip long as gallows, speeches pregnant with clouds and grammatical shadows. *La noche escondida, la máscara* of painted *palabras,* lucid *pajaros de la anochecida . . .*

He gave me a blank piece of paper. "Dare," he laughed.

When I entered his dayroom, whirring white doves, their eyes *brilliantes entre dos luces de cobre,* settled into their golden cages. I called to them, "Coo, coo," and my breath smudged the night with coal dust, *negra y pesada.*

If I write this, if I dare to imagine the moment—as I have imagined others—where a man or a woman who had no prior existence together suddenly grow ruddy on the page with the breath of life—if I dare to imagine this: myself with this poet named Pablo Neruda, the two of us together in a room—*vivendonos*—then he hasn't died yet—poetry is still possible—it is raining in the south of Chile. . . . I know the landscape. *La lluvia* of hope . . .

A woman who writes a word down is not the same as one who does not.

When I was not yet twenty-four, I followed Pablo Neruda, the world's greatest poet, into his house. He said, "A woman rarely becomes a poet because the fathers tell her to keep her body closed and the mothers agree. If you want to write, you will have to be as open as the sea. *Apertura lluviosa.*" He said, "Live in my house for a month and don't speak. *Mi casa es tu casa—miento incomunicado.*"

—*"Walking with Neruda,"* no. 1[5]

Imagine that you are the writer or artist you hope to be. It was not easy to achieve this success. You had to overcome serious difficulties. Largely through the companionship and intervention of your teacher, you had the energy to overcome the obstacles, to act differently than you would have acted otherwise. "Remember" an important moment in the relationship with your teacher that helped you overcome the difficulties.

Now it was late August. My retreat into semisolitude and literary companionship was drawing to an end. As I was gardening with May Sarton I wanted to ask her so much. The core questions were: "How did you find the courage to be so open, open in your writing, open in your conversation, open to defying convention, open to speaking the unspeakable, open to living the socially unacceptable—open?"

She answered, "One day, I realized that in three hundred years I'll be dead. There will be nothing left except what I write. That, too, will probably turn to dust. But if I write the truth, the truth as I've lived it, the truth as I've felt it speak itself through me, then someone may read it. And, if they read it, it may help them find their truth. Their lives will be enriched, as mine has been enriched, by all the deepest truths I have read. Then my words may last.

"If it all turns to dust, OK. What have I lost? The only chance that anything may last comes through the truth. To tell the truth, I must live the truth and be open about this brief and transient life."

—*Jean Katz*

Now write the account of this important moment from your teacher's viewpoint.

Joseph didn't know I [Opal Whiteley] was there, resting on the stoop in the moonlight near the center of the logging camp. I couldn't see him, but I could hear him from the moment he left his hot and stuffy trailer. Even his breathing was very loud, louder even than a bear. I would tell him later that he had scared the bears and the toads, *and* the deer *and* the crickets, *and* the birds nesting high above him, *and* the squirrels and raccoons. I don't know if the fish in the pond were also frightened. I think only the mosquitoes were curious enough to approach him, to learn something personal about him. He told me much later they had indeed sought him out that night—all that night, in fact.

I said a whispered good night to Daniel Webster III [the toad] who lived under the steps, and left the logging camp along a very quiet path toward the west as Joseph approached noisily from the east, with his light flashing nervously through the stands of birch, ash, and spruce.

In the morning I returned, just at sunup with a moist cloth, warm tea with two cups, some cookies, a few napkins, and a small bottle of calamine lotion. I was very noisy stepping on twigs, whistling at the birds and occasionally singing a little tune as I approached the camp. I wanted him to hear me so he wouldn't be afraid. I only hoped he wouldn't be upset with me because I knew this was his property now.

. . . He had been up most of the night either scratching his mosquito bites or freezing in his sleeping bag with the broken zipper. I was right about the calamine lotion; he would need that more than the tea. His face was a field of bite bumps and his eyes just stared like a frog at me. I think maybe he even jumped a little bit like Daniel Webster.

I said a very nice, "Good morning, sir," to Joseph, just as if I had expected to find him right in that spot, which, of course, I did. He finally blinked and tried to reply but at first it only came out like he had maybe swallowed Daniel Webster or one of his kinfolk.

I could see right away that Joseph had good intentions. Only good intentions could possibly explain why he tried to sleep in the woods on one of the last nights of an Indian summer that mostly slipped away every time the sun set.

And since he slept right near my old writing stoop, I felt we could be kindred spirits of a sort. As Joseph fumbled to twist his sleeping bag one way and his shirt the other, I stole a glance at the step near his sleeping place and saw a sandwich on top of a beer can. I knew he had put it there so the ants wouldn't get it. He would be a good student, I could tell right then.

I quickly estimated that his sandwich would go very well with my warm tea. He would look funny with his face daubed with white leopard spots of calamine lotion. But I would be very kindly with him and give him a personal introduction to Daniel Webster III after our woodland breakfast. I knew he would like Mr. Webster very much if only because for every meal Mr. Webster eats mosquitoes.

—Joseph MacKenzie

You and your teacher are together. Something happens. Write the story. Write another such story. And another. Until you have conviction about your friendship.

Next, write from your teacher's perspective about the relationship between the two of you. By now you know what the connection offers you. But what does it offer the teacher? Not only the teacher-student relationship per se but specifically this relationship with you. Try to write in the teacher's voice, with fidelity to his perspective, point of view, images, concerns. Tell the stories that hold your common history.

So I [Georgia O'Keeffe] am almost blind now. It is ironic. I think of Beethoven becoming deaf. Of the lucid friends who lost their minds. I cannot do what I once could do. I have to learn new things and only the young ones can teach me. The young potter said, "Keep on, keep on—you have to work at it—the clay has a mind of its own." I kept on. I make pots. This new young friend comes to me. I learn to speak about my life again. I learn to make things with words. Once I worked with my hands and my eyes but now I learn to speak. I am the clay and I speak. I am not very good at it, but my friend says, "Keep on, keep on."

—*J. D. Whitney*

We are trying to create a world in the imagination from which to draw the kinds of experiences we need in order to realize our possibilities. Increasingly isolated and overwhelmed in the public world, we inevitably sink, without the solid ground of the inner world under our feet. Through this work with our teacher, we can draw upon the kinds of experiences all of us have needed but few have encountered, in order to become the creative people we want to be. Step by step, proceeding like filmmakers or novelists who virtually create a world as the context for their art, we are also creating a fictional but viable universe in which we can live our lives. Verisimilitude is the key here. Without it, our efforts remain arbitrary.

We tend these relationships by writing about them frequently and in detail, by examining them now from one perspective, now from another. Variety, detail, repetition—these are the elements around which the verisimilitude of this relationship coheres. From these elements we gather conviction.

After we have "remembered everything," then we will able to stroll into the future, our companions by our side.

Some psychological acumen is necessary here. Create a relationship that feeds you, that gives you what you need, that actually supports you for the next steps. Try to avoid the patterns of behavior that have impeded you in the past. Because we so readily repeat in our lives what has been harmful to us, we must be aware that these repetitions are habits of the psyche and could easily contaminate the imagination if we are not aware. On the other hand, avoid so idealized and ungrounded an image that this activity of the imagination becomes a farce to which you can't give credence. Let the teacher be a teacher. Let the teachings come. Take them in—they are yours.

Think of a moment in your life when the choice you made was not, in retrospect, in the best interests of your creative self: a time, perhaps, when you didn't have enough courage, when you did something you have regretted, when your judgment of circumstances worked against the artist in you, when a choice was made, an action was taken or avoided that closed a door on your creative interests. Rewrite that

206

moment as it might have been played out if the relationship with your teacher had existed.

I woke up one morning and thought—I can't have this child. My husband said, "You'll have to get a job after it's born so we can buy a house. You'll need an advanced degree so you can do something." I thought—I can't. I have to write a poem. My mother found a crib. Someone painted it white. My friend sent a pastel mobile with tame wooden animals. I thought about blue curtains, making bedspreads, and abortions.

Pablo [Neruda] was silent. He was walking so far away from me, I couldn't hear him. My husband objected to donating more free medical care to the Black Panthers. I tried to make dolmades from scratch and located grape leaves preserved in brine at the Boy's Market, twenty miles away. I organized a write-in campaign against JFK who wasn't against the Bomb or for nuclear disarmament. My husband thought it would be nice to have teatime with the children and romantic dinners by ourselves. The new formula bottles lined up on the sink like tiny bombs. The U.S. was pursuing overground testing; I was afraid the radiation would cross the milk barrier. I had a poem in me howling for real life but no language to write in. The fog came in thick, flapping about my feet like torn bandages. It occurred to me I was afraid to have a daughter.

I called Pablo Neruda in the middle of the night as he walked underwater by Isla Negra. He moved like a dream porpoise. He seemed pregnant with words. They came out of his penis in long miraculous strings. The sea creatures quivered with joy. I said, "Pablo, I want to know how to bear the child in my belly onto this bed of uranium and I want to know if a woman can be a poet." He was large as a whale. He drank the sea and spouted it in glistening odes, black and shiny. I said, "I can't have this child," and he laughed as if he had never done anything but carry and birth children.

So I packed my little bag as if I were going to the hospital and I left a note and the Wearever pots and the sterilized nipples upon the glass missiles, and I took the cradleboard which an American-Indian friend had given me for the baby and which had made my husband snort—"You're not going to carry the thing on your back, are you?" I took some money, the car, some books, paper and pens, my walking shoes, an old, unwieldy IBM electric typewriter, my pregnant belly, a dozen cloth diapers, and I went out.

I knew how to carry a baby and how to carry a poem and would learn how to have a baby and how to have a poem. I would have enough milk for both.

And I would learn how to walk with both. But I didn't know, and didn't want to know, how to have a husband and a matched set of Wearever pots.

—*from "Something in the Belly"*[6]

Your teacher has helped you overcome impediments in the past. Imagine a moment together during which the teacher helps you solve a current problem.

What we are doing here is creating refuge in the relationship with the teacher, making community out of our connection, and gaining ease from the wisdom given to us. To take refuge, we must be vulnerable enough to admit we need refuge, and we must open ourselves to it. In these dark times, we need to know that we can find a peaceful place despite all the difficulties and dilemmas. The teacher who can give us this is a treasure.

Consider the major issues in your current life. Allow your teacher to help you consider them. See if you can create a dialogue through which you enter the depths and gain another perspective on the issues. Perhaps your teacher will find parallels from her own life that will be useful. Allow your teacher to consider the issue from the perspective of her lineage and training, of her own experience, of her alliance with creativity. Remember that a teacher rarely, if ever, gives advice, for the task is not to do but to be. Allow the teacher to illumine how you might be in this situation. Can you allow yourself to see it all from someone else's perspective? Can you tolerate the teacher's understanding?

I took a long drag from the opium pipe and sat, immobile, in the corner of the darkened room. We had come thousands of miles across the world, as far away as I could possibly get. And here at last I let go. I was sinking, felt the layers of myself slough off as skin is shed by snakes. Fyodor [Dostoevski] entered the den and sat with me. No words passed our lips for what seemed like hours, weeks. He knew not to speak. For one so masterful with words, he impressed me now more for his silences—those pregnant vessels in which the real mysteries lived. And now he was sharing mine. I noticed tears welling in one of his eyes, then in both, and then the steady stream of them from which I felt detached, apart. The moaning voice becoming wails seemed not mine either, and I rocked myself as if, incongruously, to steady a flickering light.

Fyodor did nothing, but I saw that he was crying, that his face bore a grief which frightened me for its rawness, depth, and simplicity. His was a terrible beauty, and then, as if a veil of confusion had lifted, I knew that his features were molded after mine, were, in fact, pale reflections of a grief I bore; that in this, I was in the lead, that he no longer was mentor, that the illusion had been broken, that he could not feel for me, only with me, and never to the extent I would know my own torment; that nothing he could ever give me would make this reckoning any easier. My grief was my own, and it was this awareness which made the barriers I had always felt disappear, the barriers I had shored against my presumed ruin. Well, here I was. Ruined. It felt good, it felt good. It felt good.

—*Daniel Attias*

Ruminate on the history of your relationship with your teacher, remembering moments when you were together, ordinary time and extraordinary time, so that the entire history is fresh in your mind.

Consider the history of your own life from the time you met this teacher, and unravel it. Rewrite your life history carefully, weaving the new thread of this relationship into it.

Imagine that you know your teacher so well that you even know his dreams. Dream a dream of his in which you appear.

We met by chance. I walked into an unattended garden filled with frangipani and jasmine. She [Corazón Aquino] was seated at a fragile table pouring herself tea into a cup as delicate as an eggshell. She was still inside of her body, inside of her yellow dress . . . comfortably still. I watched her perfectly shaped hands caress the tools of tea and felt at once relieved of the chaos of my life, calmed.

She looked at me and smiled.

"Tea?" she asked.

I said, "Yes," and sat down across from her on a green wicker chair. Then she handed me the cup. My hands were shaking. I tried not to cry but she was so still, so very caring in her stillness, I could relieve myself of tears. She handed me a handkerchief, which I tried to use delicately. She told me I could keep it and asked me what was wrong. Could she help? I was eleven and it was summer.

"It's not much," I said.

"Are you sure?" she asked.

"It's them," I said. "The parents," I said. "The judge and the court," I said.

"It's not much, but it really is everything," I said. "They want me to make a choice between my mother and my father."

She smiled. "Do what's best for you."

"Neither is very good," I said.

"I know," she said.

She patted my knee and filled my cup again before she had to leave the garden of green and light. She invited me to come back the next afternoon, that perhaps we could talk some more.

And so we met afternoon after afternoon in the palmy paradise for the three months of summer. Each day she listened to me, let me ask about love and fairness until one afternoon, she told me quietly, boldly, unwaveringly, without any histrionics that her husband had been killed, shot, assassinated, that her life as she knew it before that moment had been ripped from her. Shred by shred all of her values had done a pirouette, a turn in time. Whether she wanted to or not, she had had to face east and rise with the sun, take up the fragments of her beliefs and weave them into a whole, a larger fabric that would combine the integrity of what her husband stood for and her own truths. This fabric, this whole, this flag, waved proudly over the garden where they sat every afternoon.

On a regular basis, in the course of these hours together, a hand grenade would be lobbed over the garden wall by invisible hands. It would land at our feet like ripe fruit fallen from a tree. Quietly, gently, as though she was still dealing with the tools of tea, she would reach down and pick up the metallic missile, defuse it with her gentile, graceful meticulous fingers, and place it on an orderly pile of defused twentieth-century weapons next to her Victorian garden chair.

Then, on one of the afternoons, two grenades glided over the wall. One, then the next. One after the other. Thud. Thud. At that moment, she was speaking about when to take action, when she did.

Excusing herself, she reached down, picked up the first arrival and then the second. For a moment, she stood, her crisp yellow dress etched against the palmy green of the garden and the fragrance of jasmine and frangipani. She stood with a live grenade curled in the delicate palm of each of her exquisite hands. She waited quietly for a few seconds, took in the trajectory, the source, the locations of the attacker. Then she slipped out of her low-heeled pumps, stepped up onto the seat of the Victorian chair, and lobbed the grenades back over the garden wall with speed and grace and ultimate accuracy.

A human cry was heard somewhere inside of the explosion, then everything was quiet. The birds in the garden started to sing. Mrs. Aquino stepped down from the Victorian chair, brushed off her hands before she smoothed the yellow skirt of her dress and sat down. Then she looked at me and sighed, "There are times when one must be aggressive about the defense of one's boundaries."

I looked at the woman's bravery on display. "How do you know when?" I asked.

Mrs. Aquino smiled, leaned forward, took hold of my hands, put them in her hands.

"You must sit in the garden and be still with your ceremony, the orderly discipline of any ceremony you choose, and when the time comes, it will present itself as disorder . . . note, not one grenade but two . . . and so, the order in your ceremony will bristle, stand on end, bring you to your feet where you will act calmly, assuredly, accurately, unsentimentally to restore the order in the garden where you like to be still with your ceremony."

—*Joan Tewkesbury*

Write about the last time you saw your teacher.

If your teacher is no longer alive, write about his death, how you experienced it, and how it affected you.

I don't know when I first met Opal [Whiteley]; I think I met her in a very unusual way. I think she actually lived inside of me long before I ever saw her outside of me, in front of me.

When Opal came around the corner of that old cabin in the long-abandoned logging camp on my land in Oregon, I was very pleased, yet saddened too. Up to that moment, she was mine alone and I had a very strong, almost proprietary interest in her. She knew me and I had no secrets with her. As long as she lived only within me.

When Opal stood before me carrying the little tea bucket and whistling like the birds, I was delighted, absolutely delighted to see her. I smiled at her and looked in her eyes that sparkled and danced.

But I also felt that I had lost something of me in that moment. She was no longer mine alone. She had her own life. And I was saddened by my loss even as I was delighted to see her.

It would be unfair for me to skip over Opal's own sadness. Behind the sparkling eyes that invited nature to be her friend, she carried a deep sorrow. I saw that sorrow behind the sparkle; it mirrored my own. I knew she understood my sadness, just as she easily saw how very pleased I was that she was now in my life in a new way.

I was alone that Indian summer when the outer Opal greeted me. That was nothing new. We had always been alone together before that. She spoke French words with her English just as my own French-Canadian grandmother had spoken to me in Vermont when I was a little boy. I knew that *cochon* meant pig. It was very easy for us to talk in this English-French way. I didn't know all the French words, but I could guess well enough to get Opal's meaning. The secret language I had learned to speak inside of me was the same language Opal and I now used between us outside of me.

As I consider these things, I remember now—and I still can feel—that there was one special sadness I felt as soon as I saw Opal, and I still have not told her about it. I don't know if I will ever tell her.

When I saw her, I knew Opal would die. I didn't know when, but I did know she would die. Probably not any time soon but someday. What bothered me about that was that I didn't know if she and I would die at the same time. I knew I did not want to die before she died because I did not want to leave her alone, even though she would probably be just fine without me because everyone was her dearest friend. And the flora and fauna loved her dearly in return. But if I died first, I wouldn't feel right about disappearing or going on—or whatever we do when we die—without her. And I surely didn't want her to pass on and leave me here without her—friends or not.

Maybe she feels the same way about me; maybe not. I guess I will never talk about this with her; I'll just see what develops. In a way, I really like the uncertainty. It keeps me sober when I need that.

I've never told anyone about Opal. No one's ever been close enough to me to ask, or to tell. No one except Opal herself. And she doesn't need to ask and I surely do not need to tell her that she is my life—although I often do, but mostly without words, not direct words anyhow.

I still have Opal inside of me. I can feel her inside my body. A nice quiet feeling. Sometimes when it's really quiet in the city and in my head, I can actually spend some time with her and we talk. Mostly she shows me all the flora and fauna of the forest in my mind. I think she's there even when I'm busy with my work, my family, this city, freeways, and people. That's just a guess; but she is always nearby when I happen to wander in there on my own.

I don't often get to the Northwest to visit my land. When I do, it's Opal I'm really going to see. I love this being as much as I love me, sometimes more it seems. Opal thinks I'm quicker than lightning, especially when I first get to my land from the city. She gave me a name to tame me for the woodlands. She calls me Januarius Molasses McGee. That name slows me down even when I just think about it: Januarius Molasses McGee. I have another name for her, too, though I pretty much like her given name. I call her the Opal of my Eye.

—*Joseph MacKenzie*

Consider a piece of work you have been wrestling with, an aesthetic problem you have not been able to solve, a dilemma about approaching or organizing your creative work. Imagine an afternoon when your teacher engages with you over this issue.

By now you are integrated into each other's lives and have intimacy with each other. Ask the teacher to articulate the elusive point, the theme, the obsession of her lifework, so that you may come to know her and also learn how to think about your own life and work with more respect and consideration. Ask your teacher if he will answer the most difficult question: "What is it you have spent your entire life trying to do?"

Or as Kabir put the question, who is it we spend our entire life loving?[7]

I [Neruda] was a great whale in a black sea. When I spouted, the white water sprayed onto the waves in burning letters. All of history burned into the sea through this alphabet. But I was a whale and understood none of it. The water that flooded into me was all my knowledge, also all my ignorance. So it went for eons. The black sea, viscous and inky, was seared by the incomprehensible script of white lightning erupting from the top of my head.

Sometimes I wished I were blind to the light of these mysterious words and longed to navigate by sound like other whales, but I also knew that letters of fire shook the depths in thunderous crackling swells.

—*from "Dreaming of the Girl and the Sea"*[8]

What we hope to gain from the teachings and the teachers is wisdom. Not information, not knowledge, but the understanding of how things are and how one lives accordingly. More and more often, in the presence of dazzling mind, we feel a longing for a far simpler and more humble but essential intelligence.

Sometimes we have to confront ourselves and ask what it is we know. Amid the noise of contemporary life, it is difficult to assess what one knows in the way that people once knew what mattered, about weather or cows, about life and death, or even about their own nature. One hopes at one time or another to be with someone able to impart wisdom.

> *Imagine that you have reached a certain age and that someone you care about has come to you troubled. You want to give them something that will ease them but not delude them. You want to pass on some wisdom because you believe that this will help. Tell the young person two stories, two teaching stories from your own life that contain the necessary wisdom. What you know can be very small and thus be very large.*

> *After you write the stories, set them aside. At another time, reread the stories and glean the wisdom they contain. This wisdom is yours.*

The teacher can help us gather into ourselves what can be known. And the teacher can help us enter history, can orient us in a past with a future. New ideas pass through quickly and lose their power; it is the oldest wisdom that we set out to learn, each of us alone, again and again. The teacher helps us along the path, urging us on, if only by the example of his dedication. When we are the teacher, we bring the wisdom also to ourselves.

Nature: Her Secret Teachings

There is another teacher, and she is the most profound teacher of them all. This teacher belongs to all of us and gives to us all equally, though we may not equally recognize her or accept her teachings. This teacher is, of course, nature. Nothing, no one, in the human realm compares to her. When we recognize nature as the ultimate teacher, we set aside the antics and aggrandizements of human ego that plague us increasingly.

Nature is what we come out of and descend into. The middle passage is what we call our lives, and in this realm between the source and the aftermath, between the roots and the highest branches of the World Tree, we often try to forget our origins and destiny as if we sprang out of air and could become air again through effort and deserving.

Nature teaches us otherwise, says we must get our hands dirty, says we are also fire, water, and earth. Says we have a body. Says that bodies matter. Says that the tree is equal to us, also the wolf and the stone. These teachings break us down; afterward, they allow us to see.

Keep a journal of each of the four seasons. Track the shift from one time to another. Locate the beginnings and the endings of the cycles. Discover the existence of the seasons within yourself.

Here are two true stories: A boy from an industrial city was taken to the mountains for the first time. He awoke in the middle of the night and cried out in fear, pointing at the sky, "What are them things?"

A little girl found it hard to believe that milk really came from those four-legged creatures she was watching in the field. "Milk comes from bottles," she said.

Track an animal in your mind. Learn its habits. See the world through its eyes. Find it within yourself. Howl.

There are people who will never in their lives see any animals but dogs and cats outside of zoos, people who will never speak to birds, never watch a bear or elk tromp by, who will always define the wild through fear. But the wild is our nature and our essence. Not that we are wild but that we are of the wild. And the wild is not what we have come to believe it is. According to the thesaurus, the wild is predominantly negative and dangerous: barren, desert, wasteland, wilderness, rabid, savage, untamed, uncivilized, feral, bloodthirsty, uncontrolled, amuck, frenzied, inaccurate, intemperate, unwise, foolish, untrainable, rank, vulgar, freak, vicious, barbaric, corrupt, stubborn, violent.

This list of words is a narrative of our thinking. The connotations of these words keep us from ourselves. For the imagination is a territory outside of the domestic sphere. Though sometimes cultivated, it cannot be contained. It will not flourish within a prison, no matter how cultured that prison is. The imagination and the creative thrive only among the wild things. For this, nature is the teacher and the territory.

Study something wild. Learn everything you can about its nature. What does it teach you?

Each one of us can pursue nature in our own way. I believe the pursuit is essential to everyone and that the writer is bereft without knowing and understanding the natural world, without submitting herself to it.

What can we learn from nature? Everything. And what do we know without it? Nothing.

For the writer, nature's teachings are the most important teachings. There is no silence like the silence of nature. If a writer wishes to learn the lessons of solitude, he must go to the woods or the mountains or the sea.

Create solitude for yourself by meditating on something small: a wild iris, a spray of seaweed, a deserted nest, a puddle. Can you match your silence to its?

There is no ferment, no variety, ingenuity, or creativity like that of nature. If a writer wishes to learn to invent and conceive, then she must go again to the wild where invention is continually born.

Pursue the wild and chaotic. Go to the sea during a storm, get drenched to the skin, then write about it. Find words equal to the surf. Write down into the cauldron of a volcano. Let the sand of a desert storm blister your face. Sleep under the stars. Pick up your pen and wait for the first light to illuminate your journal page.

The wisdom schools of all traditions teach variations on the same theme: the sacredness of all life; compassion for all sentient beings; the oneness of the universe; the unity that is called God or the divine. This understanding of oneness belonged to the old gods of wind, corn, and fire, the deities of the rivers and trees who blessed the world and all its creations and who made no hierarchy between people and other creatures. Now perhaps only the word can bring them back with all their wisdom. In the beginning was the word. And the world emerged from it. Perhaps the poets in us can perform this miracle of creation again and then again.

Become a caribou or an iguana. Burn like a galaxy. Slink with the lions through the savannas. Be an ostrich or a crowned crane. Glide through the sea as a moray eel. Write a monologue for a hydrogen atom.

Look at yourself through the eyes of an ape or a vulture. Get out of your own skin and enter another's.

Speak on behalf of the other species. Let the wisdom of the other species emanate from you.

Wisdom and Ethics

Speaking about wisdom, we are led inevitably to speaking about ethics. What we know has real value only when it translates into how we live our lives. But ethics is not the central concern it was once. Still, it is central to spiritual practice, and all serious literature concerns itself in one form or another with ethical issues. The very need and willingness to see a character for what she is, to view her reality without judgment, this rigorous attempt to understand behavior or to accept our own shadow is the beginning of ethical practice. For the most part, ethical literature is founded in investigation and scrutiny. Contrary to popular assumption, it raises questions rather than answers them.

> *Make a list of serious ethical issues that concern you and for which you have no clear solution. Write a piece in which you explore the ethical dilemma.*

> *Write the story of the time when you had to face a serious ethical dilemma. What were the issues? How did you face them? What was left unresolved?*

We have become ignorant of the language of ethical discourse, even if we are not innocent of its dilemmas. The century abounds with horrors while our ability to deal with them diminishes. We know more now and understand less. Living in a century in which murder and torture, both in the family and at large, are commonplaces, when we have already developed the ultimate weapon on the one hand and on the other are determined to revise even the meaning of life through genetic engineering and the like, it is hardly appropriate to be so ignorant.

We have to find a new language as part of our spiritual practice. We have to ask ourselves ruthless questions, particularly about our relationship to other beings. Words can be the front line for the writer. Writing with utmost honesty, searching one's soul, admitting the inadmissible, trying on the impossible—all these are ways of going to the front lines.

> *We can think about these issues, but theory is different from experience. Take the following dilemmas and make stories of them. Do not think about what you will do. Rather write the story, find all the pain and contradiction. Don't try to solve the problem so much as put yourself in the center of the storm:*

> *You are the one with your finger on the red button. Will you drop the bomb? Write the scene in which you make a decision. What are the implications of your decision? What happens to you?*

> *Your parent, your child, or your best friend is suffering unbearable pain from an incurable disease. You are asked to help him end his life.*

> *Under cover of darkness, with many others, you are escaping from a ruthless enemy. The border is far away. The enemy is close by. Your infant won't stop crying.*

> *Your mate is dying. There may be a cure, but it has not been tested. One side effect may be unbearable pain. Anesthesia will interfere with the test. It is suggested that the drug be tried on your family dog.*

> *You are being tortured. If you speak, your cause will be jeopardized, your comrades tortured. If you don't speak, your family will be tortured.*

Your sibling has kidney failure. He cannot find a donor. You are young and an athlete. He is the father of a small child. You are the only likely prospect.

You are one of the elders of an aboriginal tribe. You are the only one who remembers all the stories. Someone from the culture that oppressed you comes to record the stories. If you tell the stories, they will be distorted, but if you don't, they will die out. What stories remain? Which, if any, do you tell?

Your family is very hungry and you have had no work for a long time. You are offered a job that will pay you sufficiently but that is morally abhorrent. What job has been offered to you? What do you do?

Your people are besieged and hungry. If they sell their land, they will not survive as a people. If they don't sell their land, they may not survive at all.

For the writer, morality and ethics are not received wisdom but must also be searched out, uncovered, tested. Like it or not, the writer cannot be innocent because she affects the world with her words. What she says or does not say becomes part of a moral climate. Even disinterest has moral implications. It was a sobering moment for me some years ago when I stood before an audience and realized that, having come to a certain age, I could no longer call myself the rebel. Like it or not, I was responsible.

At a later time, the recognition of responsibility came to me as I was writing the voice of Peter Schmidt, a fictional Nazi character surveying the horror he had helped to create. The words he spoke expressed exactly the grief I feel about ecological destruction: "I could not help myself," he (and I) grieved. "I am so ashamed. God, I am so ashamed. And I am completely responsible."

Listening to the Voices

There comes a time, even in spiritual practice, when we go on alone, when we hear the call and enter the desert of the spirit or, as Ikazo calls it, "the forest of no words." In this place, the voices come to us like the plaintive calls of the night owls on the bare branch. We know the owl is looking for its prey. We hope we are not the prey, and we know we are.

It sounds romantic to say that one is called or given a task by the spirits; this is easy to say but far more difficult to live. To be called is almost always to be broken down. For who we are, our so desperately developed identity, must be shattered so that we do not overshadow what it is that we must see and do. Too often, the self is in its own way. To write what we are given to write, we, in one way or another, must disappear.

In January 1978, I had a dream. At the end of it, a title came across the screen as if I had been watching a movie: *The Woman Who Slept with Men to Take the War out of Them.*[9] The title did not relate to the dream, and I didn't understand it, but it stayed with me. Such a line cannot be disregarded, though I confess I managed to forget it from time to time. Then summer came. With a grant from the National Endowment for the Arts, I rented a small cabin in Mendocino. I went there with a typewriter, a ream of blank paper, the title, and without an idea in my mind.

The novel was not easy to write. I was afraid, first, that I would not find the story and, second, that finding it, I would not be up to writing it. I did not know if it was arrogant or foolish of me to be so attentive to the messages of a dream. Aggrandizement, ego, inflation are the demons of writers and of spiritual practitioners. They buzz around our heads like flies. Believing we cannot write goes hand in hand with believing we've been given the Word. We are convinced we are the worst writers and believe also that we must be the best. We feel abandoned by our talents just as we believe that we have God's ear—or, better, that the gods have ours. We cannot escape this territory: we can only learn to humble ourselves and try to negotiate it with some grace.

One way or another, each poem, each book, each project carries with it an imperative from another world. We are inspired as if something strange and mysterious breathed into us, impregnating us with the divine child and making us one with the immortals. But this same moment when the gods appear can be frightening, or the task they demand, unbearable. We know, no matter how lightly we carry the task, that it will have repercussions, because we have to give our lives over to it. And, in the doing, we never know whether we are truly inspired or mad.

I won't pretend to know how to differentiate the voices—the ones that come from inflation and the ones that come from creativity—how to distinguish my own distortions and fantasies from the imperative of creative energy, how to know when to set something aside or when to devote oneself to it wholeheartedly. It is always wise to think as long and hard about any serious creative project as one thinks about taking on a new friend, about marrying, or about having a child—and then to take it on with only a modest hope for its success. Whenever a novel comes to mind, the accompanying voice says, "What are you doing for the next ten years?" Over time, contemplation helps to separate the drama of the ego with all its hopes for acclaim and accomplishment from the more workaday acquiescence of the nameless novitiate trying to fulfill her duties to the muse.

I hadn't wanted to go to the death camps in the spring of 1989. And when I came back I certainly did not want to write about it. Nor did I have any conviction that it was appropriate for me to do so. Still, when a new book returned to me again and again, more haunting than any of the desperate ghosts I had encountered in the camps, I could not refuse it.

This is an excerpt from a journal piece I wrote two months after my return:

July 22, 1989, 12 P.M. I submit. Both gripped and repelled, I submit. I expected to be released; I wasn't. To be released is as hopeless a wish as to have been born . . . what . . . an aborigine? To have been born into myth instead of history. No one born in this century is born into myth any longer. Even the wolf is born into history. I would have preferred to have been born the wolf, the bear, or the bird. I would have preferred to be a tree. Yet this is where history has brought me. There is not a single human life I would like to step into unless it is the life of a hermit in a forest which still exists somewhere.

I cannot imagine writing anything else—no story, no image, no history, no people offer themselves. Nothing distracts me from this unbearable compulsion. "You seem to have been freed," M. said yesterday, noticing that I was no longer reading books on the Holocaust. "The nausea is more extreme," I answered.

"Yes, but for the last year and a half, you couldn't resist the nausea and now you can."

We will see. I am still trying to skirt the nausea. "I have done my duty," I assert to any spirit which is listening. It is not so much an assertion as it is a plea.

The bitter gall of the Nazis repels me. I am no longer even fascinated by their behavior. I feel only repugnance, aversion, revulsion, repulsion, but I am forced toward them the way one enters the boxcar or solitary cell of this century, the ones full of excrement, ankle deep. The Nazis and the Jews, I can't escape either of them. The shadow which lost its shadow when it trampled the light and the light which loses its light when it won't look at its own darkness.

Bitterness, cynicism, despair are plagues. Knowing this does not mean that I can escape. Naming the disease is no longer the cure.

This is what I don't know: Can I write myself back to loving the world, human beings, this life?

It may be inflated to think we have been called, but it is more inflated to resist the call when it comes. Better, perhaps, to err on the side of foolishness, to look pompous or absurd, to irritate or annoy one's friends with one's arrogance than to miss the opportunity to carry something we are called to carry.

Beginning the novel, I recognized how desperately I needed to be healed and also that I couldn't bring a false light into the novel to ease my pain. Not only do I have to write the novel, I have to write it as it comes; I have to trust that there is some truth to be uncovered and that its light, if it is a light, will be sufficient.

> *Describe moments when you were called—moments in which you heeded the call and moments in which you turned away.*

> *Recall a moment in which you heeded the call. Write the story that might have occurred if you had ignored it.*

> *Recall a moment in which you ignored the summons. What would your life be now, if you had listened to it?*

The Dream World

Dreams, prophecy, visions, messages from the other realm, are as essential to spiritual practice as prayer and meditation. Through dreams we travel the night world, our soul flies out, presses against the seam of the universe, and penetrates that dark world. In the dream we climb the World Tree to the heavens or descend the stairs, careen, fall, or drown in the underworld.

> In my dream, the words, "Who? What? When? Where? Why?" repeat themselves again and again. They are the sound track of the dream and so I know this dream is from the writer or is addressed to her. The words loop horizontally while the elevator goes up and down, up and down. It does not stop. I cannot get off. There is no way to open the door. Then the elevator does stop and I exit thinking, or is it hoping, that I am at the top floor but find myself in the cavelike basement. It is dim and shadowy. I see the actors from my play, *Dreams Against the State,* in which six characters hid in the underground when dreaming became illegal. They are rehearsing the play again. The director, Steve Kent, has become a dwarf. Is this death? I wonder fearfully. Or is this finally the underworld with all its treasures and terrors? As I awaken, the following line is planted in my mind: There is a place between waking and sleeping which resembles neither of them.

The place of my dream was the dream world. And the dream world is the territory of the writer or the artist. It may happen that the writer is the citizen of no other country, but the dream world is his native land and his citizenship cannot be revoked.

Each of us knows what it is to be in exile, to be without a passport, to cross dangerous borders, to live in foreign places, because we spend part of our lives or each day in another country. But when we tell the story of our lives, we rarely refer to events in our night country. Sometimes we share a letter from that dark place, attempt to analyze the cryptic message conveyed in a peculiar grammar, in mysterious and disconcerting images. But we generally apologize for a lack of fluency, say we don't really speak the language and are suspicious, properly, of any translations. We don't admit to the world that we live in that other territory. Sometimes we don't admit this even to ourselves.

When we tell our life stories, we tell the public tale, give the everyday account that is consistent and verifiable. We do not admit that each night we become fugitives or are kidnapped across the common and guarded border to a private country where we meet everyone yet are always alone, where we traffic both with the living and the dead. Perhaps we cannot comprehend how we can be the only citizen in the country from which everyone and everything is born and into which everyone and everything will die.

List the dreams you remember.

Write your autobiography—that is, the autobiography of the dreamer—by referring only to your dreams. Tell your life story by revealing only the experiences of your dream life; include your dream family, your dream work, your dream residences, your dream aspirations and fears. Incorporate your most important dreams as events of the dream life. Do not indicate that these are dreams or dream images. Tell them as if they happened—they did. Write as if this is reality—it is.

Perhaps you can't remember your dreams. Perhaps you haven't kept a dream journal. Well, then, this is a time to begin. Put a beautiful book by your bedside, a book that announces itself as the proper container for such material, and turn to it immediately upon awakening. There you can record your dreams, whatever you remember, even the fragments, the fleeting images, the faint scent of dream left on the night air.

If you don't remember dreams in their entirety, you may still remember images. List the ones that seem most compelling, that reoccur again and again, that haunt you. Create a composite dream from these images.

Michael Ortiz Hill created a glossary of images around common themes for his book about nuclear dreams, *Dreaming the End of the World*. From it he created a collage that becomes a dream in and of itself:

Earth

A chemist hurled miniature atomic bombs at a world globe until the globe exploded. Looking down with an eye and no body at a very little blue planet. I pushed a bullet that would explode and destroy the world all around us.

Suddenly we learn that the earth is under fire, atomic bombs exploding. There is an underground city—it is inside me and it is also the earth and a garden. I flung myself to the ground and embraced the grass and soil as if I were hugging the whole earth. And in that second before death I felt peace.

Create a collage of dream images from dreams that share a common motif or from random images that occurred during a particular time.

If you remember no dreams whatsoever, fantasize five to eight dream images. Create a dream from them, using all of them, finding some way to relate them to each other, finding the peculiar transition and the startling, jarring associations.

This will be a dream in the making. It comes from the same source as other dreams, only it is happening to you now.

The dream world is another world, but it is not, necessarily, *the* other world. The dream is a dialogue between the conscious and the unconscious, not the manifestation of a separate realm but an enterprise of cooperation, whereby what is ordinarily held separate is reorganized into one unit. The dream is the fulfillment of a longing for wholeness that is characteristic of both the day world and the night world. It is the satisfying twilight or dawn that represents the coexistence of the two worlds without the loss of the identity of either. The dream world is the territory, the threshold, the common border, the liminal space. In essence, the dream is a relationship. It is a child of two distinct parents, separate from them and yet uniquely a part of each. The dreamer, then, is someone who is and who is not ourselves.

The form of the dream or the process of dream making enlightens us more about the nature of reality than does the individual content of the dream. The fact that two realms enter into daily conversation is more important, ultimately, than what they speak about. The dream may utilize imagery from the day world, events from the current life, seemingly to speak about unconscious or even past material. It may utilize an image that hides as well as an image that reveals, an image that obscures, an image that is indecipherable. It utilizes everything—anything—that comes to hand from both realms.

The dream is formed in the dream world, the place where there is a little distraction from the onslaught of ongoing events and the day world's priorities of experience, action, and response. Here the two worlds can bring together what materials they have and what gifts exist for storytelling to establish and articulate this third world, which is larger than the sum of the two.

The conscious and the unconscious meet in the dreamer, who is a hermaphrodite—the child of Hermes, the stealthy and fleet-footed god, and Aphrodite, goddess of beauty and love in her day and night aspects. Like two creative collaborators bringing what they have and also what is incomplete or needy, they become one to construct a story that is both by them and of them. Dream making emerges from a fundamental desire for intimacy, the love of creation, and the necessity to speak. The story emerges from them, but also it is a story pointing toward them. And though at any one time, the dream may point to the needs of one realm more than to the other, there is probably never a dream that does not contain some aspect of the other, whether it be in terms of imagery, narrative, or concern.

> *Write a dream as if it just happened, giving full credence to every event so that you ground it, by your attitude toward it, in the reality of the day world.*

Then do the opposite:

> *Choose an event from your life and describe it as though it had been a dream, allowing the images to tell the story, allowing the fantastic to enter—so the telling itself comes from the third world.*

Near Tübingen

It is just a barbed wire fence in the middle of a green field. There are cows, farmhouse, a rutted dirt road leading toward the fence. I hear the shrill voices of children playing somewhere nearby.

No, there are two fences running parallel as far as I can see in both directions until they disappear from my sight, into the woods at one end, over a hill at the other. Between the fences, the grass is emerald green, lush, untouched. It is soft velvet, fragrant grass, brilliant shimmering green with bright flowers blowing in the breeze. No foot has ever stepped on that exquisite carpet between the barbed wire fences.

I put the binoculars to my eyes and look across the expanse of blowing green grass to the tower on the far side of the fences. A man is in the tower, looking at me through binoculars.

Our eyes meet. I see him seeing me. His mouth opens in surprise, a sudden intake of breath as he sees me seeing him. I see his teeth, crooked, gold-filled, the stubble of his beard. The gray collar of his uniform is tight, making extra folds of whiskered skin under his chin.

I reach out, toward him, seeing my hand extend in the binocular image far, far away from my body. Across the fences and the emerald green grass between them, I stretch out my arm to touch his slicked-down hair, run my palm down the front of the stiff wool jacket. My long fingers caress his cheek, touch his lips, move again to his hair, his cheeks, his neck.

As I withdraw my hand, he follows, down the steps of the tower toward the fence. My hand is near him, but retreating. I watch through my binoculars as he follows my beckoning fingers toward the fences, the grassy stretch of green. He moves through the first fence and steps into that pristine grass, that lush meadow dotted occasionally with flowers. He moves closer to me, following the lure of my caressing fingers across the mine field.

Through my binoculars, I see his body jerk and rise into the air as the grass and dirt erupt under his feet, a flash of fire bright even in the day's clear sunlight. Slowly his arms spread, his head tips back, he rises into the sky above the fences, above the tower, above the clods of dirt and spattered flowers, flying away from me over the treetops until I can't see him anymore, even through my binoculars.

—*Judy Welles*

We cannot tell by its imagery whether a dream is speaking of the day world or the night world. A dream told in prosaic images or showing ordinary events may not necessarily be about those events. They may constitute the language that best serves the dreamer for speaking of something else altogether. This language may well be the best disguise.

Create a character who represents the conscious life and another who represents the unconscious.

Theoretically, we can't create the latter because what we mean by the unconscious is that we are unaware of it. Still, we have imagination, and it has the capacity to do what we cannot—it can fly through doors, speak in undiscovered galactic languages, spawn centaurs and unicorns, light an icy fire, and can, therefore, posit a character who speaks in the voice of the unconscious.

Create a third character who is the synthesis of the first two.

The dream is made at night when all things, all events, even the world itself drop away. This work can exist only in the most strict and absolute monogamy. The dream can come to be, the work of dreaming can only begin in the singular marriage of the two worlds. The dream allows no witnesses or other collaborators. It is not secret so much as insistently private.

Write a small play in which the conscious and the unconscious speak to each other about this realm they share, about the dreamer who is their progeny, and about the artworks they create together.

225

Each dream is a consummate work of art. And the existence of dreams is a mysterious sign that through such art, what is disconnected can be joined. The fact of dreaming—underlined by the existence of dreaming in other animals besides humans—is incontrovertible evidence that creativity is a fundamental activity of sentient beings. This universal art-making process aligns us with the gods, who engage in the wondrous play through which what is separate and incomplete is made whole.

The fear of the dream may be an expression of our fear of partnership and intimacy. In suppressing the dream, we suppress two entities: the world of the dream, which is the third world, and the knowledge of the reality of the "other" who is always within us.

We know that the day world fears the night world. But does the night world equally fear the day? When we lose a dream, is the day world moving away prematurely, abandoning its sacred partner? When no dreams come, is that a sign that the night world is withholding itself, sequestering its secrets?

The day world is other to the night world. And the night world is equally other to the day. There is no escape from this. We are both ourselves and other, inextricably and unceasingly.

Is there an odd character in your dream life who appears again and again and whom you do not recognize? Create a story that contains him and reveals him. Write a second story in which you and the character meet each other and form an unusual and unexpected alliance.

The Bomb Lost in Its Own Dark Dreaming: An Idiosyncratic Retelling of Several Dreams from the Bomb's Point of View

Basically, I'm a very simple guy. I either sleep or burst into flames. That is all. If the truth be told, I have no preference between the two.

. . . I am floating above the street—just out of sight—of downtown Jerusalem. There is a crowd below, agitated, swelling with anticipation. They expect me to descend today—but I will not. They expect either terror or redemption—or maybe, somehow, both.

. . . One man catches my eye. He is not so remarkable at first—perhaps a little more lost within the general lostness. His face is flushed, his eyes darting about looking for enemies. He is swept up in the crowd's exhilaration and fear.

Then he does an extraordinary thing: he scuttles like a crab on his hands and feet between the trees and down the cobbled alleys until he comes upon a statue of me: Christ-Vishnu, the one with the elephant trunk dangling. Such awe and curiosity overcome his face. This is as close as a human being can come to me and live.

I like this man. He clearly has a natural affinity for worshiping me.

—*Michael Ortiz Hill,* Dreaming the End of the World[10]

We often fear that the "other" will do us harm. We fear that we will be taken over, neutralized, dispossessed of our uniqueness, made to become the other, to conform to standards that, by their nature, alter who we are. Is this the night world's fear that it will decompose under the slightest surge of light?

Meditate on an image or character from your dream life that you imagine is other to the night world. Find its night-world character.

For years I carried a secret shame. All my dreams were about cars. When I dreamed that I was the first poet to have reached the moon, I found myself in a huge car lot. I dreamed about cars lost and cars stolen and cars disappeared. Cars without brakes and cars that could not negotiate hills. Cars in which no one was driving or no one was in the driver's seat. Sports cars, convertibles, and VW Bugs. There were finally enough car dreams for the dreamer to get the attention of the day-world person and ask her to relinquish her prejudice against the image. The car image served the dreamer very well. But the intolerant day-world person was left ignorant of its meaning. When I approached all the car dreams as if they were a single dream, I discovered that the cars did not represent frustration or my fears about my "drive." "Why," the dreamer asked, "would I go to such artistic lengths to speak about something so mundane and familiar?" But why, then, did the car appear? Far from representing lowly transportation, the car represented "transport," the "vehicle" to the other worlds, a magic carpet. And though I responded with ecological terror to the possibility that our culture could, in fact, make a car lot out of the moon, in the dream, the image from the underworld indicated the vast possibilities of "transport" on the poet's moon.

The day world is necessarily animated by the infusion of spirit. But what is animated is not the same as what is fixed. We cannot predict the path of what is animated, nor can it be controlled. The fixed material world must always have anxiety about its nature being transformed. Death, too, must have a terrible fear of life.

And the night world fears another kind of death. It does not have a body. It knows that it also will change fundamentally as it becomes embodied. With a body, it enters into density, and parts of itself will inevitably feel confined, reduced, even extinguished by the necessity to adhere to form.

Still, the dream could not exist without the primal force of attraction, the need of the day world for the night, the need of the "other" for the "other," and the beauty and wonder of their fusion. And because the dream does exist, it tells us something of this relationship and the nature of that reality.

> *Once again, write the autobiography of the dreamer. What are his essential concerns? What territories does she prefer? By following the chronology of your dreams, trace the dreamer's development from a young person to who he is today. What have been the most important moments in the dream?*

To understand dreams in this way is to engage in the work of bringing the two worlds into their proper living relationship. The work of reconciling this dualism of day and night, body and soul, is not primarily the task of healing an unfortunate and unnecessary wound, is not principally therapeutic, but is the given work of any person and of the artist-writer in particular. It is as natural and essential as maturity; it is also one of the practices of the path.

Visions and Voices: Invisible Encounters with Other Worlds

Old-time religion was easier. You were told exactly what to believe. Faith was required. It was all laid out. But the spiritual life is never orthodox. By its nature, the creative demands that one discover everything for oneself. Faith is rare and questionable. Skepticism is essential. It is an aid to the ego, which, without it, will expand much like a supernova and explode. Doubt is at the very core of spirituality. Hence one can never be certain if it is the Christ or the pied piper one is following. Yet too much skepticism or cynicism will destroy one's relationship to the invisible. Then the follower will suffer from denying the god. One of the functions of a spiritual practice is to develop the skill and discernment to differentiate reality from fantasy, experience from hope, truth from need.

The Jewish tradition, among others, has legends about a disagreeable beggar who comes to the door at an awkward time. Sometimes the beggar is dangerous, but sometimes the beggar is an angel. The task is to discern which is which. We define ourselves by the errors we make, by what we are willing and able to risk.

> *Write a story about the time when you took a chance and opened the door to the angel. What is the angel to you? What did you risk? What did you sacrifice? What was received?*

We are born into the day world. After nine months of dreaming, we are brought into the hard reality where things are said to be what they seem. We are brought into the world of the senses, of the verifiable, repeatable, definitive. But the night world does not disappear. And from time to time we get intimations of other extraordinary realities. In the dark, in the place where we cannot see, where our eyes are closed, we come in touch with vision.

The task of some writers is to see very, very clearly in the day world, to remove the illusions and hallucinations from that reality. The task of other writers is to see very, very clearly in the night world, to remove the veils from the invisible, the visionary, and the miraculous. And, of course, there are writers who live in all the worlds and risk the disorientation and turmoil of moving back and forth in order to fulfill the task of carrying vision everywhere.

The novel, *The Other Hand,* which I am writing now, had one of its origins in a phrase from the book of Daniel: "the magicians, the sorcerers, the Chaldeans, the astrologers, the soothsayers." According to the Old Testament, these people are dangerous, even evil. Nevertheless, the names repeated themselves over and over, charming me. I wanted to know who these people were and what realities they understood. The novel develops, in part, from my curiosity about these seers who were attuned to nonordinary reality. To have a spiritual practice is to risk that one will encounter something larger than oneself and have to wrestle with meaning that extends beyond the human.

When one's spiritual practice lies outside conventional religious belief, it can be particularly fearsome to encounter the mystical and to trust or rely on one's own unique experience. Still, such experiences exist, and the very particular form in which they appear to us may be a revelation of who we are. I believe that I will never see a flying saucer or be taken up by a spaceship from another world if only because technology is not a form in which I put much credence. When the invisible appears to me, it will come in another shape.

In 1984, the writer, Julio Cortázar, died. I had always thought that our friendship was incomplete. When he died, I felt a double loss, the loss of Julio himself and the loss of the possibility of really becoming acquainted. In truth, I felt cheated. A few days after his death, I was mourning him so fiercely that I decided to write him a letter:

Dearest Julio:

. . . I am a writing a novel, *What Dinah Thought,* about two women who are in love with dead men. These women are not mad. Once during a retreat, I looked up from the Loren Eiseley book which was absorbing me and said to the patient waitress, "I've fallen in love with a dead man."

"That's what happens when you read," she answered sagely and took my order.

I'm not mad, though I don't quite know yet how this letter will reach you. Ariel says you didn't believe in death and so I'm certain you'll return. Please don't float in through the window, that will be too melodramatic, and I will think I'm hallucinating—so much for proclamations of faith.

But you must return. It's not finished between us. Nor between you and the universe. You know too much that no one else knows. Most importantly, you know that death doesn't exist. We need that knowledge, to save us from the effects of our imagination.

Maybe you'll come as a gift. Maybe you'll pass your storytelling stick to me. I am going to sleep. It would help if you came in a dream. Come back to us, Julio, we need you here and all your secrets as well.[11]

The form in which Julio did appear was utterly convincing, if unnerving. Immediately after writing this letter, I received a call from the *L. A. Weekly* asking me if I would review something for their book section. The book they originally offered me did not interest me, and when I refused the assignment, the editor then offered *A Certain Lucas,* by Julio Cortázar.

"But he's dead," I said.

"Yes, but this was published in Spain while he was alive, and this is a posthumous translation."

Probably everyone has had communications from other worlds. Some of us are unaware of them, and others do not treat them respectfully. One goal of spiritual practice is to constitute a self that is willing and able to respond to the night realm.

List moments in your life when you have experienced the invisible, the miraculous, extraordinary reality, and so on.

What does this list reveal about you? Create a portrait of the person who sees, feels, knows things in the way you know them.

Select one experience and write about it to communicate something of what is ordinarily incommunicable. Remember the awe and wonder, fear and trembling that accompanied the experience. Pay attention to the minute details through which the moment manifested itself.

To write of such things successfully, you must admit to caring about the experience.

If only for this moment, believe that you accurately perceived something unusual or magical. Write slowly. Very slowly. Savor each word as you write it. This writing partakes of the sacred. Make the invisible visible.

"I think I see ghosts in the birch grove up the hill. Who has come to visit me this time from the great beyond? Whatever, it's greatly beyond me. I feel flatly mundane at the moment. A spiritual impasse."

Always precocious in things unseen, at thirty-four, our hero is a bit worn by the exigencies of the real world. She hadn't cared much for material things in the past. However, the mounting expenses of her small house and the loss, one by one, of clean air to breathe, decent neighbors, and intimate time with her closest friends turned the sweet ease of the past to stony flatness. It was through this she saw these spirits now.

"So?" she shouted, as she flipped through her index of familiar spirits. These, she knew, were none of them.

Who now? she wondered. Lately, she thought, even such interest had vanished.

She was coming to a fork in the road and found herself in heated debate, whether to go toward them or head back to the house along the little path she had once cleared and now walked every day. It had been so long since she had been to the birch grove.

Birch was one of her favorite trees. White, slender trunks contrasted with thin, delicate, dark-to-light variegated brown branches. In the summer, the small green leaves played with the light, dappling the ground with their game.

Now in winter, the bare branches were stark against a bright sky, mostly clear and blue. This moment, the sun intensified the overall effect by coming out from behind a clean, white cloud.

Without making a conscious decision, she had chosen. She found herself amid the birches. She let out a long, low painful sigh, "Ooooohhhh.

"Take me, you might as well. I have gotten lost again. I have lost the thread of my life."

She lay down, then, on the cold, brown earth, among the birches to wait until she knew what to do next.

The next thing she heard was her own voice. "Oh, they're wood spirits!" She didn't know what that meant except they were different and unfamiliar. Before, disembodied spirits of loved ones had come to her to relay messages.

It was wonderful to be among these gentle beings, knowing they didn't want anything of her, weren't even interested in her. They simply lived in the grove.

Later, the sky clouded over. The cold from the ground seeped through her parka. She breathed deeply and rose, stopping for just a moment to thank the wood spirits for sharing their grove with her.

—*Janet Bieber*

(In this writing exercise, participants selected a line from another poet's poem and elaborated their own poem from it. The line *I think I see ghosts in the birch grove up the hill* comes from "First Snow," by Judith Minty.)

I sometimes keep a journal of magical occurrences and synchronicities. It delights me and also helps me remember when I forget. Everyone forgets. Everyone becomes unconscious. A spiritual practice helps us remember, can act as a mnemonic. If we record the events, we will not be able to deny our experience with the other worlds.

Begin a journal of the invisible.

Spiritual experience often contradicts the known, given, and expected. It surprises us twice—in the event itself and in our acceptance of it. Through writing consciously, we can train ourselves to record what we perceive, what is true according to our understanding, despite the pressure to conform to a conventional worldview. In order to be able to see the other world, we need a well-developed vision of this one and a similarly honest, hard-nosed view of ourselves.

Write something that you never thought you would believe, understand, or see.

We change. We become people we never expected ourselves to be. Atheists all our lives, we may one day discover that we actually believe; this was my own experience. Then it can be as difficult to sustain faith as doubt. Both faith and doubt thrive within the bonds of community. The dream life is far more viable for those who tell their dreams than it is for those for whom dreaming is a secret, even forbidden, activity. But sometimes we are the only ones who see. Then we have to accept that burden.

Describe a moment when you saw something and knew what something meant that no one else knew, when you noted what others disdained or ignored. This can be a small moment, a little bit of light entering to illuminate the darkness.

When I wrote the play *Dreams Against the State*, I imagined a society in which dreaming—the inner life—was forbidden. Of course, an allegiance to other realities is always threatening to the establishment. Apostates and heretics terrify society as much, if not more so, as nonbelievers do. Sometimes we believe our own experience simply because we cannot imagine that others will believe us.

What do you imagine have been the experiences of nonordinary reality of your mother and father? Describe their spiritual lives. Imagine a moment when they were each confronted with something outside their belief system, with an extraordinary spiritual event with which they had to wrestle. In what form does the invisible come to them? How are they altered by it?

This exercise, more than most, may require you to engage in what Coleridge called "the willing suspension of disbelief." Because experiences of nonordinary reality can challenge one's worldview completely, they are often kept hidden, buried in one's psyche. Parents and children may find it equally difficult to speak of such matters to each other.

Imagine the scene when you tell the parent from whom you feel most distant a story about a spiritual experience. Explain what you mean by belief, spiritual practice, devotion. See if you can hold your ground.

I always thought that the sign of a successful life is continuity of self. I still believe this, though I now see that the core that continues from early years through old age is not always apparent. In many ways, I have become someone my younger self would not recognize and might disdain. What is finally the constant may not be known until the very end.

Imagine that you are eighty years old, aware and articulate. What do you believe that you never expected to believe? Now that you are wise, what is it that you believe? What do you understand now that you can only understand because of the experiences of your later life?

The Dark Side

The spiritual world is not necessarily full only of light. To live a spiritual life is also to reckon with the nature and meaning of evil. So much pain occurs in the world because we avoid the dark. We never feel old enough or wise enough or experienced enough to address the darker issues, yet we have no choice but to plunge in. Even though these questions may require a lifetime to answer, their consideration may also constitute a rite of passage.

Have you ever felt the presence of the demonic? What is its nature and character?

Write a dialogue with the devil in which the devil, the satanic, manifests itself.

One definition of the devil is temptation. Whenever we are tempted to do something that betrays what we believe, who we are, or those we love—whether it is a large deed or a small—we can say we are in the presence of the satanic. Satan, almost by definition, offers what we cannot resist, what we love, desire, want, or think we need, what deflects us and entices us from our path. Often, we are not even aware that an offering is being made or a bargain struck, because these deeds occur in moments of unconsciousness. So we must face our weaknesses and vulnerabilities. When we do this, we face the moments when we fall from grace. For all of us, these moments are legion.

> *Write a narrative story in the third person in which the satanic appears to you in the very particular form in which it would appear to you. What encounter transpires? What is the nature of the temptation for you?*

The moment when we face Satan, we receive the gift of the ultimate definition of self, because we know ourselves, then, at the core. I remember the moment very well when my character Dina Z. met the adversary at the Rock of Temptation where Christ had also wrestled with the devil.

> Finally you reduce yourself to the barest essentials. Your outer life has no hold on you, no thrall. Then you're ready for the biggest battle. The one in which you dare not be distracted. Then, the devil enters, dispelling all the lesser demons, and you're finally naked with your beloved. Satan! At last![12]

> *Describe a moment when you experienced moral failure or cowardice, a moment when you betrayed someone or something. A moment when you acted unconsciously.*

> *Look at the moment with compassion. How would the gods see it?*

> *Make something else of this incident. Invent a new ending.*

We cannot redeem everything, transform it, or transcend it, but there are many ways to respond to our inevitable moments of weakness and unconsciousness. And just as roses thrive on compost, just as everything rots and rises again, so does our own behavior.

The Great Teachers

There is another great teacher, and it is death. Dying, the fear of dying, preparing for dying transform us. In the face of death, we see life from another perspective. For this reason, Tibetan Buddhists consider the Chöd practice, a meditation on death that is undertaken in cemeteries, to be one of the most profound.

I say the least about this teacher and the next one—whose name cannot be uttered—because it is for each of us to discover their presence in our life. And ultimately, there is nothing anyone can say that corresponds in any way with the Presence.

What would you say if you were going to die soon?

What do you have to say to a dying person?

Imagine your death. Write its story. What do you learn from the process of dying?

Finally we have to come to the very awkward questions, the ones about the existence, nature, and presence of God and your relationship to the divine. Here, then, are some questions that you may find worth writing about again and again and again in the course of your life:

Do you have an image of the divine? What is it?

Write a story that conveys something about your relationship to God or the gods.

How do you wish to relate to the divine? Describe a spiritual practice you might initiate.

Write the story of your spiritual pilgrimage, of your struggle toward belief. Write the story of your own arduous climb up the sacred mountain. What dangers did you encounter? When did you lose faith? How did you overcome it? How has your life been changed?

Tell this story as if it were a parable intended to communicate the mystery of such encounters.

Write a prayer or a meditation that is appropriate to your beliefs and that will sustain you on a daily basis.

Prayer and inquiry. Praise and skepticism. Search and revelation. Zen Buddhists speak of the great faith and the great doubt. The writer, fully awake, is dedicated to knowing and not knowing.

This is what it means to be whole—to accept paradox and contradiction, where what is coexists with what is not, to welcome the Presence at once so far from us, so invisible, gracing us with a sign.

What follows is the beginning and the end of a most remarkable piece by Linden Chiles that was conceived in response to "Things I didn't see today." It is a fitting conclusion to this section because it is a most spiritual meditation on doubt.

For Greg Who Died

I didn't see God again today. I'm beginning to wonder if I'll ever see Him again, if He hangs out down here at all anymore. I use the expression *down here* pejoratively, of course, because let's face it, this earthly plane can be very heavy, very difficult. So maybe that's it. Maybe it's just gotten too heavy for God or should I say the gods and goddesses and they only tune in from time to time to check us out, to watch us like we watch TV to find out what's going on.

I often wonder if the people—well not people now—the BEINGS I should say, if the BEINGS on the other side, those who have passed over so to speak, if they can watch us like we watch actors on television, going through our endless ups & downs, laughing with us, crying with us, wondering what is going to happen next.

You ever think about stuff like that? I do! A lot!

But I digress. I was talking about God and how I haven't seen Him lately. But then it occurs to me that maybe I haven't really been looking—you know, deep into things, deep into other people, into people's eyes for instance. I don't look deep into people's eyes the way I used to. Seems like a rather dangerous thing to do these days. Most of us don't gaze or stare into each other very much anymore. At least I don't.

Anyway, I was talking about God and how I haven't seen Him or Her or It or whatever you want to call it—the Sacred, the Divine, the Holy, the Transcendent. I've had such a hard time with these words. I don't know what to call it. It's kind of frustrating, you know.

I really don't like the word *god*. It's dog spelled backward, which is OK but it does seem kind of odd when you think about it. At least it does to me. My problem is that the word has such a totally masculine quality to it. That's why I don't like it. It doesn't fit with my experience. I'd much rather think of God as a female if it has to have a kind of gender at all.

Actually the word should be genderless. I can't imagine the Absolute as having sexual properties, that the Source of All Being would be a male or female. God as a father is just one of those ideas I have a hard time with. It's very much part of the "white male system" and I'm surprised that more people don't question it, especially women.

Maybe we should just call God YOU. The BIG you! "Hey, YOU! I need to talk to ya. How 'bout checkin' in here for a while, maybe hang out for a bit & keep me company?" Is that asking too much? Or does it just sound totally irreverent? Maybe it does, but damn it I could never believe that God wanted us to put Him on a pedestal and worship Him and all that. You'd think He'd appreciate a little irreverence now and then. And if He loves us at all you'd think

236

He'd want to be close. Right? I'd rather think of God as my friend, my partner, not my lord & master. And I don't know about all that worship business. Doesn't smell right to me. Sounds like a big ego trip on somebody's part.

Of course, I can always say, "I am God!" Some people believe that & who's to say it isn't true? Maybe we're all God. I wonder about that when I see people talking to themselves on street corners. If it's true maybe it's just as well we don't find out.

As you can tell, I've been thinking about this stuff a lot lately and talking about it a lot too. . . . I sometimes wonder if that's why I haven't seen God, because of Greg getting killed and the effect it's had on me over the past few months.

Before Greg died, I thought I had it all figured out. I was Mr. Metaphysical. Now, I just don't know. I'm not sure about anything. Especially, the spiritual stuff. I doubt! I even doubt there is a God sometimes, this all-powerful entity, presence, force, whatever you call it, that looks after the universe. Right now, it doesn't seem like anyone is looking out for us or the universe. You know? On the other hand, I do feel that something is there. Something!

. . ."Hey God, you mysterious fellow, where are you now that I need you? How 'bout a glimpse, huh? A little something to get me through the night," as the saying goes. And now I hear my witch's voice cackling, "When you're ready to see God, you will see God."

Maybe she's right. Maybe I'm not ready. Maybe I wouldn't know it was God if He sat right down in front of me & waved a flag. It is said that the Divine is everywhere present to those who have eyes to see. So why don't I have the eyes?

What happened to all that cosmic certainty that came over me years ago? That came back to me so strongly after Greg got killed? Is it because I'm going too fast? I got busy after Greg died. I didn't want to give myself too much time to think about things. I was thinking about it too much as it was and I was scared. So I kept moving. I avoided long drives alone in a car. I couldn't meditate. I needed people around me all the time, anything to keep occupied, to keep my attention off what had happened. But it was always there. Is still always there. Like picking up a pot of boiling water that you can't put down, like a fire in the mind that never goes out.

So maybe God is just there waiting for me to slow down, biding his time so to speak. He has a lot of that. And we think we don't. So we go faster. And the faster we go the less time we have. It's one of those terrific paradoxes which abound on this plane.

And my beliefs? Have they turned to sand & slipped through my fingers? I don't know. Maybe they have. Maybe I don't need them anymore, most of them anyway & the ones I do need or like or want, I'll just keep. I mean, what the hell, if I want to believe that I have an immortal soul, that goes on through lifetimes after lifetimes, why not? I certainly can't prove that is true, but neither can you or anyone else prove it isn't true. So why not make life more meaningful, more livable, more precious. The realists call that wishful thinking and I say fine, why not? Does anyone know the truth here? Does anyone really know what happens to us after we die?

I like the idea of reincarnation. I certainly like the idea that I'm going to see Greg again. I think a person would be a fool if he didn't believe that he's going to see his loved one again. It seems to be the more sustaining way to go, since there's no proof either way. But being as I am a well-trained doubter, I have my doubts, of course. But sometimes I think I'm more the fool for that than anything else.

Yes, there's a whole bunch of stuff I'd like to believe, but maybe I don't have to believe anything, except what I see right here in front of me. Maybe I can just live with the mystery. That's something I do know, it's a mystery. A great mystery. That used to bother me, scare me. I felt it was my job as a budding young scientist to dispel the mystery, but now I see that is not possible. The wider the circle of knowledge, the wider the area of what is not known. We have immense knowledge & the mystery is greater than ever. And I don't know if the mystery of what happens after we die will ever be figured out, can be figured out, until we pass on & even then we may close our eyes for the last time & that could be the end of it all. Nothingness. A total blank.

But that possibility doesn't appeal to me. It's not a very interesting or elegant way of viewing this terrain. And God? What about that? You know, the personal God, the God you can talk to, who hears you, who loves you, who somehow answers your prayers and supplications? Again, I'd like to believe that there is such a God. But it seems more difficult. True, again I can't prove that such a being doesn't exist, but my doubts about it are what prompted this writing in the first place.

Let's just say, I have my doubts. I'm hopeful. I have experienced that personal God before. Perhaps I'll experience Him or Her again. I'm available. And I'm going to keep looking. And I'm going to continue to wonder about all of this stuff. But I'm not pushing it. And I'm trying to slow down. To make room for the presence. Maybe it will show up one of these days.

A few days after Greg died, I had this vision. I had been driving in the mountains here in Topanga, his mountains, where he used to hike, and I'd been crying in the car, crying really hard, and when it subsided I had this picture in my mind: I saw Greg & a young man standing out in front of the house, arm in arm, looking at the mountains & chatting together like two old friends, glancing at each other from time to time, smiling. The young man was Death & when he left he took Greg with him. Death wasn't the grim reaper, no skeleton in hooded cape and holding a long scythe. No, Death was a young man, blond & fair, a radiant being, warm and loving. And I was sure that my son went with him willingly.

—*Linden Chiles*

Coda: On Trees

Well, that was certainly the right place to end this section. But something has been nagging at me to be set down, and a story that wants to be told, even a small story, needs to be told.

Some years ago, I offered four meditations to a conference. The second was the following:

> *Close your eyes and imagine yourself as a tree. Imagine that your feet, planted firmly on the ground, are roots extending deep into the earth, that your torso is a trunk stretching upward, and your arms are branches reaching into the sky.*
>
> *Become the tree.*
>
> *Now this is the difficult part: let it be sufficient to be a tree. After you have come to know the tree deeply, you can practice this meditation as a bird, a stone, a star, until you can become one with all life, with all forms of being.*

After the talk, a woman stood up in the audience. "I do not want to be a tree," she said. "Women have been reduced to objects for thousands of years, and now it is time for me to declare myself an intelligent and creative being. I no longer agree to be in a vegetative state. If I am to be more than I am, it is the divine I aspire to."

On political, cultural, and psychological grounds, I agreed with her. But there was another level on which I could not agree. With much heartbreak, I recognize that the human species has contributed very little to the planet and is, of any species, the most dispensable. Indeed, our activities add nothing to the planet. We are no longer an organic part of the life cycle. We are the destructive force, taking everything, returning little. Therefore, it has merit to be a tree. It has merit to give up the species ego and recognize the value of being one with all life.

Outside the window above the desk where I am writing this book, there is an elm and, beyond it, six eucalyptus trees in a row. It was for these trees that I bought this house. Like a corona around these trees is the light of the mythic tree we have descended into the underworld for our lost souls or have ascended into the heavens to gain a vision in this journey we have taken together. This World Tree is as much the map and the territory of our journey as is the elm whose leaves are outlined against the sky.

We have told our story again and again in the course of this book; now let's tell it one last time. Perhaps this is the story that lies under all the stories and without which we will be destitute.

> *Write your story, your autobiography through the history of your relationship with trees. Or tell your life story through your relationship with a particular tree; let this moment stand for the whole.*

The Preacher's Tree

The tree was in the Methodist preacher's backyard—Brother Somebody. I don't remember his name but I do remember he was four-square against drinking, and smoking, and going to the picture show on Sunday. He preached long and hard against these and other sins to a full congregation every Sunday morning.

But in back of the parsonage was a tree that was the occasion of the most irresistible temptation and forbidden pleasures that I have ever known before or since.

I don't know what kind of a tree it was, live oak probably, but to the eight-year-old I was then, it was enormous. The preacher's son (and when I heard later about preachers' sons who deflowered virgins and led wasteful and profligate lives, I always figured I know whom they are talking about) anyway this preacher's son hammered boards up the side of the dark, rough trunk of that tree and attached a heavy rope to a branch that was about a thousand feet up in the air and at the end of the rope he made a big knot.

All the kids would go over there and stand around in the shade, hitting at the rope, watching it swing and twist, until somebody (at first it was only the boys) would work up the courage to climb up the trunk and wrap bare feet around that knot and take off out of that leafy perch, soaring into outer space, hanging on for dear life, and most probably praying not to smash back into the trunk or fall onto the dangerous roots below.

Finally, wanting to be one of the boys, I climbed those plank steps. I can still feel the splintery wood on my bare feet and the crusty surface of the trunk as I squeezed my hands and chest to it for the final ascent onto the branch. Then I crawled out onto that precarious limb, which had suddenly grown at least another two thousand feet from the ground, all the while modestly trying to tuck my sundress around my legs so the boys looking up at me wouldn't see my underpants. I pulled the heavy rope up hand over hand until I grasped the big hairy knot and then—I froze. I looked down and found it hard to remember to breathe.

"Jump! Jump!" came the cries below. "Jump!"

And then a disgusted, "What d'you expect from a girl!"

It was then I had to make the most weighty decision of my eight-year-old life. Did I jump out into the unknown or face the ignominy of sidling along the branch to the trunk and shamefully climbing those splintery steps back to the ground?

It wasn't just the jeers that made up my mind. But knowing I'd never have the courage to make a second try, I was afraid if I didn't do it then, I'd miss something. So I looked down, grasped the rope as tightly as I could, curled my toes around the enormous knot, and holding my breath, took that leap.

The ground with its man-eating roots came flying up toward me. Then the jerk! And I had to hold on with all my little-girl strength as the rope swung out and back and as if by magic didn't even touch the trunk. It never did. Not once all summer. I figured that was the meaning of science.

We spent three hot, thrilling months around that tree. Then the fall came. And the Methodists sent us a new preacher, Brother Rysinger. From a more liberal wing of the church, he didn't get all that upset about drinking and smoking and I never once heard him preaching about the dangers of going to the picture show on Sundays, but he was appalled—not to mention his fear of lawsuits—at the sight of all those children risking life and limb in his backyard. So he cut down the rope and pulled out the boards.

The tree shrank after that. It became quite ordinary. And no tree has ever seemed so wondrous, nor has been the occasion of such pleasure, forbidden or otherwise, again.

—*Loraine Despres*

Tree

Thank God there were trees at the hospital. The only way I could endure this confinement was to hide myself among the tall, stately pine trees. I would pretend I was one of the branches. Nobody could see me when I was part of the tree. I was a majestic sequoia with circles and circles of rings proving I had existed since the beginning of time. Nothing they did now could affect me. I was older and wiser than them all.

Today, especially, I wished that I really was a tree. I was so angry. Staff had stolen my beautiful brooch with its green velvet ribbon. Of course, Mom would blame me and say that I had lost it. It was so convenient for her now that I was in the hospital. Everything was my fault. She was the long-suffering woman with a crazy husband and crazy daughter.

But I didn't care because I was a tree. The trunk of my body was strong and firm. I had deep roots. My long branches prevented anyone from getting too close.

I knew it was time to return to the ward. I'd be getting locked up again if I missed curfews. I found myself shuffling back to the ward. But I didn't care because I was a tree and trees belong outside in open spaces, free and majestic, answering to no man.

—*Dánahy Sharon Rose,* In Pieces

Tree

Each Spring I climbed
To trim the new canopy of growth
From the antenna and ribbed tin roof.
Each Fall, barrels of leaves.

I returned to the mobile home park
Yesterday, discovered
All the barren heat
In rows of gray tin roofs,
The landlord
Afraid of high winds, unstable roots,
Lawsuits.

I should have been there
When they started crawling on my roof.
When all the maple could do was stand there.
While men in cantilever buckets
Rose to the top

And started to cut limb after limb.
Had I known
I would have said no.

There are moist roots
Absorbing rainwater
Trying to send sap up the stump.

—*Daniel David Saucedo*

It was November when I moved into my room on Wheelock Lane. The cold had placed its hand across the hillsides, hardening the ground and quieting the air. In fact the air had become so cold that things seemed to fall more quickly through it. I had moved from California to New Hampshire on short notice, packing my car and driving cross country. As I left the Southwest and headed towards the colder northern states, I had the feeling of a salmon in spawning as it leaves the thick, salty water of the ocean and moves its way upstream to ever colder, ever clearer water.

My room had one large window. A third-floor window that looked out onto a giant elm tree. Because the cold kept me indoors, I spent many months sitting inside my room staring out at the tree. Its blackened bark stood out in silhouette against the gray New England sky and it occurred to me that this was its mourning suit. A suit it wore every winter until in the spring, with the thawing of the frozen earth, it could finally bury its dead.

In a sense I shared the tree's mourning. I found the winter months to be filled with great periods of quiet introspection and abstinence. I thought often of the elm standing stoically with its dead, a graying layer of leaf and branch, covered by a white blanket at its feet. It reminded me of my great-grandmother when she was laid in a white silk casket and placed in the living room of the house where she was born. There she lay quietly, tending to the visitors and friends of the family. Waiting to be placed in the ground.

And in the month of March, the weather began to change. The snow melted and the sun softened the earth. As I toiled through the mud on my way to classes, the darkened earth splashing up about my ankles, the elm tree worked its roots, kneading its dead into the ground.

As quickly as the warm weather had come, the sky outside my windows exploded in green. Exploded in a release that could only happen with the joy that comes from giving the dead to the earth. From giving the dead back to life.

—*Tucker Gates*

And because the tree has been, for me, the beginning and end of creativity and practice:

She Brings Forth Green Leaves
Something settles the tight
nest of the heart,
tree scooped out
for a running creature
O! squirrel
O! eye
tell me the forest chatter.

    I think I must be the tree
     but also the hole in it
pecked out by a sharp beak
Or
am I the heart
which lives in the tree?
I am so aware of the movement

    the going back and forth
the opening and closing[13]

Epilogue

Living the Story

A man who has a vision is not able
to use the power of it until after
he has performed the vision on earth
for the people to see.

Black Elk

There is in each of us an ongoing story. It contains our meaning and our destiny. And it goes on inevitably whether we pay attention to it or not. This is our "soul story.". . . There is an ongoing drama that we do not control and into which we are drawn. And our deepest meaning is to stay with that story. Though we do not know its final outcome, nor even what will come tomorrow, there is nevertheless a great joy and a peace in knowing we are with the story. This is our soul's journey. This is what it means to "live one's soul." This is what life is all about.

Al Kreinheder[1]

A self is made, not given. It is a creative and active process of attending a life that must be heard, shaped, seen, said aloud into the world, finally enacted and woven into the lives of others. Then a life attended is not an act of narcissism or disregard for others; on the contrary, it is searching through the treasures and debris of ordinary existence for the clear points of intensity that do not erode, do not separate us, that are most intensely our own, yet other people's too. The best lives and stories are made up of minute particulars that somehow are also universal and of use to others as well as oneself.

Barbara Myerhoff

Healing unfolds through engaging our experience as a whole.

Arthur Egendorf

We are always at the edge of our lives. Writing can be the safety net into which we leap when we are jumping off the cliff into the unknown. But there comes a time when we must become the daredevil and remove the net. This is the moment when we jump, not onto the page but into our own lives. Not only to write about it but to live it. In the beginning, to write it in order to live it, and then, perhaps, to live and then write it, or at some point not to write it at all so as to live it fully. Or to live it and to write it as one action, as one practice. To live it because ultimately our life, ephemeral though it is, is the only art piece that matters.

And to live it is to claim it, no matter what it is. Not to fix it, not to alter it, not to make it something else or someone else's, simply again and again to explore it, to come to know it, to be trusted to enter into its secret recesses, and then to live it whole, wholeheartedly, from the heart.

That's all there is, really.

I was having lunch at an inn in northern England. There was a middle-aged, respectable English couple sitting at a table next to me. One could see they had been married for a long time. In my imagination, he was a colonel in the British army, someone who, having achieved something modest and satisfying in his life, was coming to the end of the public drama. I don't know what possessed him, but as he was drinking his tea and I was drinking mine, he leaned over to me and said, sotto voce, "My wife has always wanted to live in a tree."

That image has lived with me for twenty-five years. It was not her longing that moved me, it was how thoroughly she and he were embodying that image, were living it in the imagination, if not in reality. In my mind, and perhaps in theirs, she was already living in a tree, and though I saw her quite plainly sipping tea in this very, very civilized inn, I also saw her, and continue to see her, living forever in the treehouse of her imagination.

In her imagination. The imagination is, as we've said before, a real place. And the image is as real as a table or the galaxies. The image matters. Matters as much as anything matters. The image is the *prima materia*. To respect it, work with it, live with it, act upon it, finally to live it is the very core of a creative life.

One autumn, I spent the Jewish high holy days, Rosh Hashanah, with Reb Zalman Schacter in the Santa Cruz mountains. During the morning service, we read the portion of the Torah where Abraham sacrifices Isaac. At the last moment, a ram appears and Abraham understands that he has been given the ram to sacrifice instead of his son. This time as I listened, I could neither bear the thought of the sacrifice of the son, Isaac, nor the sacrificial substitution of the ram. In my mind, I called out: we must no longer sacrifice either our sons or daughters to war, to the stock market, to our hopes, for our country, or to God. Not our children, not rams, trees, or stones. The life of everything must be guarded equally and resolutely.

That afternoon we went to a small lake to perform *Tashlikh*, the ritual purification. Asked to address the waters, I requested they accept what was too heavy for us to carry, what we shouldn't carry, and what we couldn't carry. For myself, I prayed to relinquish all that was in me that was opposed to life. In practical terms, I asked to be able to give up all my unnecessary ties to the wrong collective, the wrong value system, the wrong ways of living.

Returning from the lake, I noticed, with awe, a tree that resembled an Asherah. Tree trunks with two limbs extended upward resembling women with their arms raised overhead were traditionally likened to that ancient Hebrew goddess. The two limbs of this particular tree were each split in half again, so that I was looking at a triple Asherah, a triple goddess, the feminine equivalent of the Trinity.

Approaching the tree, I noticed that a few dozen rusted nails were embedded in the wood at the second split. My first act, then, of the new year was to remove the nails. Though we are not responsible for nailing Christ to the tree two thousand years ago, we are increasingly responsible for the crucifixion of nature.

The image of the nail in the tree transcends the rusty nail and the living tree. Extracting the nail was more than a physical act. I felt as if I was confronting the very first Tree of Knowledge, was meditating upon the kabbalistic Tree of Life, or traveling, as the shamans do, up and down the World Tree. For in that action I was transported both down into the soul's realm of the underworld and into the upper branches of the spirit.

I had not expected to have my prayers answered so quickly. Intuitively, I understood that removing the nails was a means of shifting my identification from the human realm. I was rejecting the human purpose, identifying with the tree itself, which had been wrongfully impaled. By removing the nails, I was beginning to remove the impediments between myself and my real life. The image of that tree and of the nails, embedded and removed, will be with me until I die, part of the larger story that, I hope, I will recognize at the very end of my life.

The image, the myth, the story, the gesture, the ritual, the ceremony—they are similar; all are aspects, all events of the imagination. They are variations on the myriad faces of the gods. Living with them, among them, enacting them, means living in the belly of creation. This life has integrity because the image reverberates through all the worlds, is as meaningful in the day realm as it is in the night realm. It aligns all the worlds—personal, political, psychological, aesthetic, spiritual—that we inhabit.

When we live the story, when we live the imagination, a tree is a tree, is purchased at a nursery, needs good soil, fertilizer, and water, it comes from a seed, bears fruit, and nurtures in that deep sense, but also it is the Tree, the realm of the gods, an element of the sacred grove. It is, as are our lives, both ordinary and numinous.

Once a Native American came to me in a dream and taught me a simple rain dance. When I awakened, I practiced the dance, and some hours later, I watched the rain pattern the water of a swimming pool. For a few days afterward, I could not refrain from telling the dream, even teaching the dance to friends and students. That was the winter of the floods in Topanga and Los Angeles. Though I am not so arrogant as to feel that I had the power of making rain, still I felt responsible, suspecting that I had betrayed an unspoken sacred trust.

Many summers later, traveling in the Southwest, I was confounded by the odd visual conjunction of blue hills, desert, and miniature twisted groves, by the juxtaposition of piñon, juniper, and cottonwood against red stone and wildflowers. I was disturbed by this vista: by the bare, harsh, rough hills; the open, splayed plain of brush; the palette of beige, pink, red, brown rock; the dusty sage; by everything muted by powder, dust, heat; by everything modulated by the patina of stone. The land did not conform to any principles of beauty that I had been taught. Still, this desert insisted that it was beautiful, that it resembled the desert of my people, and I had, therefore, to claim it as my own.

I tried to reject it, calling it ugly. But it demanded, nevertheless, that I take it in. It is so ugly, I thought. Then: ugly but mine. Thereupon, as spontaneously as a transformation in a fairy tale, it was beautiful. The frog, the bear, the beast of the desert had become a prince. The land had seemed ugly only as long as I kept it outside myself. When I was willing to recognize it in my heart, its beauty became manifest. And so I came to accept that harsh, dry plain, that mosaic of sand, disintegrating rock, unremitting sun, and fierce desert, as the beauty that had been given to me, was mine, always had been and always would continue to be mine.

Michael and I had been traveling to the Lightning Fields near Quemado, New Mexico. Because of the unusual amount of rain in the area, an environmental artist has erected a hundred metal rods over an area of a square mile to attract lightning. We were left overnight at a small cabin where we hoped to see the unusual display as lightning struck one rod and leapt to all the others. To pass the night hours while we were waiting, I told Michael about the dream, speculating about performing the rain dance to attract a storm.

Perhaps it was the landscape that suggested that this was a test. I stopped myself in time, realizing that, once again, I was not respecting the dream. I finally understood that magic is never to be used lightly, if it is ever to be used at all. Though nothing in the dream had admonished me to be silent, I now perceived that only a few have been given the right to make rain. Despite the dream, I was not one of them. I didn't have the proper spiritual practice through which to prepare myself for such a serious act of imagination. Only those designated know when the need is great enough, can evaluate the larger and future consequences, and can determine whether permission to proceed has been clearly given.

Ashamed that I had been playing with rainmaking for our entertainment, I spent the rest of the night repenting this and the earlier breach of faith. The rains did not come, and the next day we traveled north toward Mesa Verde.

The following morning, Michael felt strongly that we should hasten to Canyon de Chelly. I hesitated, but he was adamant, so we heeded the call.

We doubled back and drove through Navajo country. Now we watched the mysterious patterns of black rain falling in the distance, marveling as they were illuminated by pitchforks of light. But when the unmarked roads turned to clay, we became concerned that we were lost. Approaching a rise, we came upon a Navajo man and asked for directions. He responded by asking us to give him a ride to the camp where his people pastured their livestock for the summer. We proceeded as he directed, turning off onto an exceedingly narrow lane to take the man to his door. Soon we came upon a compound with a few houses and hogans, and at the man's insistence we went in to meet his mother.

When we entered the house, his mother was weaving a red, black, and white rug. She showed us other rugs, photographs, objects on the walls of the two rooms. "I am so glad you are here. This is how we live. We want you to know this," she said.

While Michael got piñon nuts from the car to leave with them as a gift, I asked for directions again. She gave them vaguely, waving her hands wildly, "Left, left, left, then right, right, right." She was deliberately imprecise, and it amused them both. Then—it was mysterious even in the moment—she looked directly into my eyes, and with a seriousness that could not be mistaken for road directions, said, "Don't worry, you will get there. You will get where you are going."

By the first crossroads we were completely confused. I recounted what had transpired, and we proceeded as best we could. After a few turns, we came, again, upon an Indian man walking along the road. As we were involved in an intimate conversation, we hesitated before stopping, knowing he would ask us, as he did, for a ride. He had been walking for ten miles and had another ten to go, he said, when we asked for directions.

After a very few minutes, the road changed. It must have rained profusely because it had become a sea of mud. The thick red clay was sleek as oil, the ruts peaked wavelike, four, five, six inches deep. The car, unable to hold the road, slid in one direction, then another. Sometimes we went down inclines sideways, barely missing ditches, boulders, overturned logs. The Navajo man said nothing. My terror of heights returned. When the road edged along a cliff, I insisted that we stop. I entreated Michael to abandon the car as fear overwhelmed me. Pulling on my old cowboy boots, I got out to walk. In the far distance, some ten miles away, I could see lights. The Navajo said nothing, sat serenely in the back of the car, eating piñon nuts. We developed a pattern of driving and waiting. Michael would drive until he came to a place where I would not be afraid and would wait for me there. When the road approached cliffs again, I walked. And so we proceeded for about seven miles.

When we arrived at the man's house, he thanked us, took a package of piñon nuts, and waved us on. Immediately after we turned the next bend, we were on a dry road that looked like it had never seen rain. In moments we were on the paved highway to Canyon de Chelly.

It was almost sunset when we arrived. Michael asked me to close my eyes and led me blind to the rim.

There I opened my eyes to the presence of absolute beauty. Soft, red clay walls were luminous in the fading light. A thousand feet below, a glistening snake of a red clay river twisted through the small milpas of maize, which had been worked for more than a thousand years. The brush and junipers curled like the pubic hair of the Mother on the ledges, and the cottonwoods beside the river gleamed blue-green, an underwater hue, phosphorescent with the light of another world. I stood on the edge thinking of the Israelites as they first came upon the Promised Land. This was a sacred vision of paradise.

Where the sun was setting, the rain fell before it in a curtain of gold. This, I thought, is how sacred texts describe the appearance of God, in a shower of golden light. I was filled with awe. To the east where the rain fell in black streaks against the darkening sky, wild explosions of lightning blasted the earth—another face of God. As if this were not enough, a brilliant rainbow appeared to the south, and beside it a gleaming, burning eye of platinum fire. Magenta followed, then rose, and then all the wild colors of approaching night. Every face of the Sky God appeared in all its glory. I saw the face of the Sky God pressed against the glorious body of the Earth Goddess, and I knew that the gods exist. And I thought, I must not doubt again.

Over the course of history, moments of such beauty have inspired that leap of imagination that asserts the presence of the divine. People have staked their lives—and the lives of others, as well—on such visions. Such a moment might have caused Noah to assume the rainbow was a covenant between him and an immanent God. It is so simple and so difficult to believe.

We had come to the rim at the very edge of time. Had we come earlier, we might not have stayed to see the sky explode. If we'd come only a minute later, we would not have seen the unearthly light. Because we were there at that precise second, I could not doubt that we had been led most carefully, through a conjunction of simple events, to a moment of revelation.

The next day, we rose at dawn to see the sunrise and descend down into the canyon. When we arrived at the edge, we were greeted by two goats who nuzzled us affectionately as we fed them crackers, their bells breaking the silence. Ordinary as the moment was, it was also miraculous, as if the goats were there to invite us out of ourselves back into the natural world.

Michael and I spent the day in silence together. As we walked in the warm mud of the shallow river, a chant repeated itself with the rhythm of my steps: "Walking on the dark red body of the Mother, at last." In the quiet mystery of the body of the canyon, something opened in me. Then, while meditating at the end of the day, I received a teaching from the "peace that passeth understanding"—a gift from the canyon floor and the primal, red river of clay where I had immersed my feet:

This beauty comes out of a great heart.

Love is the very heart of beauty. Love had created this landscape. Love was manifested here in the earth and stones. Skill, technology, aesthetics, mind cannot achieve such radiance. The world is not a separate object but the living manifestation of a love so profound it requires form. Love and form are not distinct from each other but are different faces of the divine presence.

I changed my meditative practice accordingly. After a period of stillness, I began to focus on the heart. No action taken, no word spoken, no writing initiated, no healing attempted without asking for my heart to open. Nothing that did not come out of love. Not an instant to be lived without attending to the heart. Nothing without the heart and nothing that did not serve the heart.

I also felt I had been given questions to ponder:

Had we been tested?

Had we heeded a call?

Were the three Navajo people we met real beings?

Had we been lost?

What might have happened if we had refused either of the men a ride?

Was the second man a guide through the ordeal of reaching the canyon?

What did the mother mean when she said, "Don't worry, you will get there"?

Is our suffering a consequence of ignoring what is being asked of us? Would I fall into doubt again?

The gods come to us in the forms we recognize. Once again, the gods had come to me in story.

I do believe that story is a pattern from the other worlds and that it gives coherence to our lives. The constant awareness of the possibility of story awakens us to the mystery that is always around us. Story is a grid, an archetypal narrative, a divine scaffolding that organizes experience into a complexity of meanings and forms. The life that may otherwise appear to be unbearably random or intolerably chaotic becomes whole when made known through the revelation of the intrinsic narrative.

Flailing around in the flotsam and jetsam of daily life, we may be unaware that we are engaged in a descent into the underworld or in an arduous attempt to find the entrance to paradise, but this is what we are doing nevertheless. Story is the template by which the most prosaic or mundane may be understood also as the soul's search for the ephemeral but redeeming moment of vision. There are mythic patterns under all of our lives. Each one of us, often unbeknownst to ourselves, is engaged in a drama of soul that is not reserved only for gods, heroes, and saints. Story is one bridge between the human realm and the divine. At Canyon de Chelly, story appeared—the messenger of the divine.[2]

This lived story has a sequel to it. In Greece, enacting the Eleusinian Mysteries in 1990, we were all aware of the extensive drought. Water was being delivered to some of the islands that no longer had any of their own. The extremity of the dry spell reminded us of Demeter's original grief, which had led her to withhold spring from the barren earth. This drought seemed like another expression of that same grief. Aware that Demeter had also cursed the earth when her sacred groves were cut down, we lamented the trees that have been devastated in this century. Individually and collectively, we mourned the state of the earth and prayed for rain. As the very last ritual act of the mysteries, we departed for Cape Sounion to see the sun set in the water before the magnificent and lonely temple of Poseidon. But this last day, most unseasonably, the sunset was hidden in clouds. There was nothing to be done but to conclude the rite prematurely by reading to each other from an ancient account of the end of the mysteries, which had always been kept secret on pain of death:

> At the very moment when the cries were heard, a light flashed from
> the bay from Eleusis: the light from the sanctuary . . . the fire that is-
> sued from the sanctuary could not remain a secret.[3]

As the word *light* was spoken, lightning struck, lit up the sky, and the rain came down. The ancient final words of the mysteries streamed out of our mouths: "Hye. Kye," we exclaimed in the manner of all those generations of initiates who had practiced the rites for over two thousand years. "Hye. Kye! Rain. Be fruitful!"

The gods of the mysteries asked that we live the myths for our own sakes. If we live the myth, they promise, we will gain our souls. To live the myth, to live the story, is to know the image as the *prima materia* of our lives. It is, at last, to live the transcendent reality incarnate, to be fully alive in all the worlds.

Now, here is a last story with which this book comes to an end:

Many years ago, Barbara Myerhoff was teaching a class at the University of Southern California in urban anthropology. As part of the course, the students were required to interview someone very different from themselves, someone with whom they would not normally converse. One young man in the class, who had lived an unusually protected and insulated middle-class life, was having such great difficulty in finding a subject that he considered dropping the course. However, the day the paper was due, he arrived in the class ecstatic.

"I was at my wit's end," he said, "when it occurred to me to interview our Guatemalan housekeeper. Naturally, I was very nervous because I had never really spoken to her, and it was rather late at night. But as I had to do the paper, I went to her room and knocked at her door. When I entered, I explained my need, asking if it would be a terrible nuisance for her to tell me something about her life. She looked at me strangely and my heart sank. After what seemed a very, very long time, she said quietly, 'Every night before I go to sleep, I rehearse the story of my life, just in case someone should ever ask me. *Gracias a Dios.*'"

Notes

Part I: On Creativity

1. Ellen Bass and Laura Davis, *The Courage to Heal: A Guide for Women Survivors of Child Sexual Abuse* (New York: Harper & Row, 1988), p. 133.

2. Deena Metzger, "Shadow Letters: Self-Portrait of a Woman Alone," from *A Sabbath Among the Ruins* (Berkeley, CA: Parallax Press, 1992).

3. Deena Metzger, "Provincetown, Holly" from *A Sabbath Among the Ruins*.

4. Lewis Hyde, *The Gift, Imagination, and the Erotic Life of Property* (New York: Vintage, 1979).

5. Deena Metzger, "The Woman Who Swallows the Earthquake Gains Its Power" from *Dark Milk* (Los Angeles: Momentum Press, 1978), p. 39.

6. Deena Metzger, "So Much of Women in This Uneven Grass" from *The Axis Mundi Poems* (Los Angeles: Jazz Press, 1981), p. 23.

7. Deena Metzger, "No Words for Rumi" from *Looking for the Faces of God* (Berkeley, CA: Parallax Press, 1989), p. 83.

Part II: On Story

1. Deena Metzger, "The Trees Ask Me Home" from *Looking for the Faces of God* (Berkeley, CA: Parallax Press, 1989), p. 37.

2. Joseph Chilton Pearce, *Magical Child Matures* (New York: Bantam, 1985), 66; Frances Wickes, *The Inner World of Childhood* (New York: Appleton-Century-Crofts, 1968).

3. Deena Metzger, *The Axis Mundi Poems* (Los Angeles: Jazz Press, 1981).

4. Metzger, *The Axis Mundi Poems,* p. 23.

5. Brenda Peterson, *River of Light* (Saint Paul, MN: Gray Wolf Press, 1978), 214–215.

6. Metzger, "Become One with Me" from *Looking for the Faces of God,* p. 88.

7. Diane Wolkstein, *The Magic Orange Tree and Other Haitian Folk Stories* (New York: Alfred A. Knopf, 1978).

Part III: The Larger Story: Archetypes, Fairy Tales, and Myths

1. Margaret Atwood, "Procedures for Underground" from *Selected Poems 1966–1984* (Canada: Oxford University Press, 1990), p. 122.

2. Victor Perera and Robert D. Bruce, *The Last Lords of Palenque: The Lacandon Mayas of the Mexican Rain Forest* (Boston: Little Brown, 1982).

3. Perera and Bruce, *The Last Lords of Palenque,* p. 289.

4. Carey F. Baynes, trans., *The I Ching or Book of Changes: The Richard Wilhelm Translation,* Bollingen Series 19 (Princeton, NJ: Princeton Univ. Press, 1977), p. 682.

5. Title taken from the poem, "I Will Come Back" from *Las Piedras de Chile,* by Pablo Neruda.

6. Barbara Myerhoff, "Life not Death in Venice: It's Second Life" from Victor Turner and Edward Bruner (eds.), *The Anthropology of Experience* (Urbana and Chicago: Univ. of Illinois Press, 1986).

7. Barbara Walker, *The Woman's Encyclopedia of Myths and Secrets* (San Francisco: Harper & Row, 1983), p. 821.

8. Deena Metzger, "The Descent of Rain" from *A Sabbath Among the Ruins* (Berkeley, CA: Parallax Press, 1992), p. 46.

9. Deena Metzger, *Skin: Shadow/Silence* (Reno, NV: West Coast Poetry Review, 1976), p. 78.

10. Metzger, "Eve Awake" from *A Sabbath Among the Ruins,* p. 40.

11. Alwyn Rees and Brinley Rees, *Celtic Heritage: Ancient Tradition in Ireland and Wales* (Thames and Hudson, 1989).

12. Deena Metzger, *What Dinah Thought* (New York: Viking/Penguin, 1988), p. 5.

13.   Metzger, *What Dinah Thought,* p. 187.

14.   Deena Metzger, "Returning: The Eleusinian Mysteries," *Theaterwork,* vol. 2, no. 5 (July/August 1982): pp. 42–44.

15.   Deena Metzger, *The Axis Mundi Poems* (Los Angeles: Jazz Press, 1981).

Part IV: Writing as a Spiritual Practice

1.   Genesis 31:18.

2.   Joseph T. Shipley, *Dictionary of Word Origins* (Patterson, NJ: Littlefield, Adams, 1964), p. 44.

3.   Opal Whiteley, "The Story of Opal: The Journal of an Understanding Heart," *Atlantic Monthly* 125 (March 1920): pp. 289–298. Recently her journals have been reissued: *The Singing Creek Where the Willows Grow: The Rediscovered Diary of Opal Whiteley,* presented by Benjamin Hoff (New York: Warner Books, 1988).

4.   Luis Poirot, *Pablo Neruda: Absence and Presence* (New York: Norton, 1990).

5.   Deena Metzger, "Speaking with Neruda" from *A Sabbath Among the Ruins* (Berkeley, CA: Parallax Press, 1992), p. 102.

6.   Metzger, "Something in the Belly" from *A Sabbath Among the Ruins,* p. 104.

7.   *The Kabir Book: Versions by Robert Bly,* no. 23 (Boston: Beacon Press, 1977), p. 52.

8.   Metzger, "Dreaming of the Girl and the Sea" from *A Sabbath Among the Ruins.*

9.   Deena Metzger, *The Woman Who Slept with Men to Take the War out of Them* (Berkeley, CA: Wingbow Press, 1983).

10.   Michael Ortiz Hill, "The Bomb Monologue" in *Dreaming the End of the World, The Sun,* no. 171 (February 1990).

11.   Deena Metzger, "An Open Letter to Julio Cortázar," *L. A. Weekly* (July 20–26, 1984).

12.   Deena Metzger, *What Dinah Thought* (New York: Viking/Penguin, 1988), p. 187.

13.   Deena Metzger, *The Axis Mundi Poems* (Los Angeles: Jazz Press, 1981), p. 19.

Epilogue: Living the Story

1. Al Kreinheder, *Body and Soul* (Toronto, Canada: Inner City Books).

2. A version of this story was published as "Miracle at Canyon De Chelly," *The Sun,* no. 146 (January 1988): pp. 12–14.

3. A retelling of the miraculous tale as recorded in Plutarch's life of Themistokles (15) from C. Kerenyi, *Eleusis: Archetypal Image of Mother and Daughter* (New York: Schocken Books, 1977), p. 10.

Other Works by Deena Metzger

PROSE

Skin: Shadows/Silence

What Dinah Thought

Tree

The Woman Who Slept with Men to Take the War Out of Them

The Other Hand (forthcoming)

POETRY

Dark Milk

The Axis Mundi Poems

Looking for the Faces of God

A Sabbath Among the Ruins

PLAYS

The Book of Hags

Not as Sleepwalkers

Dreams Against the State

Photo by Cathleen Rountree